Through the Christian Year with Charles Wesley

Through the Christian Year with Charles Wesley

101 Psalms and Hymns

MURRAY R. ADAMTHWAITE
Foreword by Alan R. Harley

WIPF & STOCK · Eugene, Oregon

THROUGH THE CHRISTIAN YEAR WITH CHARLES WESLEY
101 Psalms and Hymns

Copyright © 2016 Murray R. Adamthwaite. All rights reserved. Except for brief quotations in critical publications or reviews, no part of this book may be reproduced in any manner without prior written permission from the publisher. Write: Permissions, Wipf and Stock Publishers, 199 W. 8th Ave., Suite 3, Eugene, OR 97401.

Wipf & Stock
An Imprint of Wipf and Stock Publishers
199 W. 8th Ave., Suite 3
Eugene, OR 97401

www.wipfandstock.com

PAPERBACK ISBN 13: 978-1-4982-3756-7
HARDCOVER ISBN 13: 978-1-4982-3758-1

Manufactured in the U.S.A. 03/08/2016

My thanks go to the following agencies in granting permission to publish material in this book:

1. Methodist Church House, 25 Marylebone Rd, London, for permission to republish Charles Wesley's hymns from the George Osborn Edition of 1868–72.
2. The Museum of Methodism Wesley's Chapel, City Rd, London, for permission to use the John Russell portrait of Charles Wesley as a cover picture.

This volume is dedicated to my father, Rev. John C. Adamthwaite, who labored in the Gospel from 1938 to 1998 in the Methodist Church of Australasia, and later in the Uniting Church of Australia; and to my mother, Mrs. Emily Adamthwaite, who faithfully stood by him through all those years. Also to my wife, Corrie, who has encouraged me through to the completion of this project.

Contents

Tunes Included | ix
Foreword Alan R. Harley | xi
Preface | xvii
Acknowledgments | xix
Abbreviations | xx

Part I: Introduction to Wesley's Hymns
  1 Setting the Scene | 3
  2 A Short Biography of Charles Wesley | 14
  3 Notes on Charles Wesley's Sacred Poetry | 33
  4 Music for the Hymns | 42

Part II: Psalms and Hymns arranged according to the Christian Year
  Psalms and Hymns with Introductory Notes | 53
  A. Morning and Evening | 53
  B. On the Importance of Studying Scripture | 60
  C. Prayer | 67
  D. The Lord's Day | 71
  E. Christmas | 76
  F. Epiphany | 86
  G. Good Friday | 91
  H. Easter Sunday | 102
  I. Ascensiontide | 112
  J. Whitsuntide (Pentecost) | 119
  K. Trinity Sunday | 129
  L. From Trinity to Advent | 154
  M. The Lord's Supper | 168
  N. Advent | 177

  O. New Year | 188
  P. General Devotional Psalms and Hymns | 194

Part III: Theological Issues and Themes in Christian Experience
  A. Theological Issues | 213
    1. Wesley and Incarnational Theology | 213
    2. Theopaschitism | 217
    3. Perfectionism | 221
    4. Arminianism | 231
  B. Christian Experience in Wesley's Hymns | 237
    1. The Hidden Life | 237
    2. The Role of Feeling | 243

First Line Index of Psalms and Hymns | 251
Wesley Hymns in the Wesleyan Hymn Book (USA) | 255
Appendix: John Cennick's Hymn on the Second Coming | 257

Bibliography | 261

Tunes Included

Bradford
Gopsal
Dying Stephen
Praise

Foreword

IN THE MID-1970S I attended a conference of the Canadian Methodist Historical Society. It was held in Toronto's Emmanuel College, the training institution of the United Church of Canada, a church formed in 1927 by the union of Methodists, Presbyterians, and Congregationalists. In one of the discussion periods, a delegate drew the attention of the group to the hymn book of the United Church. "This church claims to be in succession to Methodism," she said, "But in this book there are only two hymns by Charles Wesley, one of which is a Christmas carol."

Sadly, similar observations could be made of the hymnody of other denominations claiming to derive from the Wesleys and their movement. Many churches that claim to stand in that tradition resemble other evangelical traditions whose worship fare is almost exclusively contemporary. For them too, that carol is all they know of Charles Wesley.

Yet Charles Wesley was a genius. Bach was able to produce a new cantata every week and Wesley's work stands in a similar category. His poetry was prodigious, elegant, and biblical. His thousands of hymns and poems reflect a vast knowledge of the Old and New Testaments and the Book of Common Prayer. Like authentic Methodism itself, they stand as a *via media* between the stately, yet biblical worship of Reformed Anglicanism and the warm-hearted and evangelical religion of the eighteenth century revival.

The great truths of the gospel were preached by Whitefield and the Wesley brothers, and when they preached the gospel there was little to distinguish them one from the other in what they believed. This gospel was put into song by Charles Wesley. All the dominant beliefs of early Methodism, both Calvinistic and Wesleyan, are to be found in his poetry. Their birth within revival is reflected in the dominance of "me," "my," and "mine." They echo the belief of Luther that "the heart of religion is in personal pronouns." They are the work of someone who knew what it meant to be converted, to experience the inner testimony of the Holy Spirit to his conversion, and who was seeking to experience that for which the Book of Common Prayer prayed, viz. that God would "cleanse the thoughts of our heart by the inspiration of the Holy Spirit that we may perfectly love Thee and worthily magnify thy name."

Charles Wesley's hymns are songs of testimony. They also are songs of exhortation, reflecting the cry of the evangelist—"O that my Savior were your Savior too." In addition, his hymns constitute a treasury of devotion. I have in my possession of copy of "A Collection of Hymns for the use of the People Called Methodists," compiled by John Wesley. My copy was printed in 1876 and the vast majority of its hymns are by Charles Wesley. This hymnal is my prayer book. I use it daily, along with Scripture, in my devotions. I so often have to pause to write out a verse or a couplet. Here are two random examples:

> *Thou callest me to seek thy face,*
> *'Tis all I wish to seek;*
> *To attend the whispers of thy grace,*
> *And hear thee inly speak.*
>
> *. . .*
>
> *Hourly within my soul renew*
> *This holy flame, this heavenly fire;*
> *And day by day be all my care*
> *To guard the sacred treasure there.*

In addition to beautiful words and expressions such as "whispers of thy grace" and "hear thee inly speak," the lines reflect deep and biblical spirituality and good theology. Wesley links human responsibility to God's prior grace. The believer is called to "guard the sacred treasure," but God must first "hourly . . . renew this holy flame."

Even as John Wesley's "perfectionism" is clearly balanced in the prayers he wrote for individuals, families, and children, in which there is opportunity for heartfelt confession, repentance, and the appropriation of God's forgiveness, so also in Charles Wesley's hymns. He wrote (in words quoted by his brother in Sermon XIV):

> *I sin in every breath I draw*
> *Nor do thy will, nor keep thy law*
> *On earth as angels do above;*
> *But still the fountain open stands,*

> *Washes my feet, my heart, my hands,*
> *Till I am perfected in love.*

The last line of that verse is welcomed by those whose theology embraces the Methodist doctrine of Christian Perfection. It can be sung with equal fervency by believers for whom such language rightly belongs to that time when "we shall be changed, for we shall see him as he is"; at that time "when we cast our crowns before him, lost in wonder, love and praise." However we interpret it, Wesley's spiritual quest was pursued with the awareness of his utter, continual dependence upon Christ.

> *O may the least omission pain*
> *My re-awakened soul;*
> *And drive me to the grace again,*
> *Which makes the wounded whole!*

These hymns also are the reflection of a Christian who knows something of that "joy unspeakable and full of glory." Here is yet another random example:

> *. . . The opening heavens around me shine*
> *With beams of sacred bliss;*
> *If Jesus shows his mercy mine,*
> *And whispers I am his.*
>
> *My soul would leave this earthly clay*
> *At that transporting word;*
> *Run up with joy, the shining way,*
> *To see and praise my Lord.*

Yet the man who penned these sentiments was not a medieval mystic; he was very much the Anglican, of "high church" leanings, who possessed a solid foundation in theology. Even his best-known hymn, "Hark! The Herald Angels Sing," reflects this. The carol is so well known that the theological depth is generally missed. According to Wesley (as well as Scripture and Creed), the baby of Bethlehem is "the everlasting Lord" and yet "offspring of a virgin's womb." He is "the Godhead" who is "veiled in flesh." He is "the incarnate Deity," "our Immanuel," "the heaven-born Prince of Peace."

Originally this carol concluded with a prayer, not now found in most hymnals, even the fine 1933 *Methodist Hymn Book*. The words are now to be found in the body of this book. (Note that Wesley wrote this carol not as it is sung today, with 7.7.7.7.D. meter, i.e., eight lines to the verse, but 7.7.7.7., or four lines per verse, and without the refrain).

But the high church Anglican theologian was very much a son of the Reformation. His hymns reflect his acknowledgement of his utter helplessness and dependence upon God and his grace. His works are peppered with such lines as:

> *Father, I stretch my hands to thee;*
> *No other help I know;*
> *If thou withdraw thyself from me,*
> *Ah! Wither shall I go.*

And again:

> *At last I own it cannot be*
> *That I should fit myself for thee;*
> *Here, then, to thee I all resign;*
> *Thine is the work, and only thine.*

Unlike many who claim to be their followers, John and Charles Wesley said little about "free will." Their favored term was "free grace" with its corollary, "the freed will." While parting company with Whitefield over the doctrine of Predestination, they nevertheless believed that in all of our salvation God had to work preveniently. J. I. Packer described John Wesley as "an inconsistent Calvinist," and Wesley averred that he was "a hair's breadth from Calvinism." The "inconsistent Calvinism" of the Wesley brothers arguably was no more so than the position of many of today's "moderate Calvinists" who reject the first three of the so-called Five Points of Calvinism while holding to the fifth. No one, the Wesleys believed, had any ability to turn to God. They were not Pelagian in any sense. Even the Arminian designation has to be employed with caution. Their high view of grace would put them at odds with many who style themselves Wesleyan/Arminian and who appear to make the sinner rather than the Spirit the "prime mover" in salvation. Wesley's "And can it be?" is as strong an affirmation of the prior grace of God as Newton's "Amazing Grace," or even Toplady's "Rock of Ages," written by one who opposed the Wesleys for their Arminianism. Contrary to the view of some, to be semi-Augustinian, as were the Wesleys, does not make one semi-Pelagian. They agreed wholeheartedly with Augustine and Calvin—salvation is all of grace. But they did not see Double Predestination as the necessary corollary to *Sola Gratia*. A host of Wesley hymns affirm that salvation is all of grace: "Jesu, Lover of my soul," with its "plenteous grace in thee is found, grace to cover all my sins," is one such.

Much more could be said, but that would be an indulgence on my part. My task is to introduce a well-written book which considers the hymnody of Charles Wesley from several aspects—doctrinal, technical, historical, biographical, and practical. As its title suggests, it is designed, among other things, as a resource in the leadership of worship. I know of no other volume such as this. It is a book for pastors, teachers, and musicologists.

Because of the breadth of his thought and the brilliance of his poetry, the works of "the sweet singer of Methodism" soon found their way, in an earlier age, into the hymnals and songbooks of a wide range of denominations and movements. It is my fervent desire that Murray Adamthwaite's delightful and richly informative book will be used by God to cause God's people to rediscover the hymns of Charles Wesley as a source of blessing in private devotion and corporate worship.

—Alan R. Harley, ThD
President, Tyndale College, Sydney
Former Vice Principal, Booth College, Sydney
Former Dean, Wesley Institute, Sydney

Preface

THIS COLLECTION OF HYMNS and psalm versions by the renowned Charles Wesley is dedicated to the Christian public, and even to those who make no profession of Christianity, but who harbor a liking for his verse which has become famous the world over. I have long contemplated a particular and so far unique collection of Wesley's hymns for a number of reasons, as outlined below. However, before I give those reasons there is a word of caution: I do not claim to be any sort of "Wesley specialist." My proper field is elsewhere. I only share my love of his hymns as an aid to devotion, born of my early years in the old Methodist Church of Australasia, through whose ministry I came to Christ.

Moreover, this selection does not claim in any way to be comprehensive, or even fully representative of his total output of sacred verse. There have been only three basic criteria of selection, viz. the Christian Year, bringing to light some unknown compositions, and hymns of rich devotional content. This, I believe, is being faithful to Charles Wesley as a staunch Churchman of the Established Church of England. The Revival of the eighteenth century, in which he played a prominent part, he saw as a movement of evangelical renewal and improvement within his beloved communion, and a recovery of its Protestant heritage combined with the piety and zeal of the Moravians—who had made their presence felt in England in the early eighteenth century. As a Churchman he opposed strongly any move for Methodism to separate from the Church of England, and was accordingly alarmed when his brother John began to ordain evangelists and superintendents for the work in America. "Ordination is separation," he insisted.

As a minister of the Church of England, Charles remained devoted to the classic Christian Calendar, and accordingly published a collection of *Hymns on the Great Festivals, and Other Occasions* in 1746. From this and other early collections came some of the famous hymns for Christmas, Easter, Ascension, and Whitsun, which are still known and sung around the English-speaking world, and with many others have been translated into many languages for worship in countries and cultures unknown to Wesley in his time. Whether the reader shares his commitment to the Christian year or not, it is hoped that all will find this selection to be of spiritual profit.

Acknowledgments

SEVERAL PEOPLE HAVE MATERIALLY assisted in the preparation of this project whom I wish to thank:

Mrs. Rosslyn Devenish, former Librarian of the Melbourne School of Theology (MST), plus other members of her staff, for making available the Charles Wesley volumes from the Renshaw Collection at the Library, and rendering other assistance when necessary.

Rev. Dr. Alan Harley, President of Tyndale College, NSW, who also gave me encouragement for the volume to be published, provided useful suggestions, and has kindly written a Foreword.

Rev. Dr. Allan Harman, former Principal of the Presbyterian Theological College, Melbourne, who read the manuscript and made useful suggestions for its improvement and has kindly written a commendation.

Rev. Dr. Dallas Clarnette, formerly a minister of the Methodist Church of Australasia, but now a minister of the Presbyterian Church of Australia, who gave me much encouragement upon reading the manuscript and has written a commendation.

Rev. Peter Hastie, Principal of the Presbyterian Theological College, Box Hill North, Victoria, who has kindly written a commendation for the volume.

Rev. Ken Brown, pastor of Somerville Presbyterian Church, who made useful suggestions for the improvement of the manuscript.

Dr. Barry Horner, who from his residence in Arizona, USA, encouraged me in the project and made useful suggestions. He has also written a commendation which appears at the conclusion of the book.

Dr. Yuk C. Liong, of the Melbourne School of Theology, who gave me much encouragement for the project and made some useful suggestions.

Mr. Maurice Arnold, my long-time friend and colleague, who kindly did preliminary proofreading of the manuscript.

Abbreviations

1904 MHB	Bridge, Sir Frederick, music ed. *The Methodist Hymn Book with Tunes*. London: Wesleyan Conference Office, 1904.
1933 MHB	Wiseman, Rev. F. Luke, ed. *The Methodist Hymn Book for Use in Australasia and New Zealand*. London: Methodist Conference Office, 1933.
CSWT	The website of The Center for Studies in the Wesleyan Tradition, Duke Divinity School: http://www.divinity.duke.edu/initiatives-centers/cswt/wesley-texts.
CWJ	Wesley, Charles. *The Journal of Charles Wesley (1707–1788)*. The Wesley Centre Online. http://wesley.nnu.edu/charles-wesley/the-journal-of-charles-wesley-1707-1788.
EEC	Ferguson, Everett, ed. *Encyclopedia of Early Christianity*. New York: Garland, 1990.
H&B	Hildebrandt, Franz, and Oliver A. Beckerlegge, eds. *A Collection of Hymns for the Use of the People Called Methodists*. The Works of John Wesley 7. Oxford: Clarendon, 1983. Reprint, Nashville: Abingdon, n.d.
HFL	Joint Hymnal Commission. *Hymns of Faith and Life*. Winona Lake, IN: Light and Life / Marion, IN: Wesley, 1976.
Julian	Julian, John. *Dictionary of Hymnology*. 2 Vols. Reprint, Grand Rapids: Kregel, 1985. First published 1907.

JWJ	Wesley, John. *The Journal of the Rev. John Wesley, A.M.* 4 Vols. London: Wesleyan Conference Office, 1903.
KJV	King James Version.
Lampe	Lampe, G. W. H., ed. *A Patristic Greek Lexicon.* Oxford: Clarendon, 1961.
Manning	Manning, Bernard L. *The Hymns of Wesley and Watts.* London: Epworth, 1942. Public Domain reprint, n.d.
NIDCC	Douglas, J. D., ed. *New International Dictionary of the Christian Church.* Exeter, ENG: Paternoster, 1974.
NPNF	Robertson, Archibald, trans. *The Nicene and Post-Nicene Fathers.* Series 2, vol. 4. Reprint, Grand Rapids: Eerdmans, n.d. First published 1891.
Osborn	Osborn, Rev. G. *The Poetical Works of John and Charles Wesley.* 13 Vols. London: Wesleyan-Methodist Conference Office, 1868–72.
RTR	*Reformed Theological Review.*
Scripture Hymns	Maddox, Randy L., and Aileen F. Maddox, eds. *Scripture Hymns* (1762): The online edition of Charles Wesley, *Short Hymns on Select Passages of the Holy Scriptures.* 2 vols. Bristol, ENG: Farley, 1762. From: https://divinity.duke.edu/sites/divinity.duke.edu/files/documents/cswt/63_Scripture_Hymns.

All Scripture quotations are from the *New American Standard Bible*, The Lockman Foundation, Zondervan, 1999, unless otherwise stated.

PART I

Introduction to Wesley's Hymns

1

Setting the Scene

1. THE MAIN REASONS FOR THIS VOLUME

INTEREST IN CHARLES WESLEY, even more than his brother John, continues unabated for both scholars and the rank-and-file, with more books being published[1] and Wesley Study Centers turning out on-line material on a regular basis.[2] The reason for this is not hard to discern: there is a depth of both theology and devotion in his hymns that few, if indeed any, have ever matched, and certainly not to his volume of verse. Even as literature Wesley's hymns are up with the very best of English poetry, and although there is a romantic streak to his verse, his Christ-centered commitment enables him to rise above the secular romanticism of Shelley, Keats, or Wordsworth.[3] So what contribution does this volume make, one may ask? Several reasons arise here, not necessarily in order of importance:

1. A love of Charles Wesley's hymns, and a regard for him as probably the greatest hymn writer of all time, both for the sheer volume (around 7500—the estimates vary[4]) and the high quality, whether for their

---

1. For example, Tyson, *Assist Me to Proclaim*.

2. See Northwest Nazarene University, The Wesley Centre Online, http://wesley.nnu.edu/charles-wesley; see also, CSWT, https://divinity.duke.edu/initiatives-centers/cswt/wesley-texts/wesley-works-editorial-project.

3. As discussed in H&B, 38–55.

4. Rattenbury, *Evangelical Doctrines*, 20, gives a total figure of 7300.

rich devotion, for their doctrinal orthodoxy and theological depth, or for their literary merit. As to the latter, my own view is that Charles Wesley ranks high in the annals of English poetic literature; he is "up there" with Dryden, Shelley, Keats, Tennyson, and Wordsworth, but secular literary critics are usually loath to grant him that honor, probably due to a dislike of his robust evangelical Christianity. Whatever, it is my conviction that in the current Christian climate Charles Wesley is being forgotten, and such a loss is to the serious detriment of the Christian church. Contrary to those who allege that the church must "move on" from the past, I firmly believe that Wesley's hymns are too precious to be consigned to the dustbin of history.

2. The following is confessedly a negative point, but in the light of today's worship scene, necessary. I have a firm conviction that hymn singing generally has seriously declined in Christian worship today, as reverence, doctrinal orthodoxy, and Scriptural piety and devotion have correspondingly declined. This in my view is an index of the spiritual poverty of the contemporary church. There are two reasons for this move away from "the old hymns": the first is the decline of appreciation for poetry and its essential features. However, for both John and Charles Wesley, poetry was the handmaid of piety (see below), and if that is true then as genuine poetry has declined, so too has genuine piety. Here Wesley's adherence to rhyme, meter, rhythm, and accent will strike many a modern reader as strange, in contrast to what passes for poetry today, which displays little or nothing of these features, especially the so-called "blank verse," which seems to be merely a set of brief one-liners arranged one under the other. Then on the musical side we have on one hand the dry pomp and ritual of liturgical churches, where missing are the solemnity, piety, and evangelical fervor evident in Charles Wesley's hymns. And on the other there is the "contemporary music" of the mega churches, where a few lines are repeated endlessly—and one suspects mindlessly, and combined quite often (let us be candid) with singers sensuously gyrating on the stage to the twang of guitars and the thump of drums. In short, worship has become performance and entertainment to a large degree, to the detriment of reverence for a holy God, and corresponding erosion of the cry of a sinful heart (cf. Isa 6:1–7). It is therefore hoped that this volume will renew interest in the real Wesley, in reverent and humble

worship, and in congregational hymn singing in general, in response to God's revelation.

3. In regard to content, there is in Wesley's hymns a firm adherence to both sound doctrine and a deep but healthy devotion and piety (in the best sense of the term). As one surveys his hymns, all the great doctrines of the Christian faith are set forth in clear language: the Trinity, the Divine plan of redemption, the Incarnation of the Son, the Cross and Atonement, the Resurrection and Ascension, the Second Coming, the Holy Spirit's work, the Holy Scriptures, the Christian life in its various aspects, etc. His hymns taken together are a veritable confession of faith in verse. This is in line with Paul's admonition that our praise in song is for "teaching and admonishing one another with psalms, hymns, and spiritual songs, singing with thankfulness in your hearts to God" (Col 3:16). Therefore, a recovery of Wesley's hymns will assist greatly in a recovery of doctrinal orthodoxy and understanding of our great doctrines. Bernard Lord Manning commented on Wesley's hymns as follows:

> ". . . their faithful, moving, but utterly unsentimental record of every phase of religious feeling. There is no mood of the Christian soul that is not reflected in Wesley's hymns."

But to that Manning also added,

> "The heart of Wesley's religion is sound doctrine."[5]

4. As a corollary to Point 2, this volume is intended also for a recovery of our Christian heritage. While the Reformers rejected tradition as an authority alongside Scripture, they always appreciated that Christians stand on the shoulders and receive the legacy of those who have gone before. Protestantism at its best has always appreciated heritage, and says with the Psalmist, "The lines have fallen to me in pleasant places; I have a goodly heritage" (Ps 16:6 KJV). However, we live in a day when heritage and tradition are deemed of little value, and peremptorily discarded. An Athenian love of novelty is abroad instead (cf. Acts 17:21)—all too often novelty for its own sake. While the above is not intended in any way to denigrate such fine modern hymns as *In Christ alone*, or *From heaven He came, helpless Babe*, it is my sincere belief that a study of Wesley can help recall us to true worship, a true

---

5. Manning, 72, 75.

Part I: Introduction to Wesley's Hymns

evangelical spirit, and an appreciation and recovery of our rich heritage to combine with the modern ethos.

One should note at this point that while Wesley's hymns had a wide acceptance in Methodist circles, being part of their standard repertoire, they are not specifically Methodist but belong to the entire Christian world. They will be found in the hymnals of many denominations (even Roman Catholics!), as well as non-denominational collections; hence this volume is dedicated to an ecumenical cause, with "ecumenical" used also in the best sense of the term.

5. Even apart from a hymn singing emphasis, Wesley's hymns have long been used as an aid to devotion. The Editorial Committee of Wesley's 1780 *Collection* with the added Supplement (publ. 1877) expresses this sentiment:

> "The 'Collection' of 1780 has been circulated by millions, and has been recognized as a priceless treasure, not only by Methodists, but by many other disciples of the One Master. As a testimony to Scripture doctrine and Christian experience, as a monument of piety, a manual of devotion, and a bond of fellowship, it can never cease to be precious to all who cherish the spirit of its authors . . ."[6]

Similarly, the Preface to the 1933 *Methodist Hymn Book* expressed the same desire:

> "The Hymn Book, like its predecessors, is intended for use in private devotion as well as in public worship."[7]

We can be sure that John Wesley also had this in mind for the 1780 *Collection*, even if he did not say so explicitly in his Introduction. Beckerlegge expands accordingly:

> ". . . there is massive evidence that Methodists have always so used their hymn-book . . . The biographies of Wesley's early preachers, as well as the later memoirs, and obituary tributes in nineteenth century magazines, all bear testimony to the part played by the hymn-book in Methodist devotions."

Then he goes on to list some prominent examples.[8]

6. Wesley, *Collection with New Supplement*, iv.
7. 1933 *MHB*, iv.
8. H&B, 66–67.

Setting the Scene

It is my prayer that this sample of both Wesley's better known hymns, and also those which have now sunk beneath the proverbial ocean, can serve the Christian faithful in their devotions, in their grasp of Christian doctrine, in an appreciation of verse (which is dying in the West), and above all, in pointing us to the Lamb of God whom Wesley delighted to proclaim.

6. It is not generally known that Wesley produced verse renderings of a majority of the Psalms, in all 110 of the 150. Indeed, many of these only emerged after Wesley's death in 1788, and appeared in various issues of *The Arminian Magazine*, which John Wesley launched in 1778. Meanwhile, others turned up in a manuscript in the possession of Rev. Henry Fish in 1854. These productions are hardly known: a few (eight in all) made their way into the classic 1933 *Methodist Hymn Book*, but the many others have disappeared entirely from view, such that most people are unaware that these Psalm versions even exist. While Wesley's hymns are replete with Scriptural quotations and allusions, he loved the Psalms, and like Isaac Watts before him (who produced his own Christian paraphrase in 1719), he desired to breathe into them the Christian content for which the New Testament's use of the Psalms gives clear warrant. This volume therefore seeks to bring to light some of Wesley's Psalm renderings for the Christian public as a further aid to devotion and guide to the New Covenant dimension of the Psalms.

7. One may ask, notwithstanding Wesley's own commitment to the Christian Year, why such a criterion has here been adopted, especially when my own position is Nonconformist and non-liturgical. In reply, we can observe that most churches today have adopted at least the basic elements of the Christian Year, i.e., Christmas, Easter, Pentecost, and perhaps Trinity Sunday and Advent. True, the Christian Calendar has no explicit Scriptural warrant, but rather belongs to Christian tradition, yet even among those for whom tradition carries little weight the Christian Calendar is often defended on pragmatic grounds, whether as a useful evangelistic opportunity, or so that the major points of Christianity receive their due and regular emphasis. The Church historian Philip Schaff puts it this way:

> "The church year is, so to speak, a chronological confession of faith; a moving panorama of the great events of salvation; a dramatic exhibition of the Gospel for the Christian people. It secures to every important article of faith its place in the cultus of the

church, and conduces to wholeness and soundness of Christian doctrine, as against all unbalanced and erratic ideas."[9]

Charles Wesley, the Anglican churchman, would have endorsed this thoroughly.

However, the "Christian Year" should not be restricted to the specific seasons such as Christmas and Easter. The Christian lives each day at a time: "Thy mercies are new every morning; great is Thy faithfulness" (Lam 3:23); hence there is section for the morning and evening of each day, and Bible study and prayer appropriate thereto; then there are hymns for the Lord's Day, New Year, the Lord's Supper, plus devotional psalms and hymns for use throughout the year. In all, there are some twenty-one psalm versions, and eighty hymns in this collection.

2. A FEW CAVEATS TO THIS SELECTION

1. In making a selection, even according to the criterion of the Christian Year, I am well aware that there will be some who will criticize the selection: "Why did you include A and B, and why didn't you exclude X and Y?" they will object. The intent, as stated above, is to make a blend of the well known hymns, the lesser-known, and also the totally unknown (except to certain scholars)—but all of which should be known because of their theological content and their ability to take the reader, and more particularly the singer, on a "flight to the skies," as in the following verse:

   With the Spirit remove
   To Zion above,
   Triumphant arise,
   And walk with our God, till we fly to the skies.[10]

   Bernard Lord Manning writes this of Wesley:

   "There is the solid structure of historic doctrine, there is the thrill of present experience, but there is, too, the glory of a mystic sunlight coming directly from another world. This transfigures

---

9. Schaff, *History of the Christian Church*, 387–88.
10. Osborn, vol. 4, 204.

history and experience. This puts the past and present into the timeless, eternal NOW."[11]

2. As noted, I am no Wesley specialist, but that does not mean I have ignored some major theological discussions by those who are. Theological issues do arise in Wesley's hymns, notably the Arminian "General atonement" view—particularly in his early compositions, the adoption of his brother's perfectionism in his hymns on holiness and the Christian life, and the alleged Theopaschitism in his hymns on the Atonement (see Part III). I have included short discussions of each of these issues, plus some lesser matters as and when they occur. In a positive vein, I have also discussed two matters relating to the devotional life: viz. the "hidden life" (Col 3:3), and the role of feeling in his hymns. However, while these discussions are incidental to the main devotional purpose of this volume, since it is not intended as any sort of scholarly analysis of Charles Wesley's theology, the discussions are intended as a guide to understanding and appreciating Wesley as to his theology and his devotion to Christ.

3. Following the qualification regarding theology, neither is it my purpose to comment on the literary precursors of Wesley's verse. That has been done quite ably in the essays contained in the Hildebrandt and Beckerlegge edition of the 1780 *Collection* of Wesley's hymns, and the works cited therein.[12] There will be the odd comment in this regard, but otherwise I leave the reader to consult this work for more information. Suffice it to say, a study of these literary analyses will result in a greater appreciation of Wesley's genius, and in turn point the reader to the God whom he served.

4. It will be readily apparent that I do not hold with the so-called "Purity of worship" position (Psalms only; no hymns, no instruments) of some highly conservative Reformed denominations. However, in those circles there is still an appreciation of Christian verse for devotional purposes, even if not for public worship. I would, therefore, commend this work to people of that persuasion in the hope that they will still benefit from this collection for their devotional reading and reflection.

---

11. Manning, 29.
12. H&B, 38–55.

Part I: Introduction to Wesley's Hymns

3. POINTS FOR GUIDANCE

1. In choosing and collating the psalms and hymns in this collection, I have sought first the original text of what Wesley wrote, which is the primary text reproduced. For this I have used extensively the complete set of Wesley's verse in the thirteen-volume edition of *The Poetical Works of John and Charles Wesley*, collated and edited by Rev. G. Osborn DD, dated 1868–72, now in the Renshaw Collection in the Library of the Melbourne School of Theology.[13] Where differences occur in modern versions as contrasted with the original text, I have sought to draw attention to them and explain as best as possible in notes after the original text. In this I am acutely aware of John Wesley's stricture in his Preface to the 1780 *Collection*, as follows:

   > "Many Gentlemen have done my brother and me (though without naming us) the honour to reprint many of our hymns. Now they are perfectly welcome to do so, provided they print them just as they are. But I desire they would not attempt to mend them—for they really are not able. None of them is able to mend either the sense or the verse. Therefore I must beg of them one of these two favours: either to let them stand just as they are, to take them for better for worse; or to add the true reading in the margin, or at the bottom of the page; that we may no longer be accountable either for the nonsense or for the doggerel of other men."[14]

   For all, that, however, certain changes over the years (not all) have been for the better. Some of the more significant alterations are noted at the end of the hymn in question with an * or †. The most obvious example is the now commonly sung version of *Hark! the herald angels sing*, from the lines which Wesley originally wrote (on which see below). We need only observe that John Wesley himself was not above correcting his brother's lines when he believed it necessary.[15]

---

13. The caveats on the Osborn Edition as published on the CSWT website, https://divinity.duke.edu/initiatives-centers/cswt/wesley-texts/poetry-hymn/osborn-collection, are well taken. However, as they do not substantially affect the textual issues of Wesley's hymns, I have used extensively the Osborn Edition as a satisfactory source.

14. H&B, 75.

15. Ibid., 59–60. Allan Harman notes also the same penchant on John's part for altering his brother's lines where he saw fit. He cites his objection to verse 2 of "Love Divine, all loves excelling," on which more below in the preliminary remarks on this hymn. See

Setting the Scene

Apart from alterations Wesley's hymns have suffered from undue truncation over the years: quite beautiful verses have been omitted (notably the final verse of his famous Easter hymn, i.e., *King of glory, soul of bliss*), while at times, for example, four-line verses have been combined into eight-line stanzas, or vice versa, usually dictated by rather strange tune settings.

Furthermore, since Wesley's original version will often contain many more verses than the abridged versions that are sung today, I have, with some exceptions, reproduced in entirety the original set of verses. Where I have included verses not in later versions my referent will be the 1933 *Methodist Hymn Book*, and those verses omitted from this latter collection will be noted with a raised #. At times I omit some verses myself, often because they are either dated, or fail to represent Wesley at his best, but I indicate as much where omissions occur.

Above all, I have been concerned in the interests of accuracy, of faithfulness to both of the Wesleys, and with a desire simply to put the record straight, to "print them just as they are." Therefore, let those who with the modern idiom in mind wish to alter them, be aware of what Wesley originally wrote.

2. The reader will note from time to time in Wesley's hymns—apart from the "Thou's" and "Thee's" with their associated verb forms—various archaic words and phrases, such as "vouchsafe," "vesture," "plenitude," "antepast," "ken," "repast," "succor," "surety," "yon azure height," etc.; and furthermore, words which have changed their meaning (at least somewhat) from their eighteenth century meaning, such as "meet," "need," "legislative" (as in Psalm 19), "inured," or "odor." A short glossary of the main archaisms appears below; otherwise, where such archaisms occur I have indicated the meaning in a note below the relevant psalm version or hymn. All this said, however, I have decided to leave them as they occur, with the proviso that readers of a poetic bent may wish to alter the wording—within limits—to something more acceptable in a modern idiom, as indicated above.

3. I have included verse numbers, but where (occasionally) an excerpt is featured I have usually begun from number 1; and again where verses have been omitted I have accordingly resumed the numbering as per Wesley's original. In regard to Wesley's Psalm versions, the reader will

---

Harman, "Impact of Matthew Henry," 6 n. 13.

find it useful to have Bible open so as to match the Biblical text (in particular the King James Version) with Wesley's paraphrase. However, I have also indicated with each selection the meter so that those who desire to sing them can fit an appropriate tune for this purpose.

4. Finally, the issue of tunes. While this book is mainly for reading, some may indeed wish to hum them to a tune, to follow them to the accompaniment of a tune, or even to sing them themselves. Accordingly, I have indicated suggested tunes with each selection, one of which will be the set tune in the 1933 *Methodist Hymn Book* (hereafter 1933 *MHB*) if the selection occurs therein. In these tune settings I have normally avoided tunes in minor keys, although I well recognize that a number of tunes in minor keys, such as "Marienbourn," were part of the original *Foundery Collection* of 1742. Furthermore, I would refer the reader to the excellent and comprehensive set of hymn tunes on-line at:

http://www.smallchurchmusic1.com/

—then go to "Selection criteria," type in the name of the tune, or first line, you want, and click "Go." You will have there an organ version, plus quite often a piano version, or sometimes even a band or vocal rendition.

4. ARCHAISMS OCCURRING IN WESLEY'S VERSE

Word in text	18th century meaning	Modern meaning
Antepast	foretaste	—not used
Azure	lapis lazuli; color of blue	—occasionally used
Fain	willingly, gladly (adverb)	—not used
Filial	of the relationship of son to father	—rarely used
Inure	to accustom, habituate; to brand	to put into operation
Ken	sight or view of something	know
Legislative	enacting laws	binding/demanding by law
Meet	suitable, fitting, proper	to encounter, welcome
Need	to lack	to require
Odor	smell (either sweet or putrid)	a foul smell
Plenitude	fullness, abundance	—not used
Pompous	with pageantry and splendor	full of self-importance

Setting the Scene

Repast	food for a meal	meal (but rarely used)
Succor	help, assistance, shelter	—occasionally used
Surety	guarantor; pledge, bond	safety; certainty
Unction	an anointing (by the Spirit)	—occasionally used
Vesture	clothing	—occasionally used
Vouchsafe	allow as an act of grace	bestow a benefit

2

A Short Biography of Charles Wesley[1]

BIRTH AND EARLY LIFE

CHARLES WESLEY CAME INTO the world on December 18, 1707, to Samuel and Susannah Wesley, the eighteenth in a family of nineteen children (only ten of whom survived infancy); and since he was born prematurely he was not expected to survive, but he came through just the same. Charles came from a family with deep Puritan roots: his paternal grandfather was John Westley, a Puritan minister and associate of the Puritan evangelist Joseph Alleine, who, having been ejected from the Church of England under the Act of Uniformity in 1662, ministered to Puritan congregations in the southwest of England during the Restoration period, at the risk of imprisonment by the authorities. However, his son Samuel Westley eventually broke with the Puritan tradition, dropped the "t" from his name, and moved back into the Established Church.

His grandfather on his mother's side was even more illustrious: Dr. Samuel Annesley, an outstanding scholar known colloquially as the "St. Paul" of Nonconformity. He organized the first ordinations of Dissenting pastors after the Toleration Act of 1689, which allowed Nonconformists to establish their own chapels and support their own pastors. However,

---

1. For the material in this section, *inter alia*, I am indebted in particular to (i) Charles Wesley's Journal (CWJ); (ii) Dallimore, *Heart Set Free*; (iii) Mohan, *Heart Set Free: Life, Ministry* (DVD).

Susannah also moved back into the Established Church, but sided with the "Non-Juror" High Church party who refused to take the oath of allegiance to William III. Susannah's adherence to the Arminian High Church views of seventeenth century Anglicanism (traceable to Archbishop William Laud during the reign of Charles I) was to influence John and Charles in their later years, albeit not the sole influence. Samuel and Susannah were married on November 11, 1688, right at the time of the Glorious Revolution, which ousted the Catholic James II and brought the Dutch Protestant William III to the throne.

Samuel Wesley, after serving several small parishes, finally settled into the benefice of Epworth in 1697, where a sizeable part of his family were born and raised. Samuel was a strict disciplinarian, even imperious, in his dealings with parishioners and the populace of Epworth, and as a result he made many enemies. At least twice the latter conspired to burn down the Rectory, and on one famous occasion in February 1709, they succeeded. However, while the family managed to flee the burning building, the young John was left behind in an upstairs bedroom, and when he appeared at the window there was consternation from his mother. Some bystanders then climbed shoulder upon shoulder to form a human ladder and rescue the boy. Ever after John believed that the Lord had "plucked him as a brand from the burning" (Amos 4:11) for a special work.

In the Wesley household Susannah took special care for her children's welfare. Here she followed her father Dr. Annesley, who taught that families should be as ordered mini-commonwealths and well-disciplined churches. She believed that children should be given a well-structured routine of learning, exercise, prayer, and Bible study, with a firm but fair use of the rod. Susannah's kitchen at Epworth she set up as a classroom; then in the evenings she would have each child come to her on a one-to-one basis for instruction in the Scriptures and holy living. Daily school was two periods of three hours each, and each opening and closing with prayer and the singing of psalms. The rod was indeed used strictly, but at the same time obedience was commended and encouraged. Her aim was "to conquer (but not destroy) their wills and bring them to an obedient temper," thereby learning the seriousness of life. Charles learned the basics quickly, while his father taught him Greek and Latin, and also the classics.

After the fire of 1709, Mrs. Wesley was forced to place the children in foster homes. However, when it came time for their return she observed in them speech and manners unbefitting a Christian home. Hence she organized—and supervised—an even stricter regime of study and discipline. This rigorous round of educational, moral, and spiritual discipline was to serve the two brothers well in later years.

SCHOOL AND UNIVERSITY

Samuel Wesley sent all his sons to school, and in 1716 Charles arrived at Westminster School in London. He excelled at his studies there, and became a King's Scholar. On the strength of that he obtained a scholarship to Christ College, Oxford, where he again excelled, obtaining his BA in 1730, and his MA in 1733. His specialty was the Greek and Latin classics, and poetry, for which he had a natural talent. However, at Oxford Charles fell in with the worldly life of undergraduates, but still later saw the need for a disciplined spiritual life, so he gathered together several friends for intense rounds of prayer, fasting, poor relief, and the weekly sacrament. His brother John, with his leadership skills, soon took on the leadership of this Holy Club, derisively called "Methodists" by outsiders. Rigorously ascetic, and not evangelical, it reflected the mystical and moralistic "Caroline High Churchism" of the period. None of them yet knew true saving faith or free justification through the finished work of Christ. One of their number, George Whitefield, even injured his health with the rigorist practices, but in 1735 he came to saving faith and conversion after reading Henry Scougal's work, *The Life of God in the Soul of Man*. After ordination in 1736 he began his lifelong preaching ministry, and saw multitudes come into the Kingdom as a result.

MISSION TO GEORGIA

After Charles graduated from Oxford in 1733, he stayed on as a tutor, but after his father died in 1735 he sought Holy Orders (ordination), first as a deacon, then a week later (!) as a Church of England clergyman. Shortly before this, Sir John Oglethorpe, the governor of the new American colony of Georgia, approached both him and John regarding the posts of missionaries to the newly established colony, to which they agreed, and their mother Susannah, although now widowed, concurred. Accordingly, and with much optimism, they set sail from England on October 22, 1735.

On Wesley's voyage to Georgia, inner uncertainties about his salvation became evident: the several storms showed that he was afraid to die.

Once when the twenty-six Moravians on board had just begun a worship service a severe storm ensued, yet they continued singing while the other passengers screamed in terror. The two Wesleys inquired of their leader: "Were his people not afraid to die?" He assured them they were not, at which the two marveled. When the ship arrived at Savannah, John began a conversation with the Moravian pastor, Augustus Spangenberg, as to what was wrong with himself. He asked Wesley in response, "Does the Spirit of God bear witness with your spirit, that you are a child of God? Do you know Jesus Christ?" Wesley realized that his replies were vain: in spite of his great learning and outward piety he had no assurance of salvation.

The American mission was a failure: both tried to run the entire colony along the rigorist lines of the Oxford Holy Club! Their conduct of ministry provoked strong suspicion and anger from the colony's governor, Gen. James Oglethorpe—so much so that Charles became ill, and he returned to England after a mere six months. John stayed on, but became the subject of a legal suit, causing him to leave the colony. A Georgia magistrate even wrote bluntly to John:

> "I like nothing you do. All your sermons are satires upon particular persons . . . Indeed, there is neither a man nor woman in the town who minds a word you say."[2]

When Charles and John returned dejectedly to London in 1737, they met the Moravian Peter Böhler and the Fetter Lane Society of Moravians, who showed them the way of pardon and peace with God through the blood of Calvary, received by faith apart from works and moral performance. From here they both sought this faith which saves.

EVANGELICAL CONVERSION

Near the site of what in the eighteenth century was the Moravian Meeting House stood the home of John Bray, in Little Britain, off Aldersgate Street. There on May 21, 1738, after Bray read to him Psalm 32, and as Charles struggled through that day he came to a knowledge of saving faith and justification through the blood of Christ. "I do believe," he exclaimed. Charles recorded of Bray, "He knows nothing but Christ, yet by knowing Him knows and discerns all things."[3]

2. Dallimore, *George Whitefield*, vol. 1, 149.
3. Dallimore, *Heart Set Free*, 59–61.

Part I: Introduction to Wesley's Hymns

Three days later, Charles's brother John came to a similar experience in the Moravian House:

> "In the evening I went very unwillingly to a society in Aldersgate Street, where one was reading Luther's Preface to the Epistle to the Romans. About a quarter before nine, while he was describing the change which God works in the heart through faith in Christ, I felt my heart strangely warmed. I felt I did trust in Christ, Christ alone, for salvation: and an assurance was given me, that he had taken away my sins, even mine, and saved me from the law of sin and death."[4]

The doctrine which brought about the breakthrough was that central emphasis of the Reformation, justification by faith alone, as expressed in both Luther's Preface, and in Article XI of the Thirty-nine Articles:

> "We are accounted righteous before God, only for the merit of our Lord and Saviour Jesus Christ by faith, and not for our own works or deservings: wherefore, that we are justified by faith only is a most wholesome doctrine, and very full of comfort, as more largely is expressed in the Homily of Justification."

This had been obscured almost entirely in the Restoration Church of England, under the widespread influence of the views and policies of Archbishop Laud, and later, of Archbishop John Tillotson, who occupied Lambeth Palace from 1691–94, and whose sermons were little more than "God and morality." Another problem was the widely held doctrine of baptismal regeneration, whereby the mere performance of the baptismal rite (Latin *ex opere operato*: "by the act performed") in infancy made the recipient a regenerate Christian. Thus an easy moralism prevailed, whereby people were cosy in the sanguine belief that because they were baptized, were part of a "Christian country," and "did the decent thing," they were Christians and all was well.

It was in one way a serious struggle for Wesley to divest himself of this all-pervasive outlook and embrace "faith alone" as the way of salvation.[5] All that memorable day (May 21st) the Holy Spirit "strove" with his own spirit until in the evening he could testify (as he indeed wrote):

---

4. JWJ, vol. 1, 97, entry for May 24, 1738.

5. Rattenbury, *Evangelical Doctrines*, 250–54, makes the same basic point, albeit from a different perspective.

"I now found myself at peace with God, and rejoiced in the hope of loving Christ . . . I saw that by faith I stood; by the continual support of faith, which kept me from falling . . ."[6]

He could—and did—now confess:

No good word, or work, or thought
Bring I to gain Thy grace;
Pardon I accept unbought,
Thine offer I embrace;
Coming, as at first I came,
To take, and not bestow on Thee.

Saviour, from Thy wounded side
I never will depart;
Here will I my spirit hide
When I am pure in heart:
Till my place above I claim,
This only shall be all my plea.[7]

CHRISTIANITY IN THE EARLY EIGHTEENTH CENTURY

Apart from the doctrinal declension noted above, there was a serious moral and spiritual decline. In the aftermath of the Restoration period (1660-89), the Church of England, having thrust out 2000 of the Puritan clergy in the "Great Ejection" of 1662, "like a torpid sloth, existed indeed, and hung on the State tree, but scarcely lived, moved, or breathed."[8]

Among the clergy were the widespread abuses of multiple benefices, absenteeism, and irreligion. Clergy, seeking to be "moderate," who gave lip service only to the Church's doctrines, often forsook their congregations as they served their own pursuits and hobbies. Deism—the view that God

---

6. CWJ, May 21, 1738.

7. *Hymns and Sacred Poems*, 1742, entitled "After a Relapse into Sin"; Osborn, vol. 2, 201; no. 168 in the 1780 *Collection*; 1933 *MHB*, no. 365. John Wesley proclaims this as "the doctrine which I have constantly believed for near eight and twenty years," and goes on to cite from the Homily on Justification in the Anglican Standards. (Sermon 20, "The Lord our Righteousness," cited in H&B, 290-91, note to Hymn 168).

8. Ryle, *Light from Old Times*, 292. Ryle (an Anglican bishop) writes of the Puritan clergy, "Many of these 2000 were the best, the ablest, and the holiest ministers of the day" (ibid., 316), and that the ejection "did an injury to the cause of true religion in England, which will probably never be repaired . . ." (319).

made the world and then left it to run itself by natural law—now produced widespread unbelief in any form of Christianity, especially miracles and the supernatural, and "natural religion" was promoted instead. Hence people deserted the Church in droves: a congregation at St. Paul's Cathedral might number a couple of dozen—on a red-letter day!

Christianity also became the butt of sarcastic humor: the charming Lady Mary Montagu, a friend of the widowed Sarah Churchill and a witty aristocrat, joked that Parliament was considering a Bill to have the word "not" taken out of the Commandments, and placed in the Creed, so as to be more in keeping with the times.

Another feature of the period was an irreligious "no popery," i.e., a political "Protestantism," motivated by fear of Roman Catholicism, from folk who never went to church themselves, who knew little of the theological issues involved, but hated and feared anything remotely Catholic. This was a hangover from the Restoration period in particular when the "Popish Plot" of 1678 (which later turned out to be a hoax), and the tyrannical reign of James II (1685–88) struck panic and terror into the hearts of many. It was therefore easy for anyone with political—and personal—motives to play the "Papist" card to stir up strife, spread scare stories, and ruin anyone's reputation.

Above all was a pathological fear of "enthusiasm"; what today we would call "emotionalism" or "fanaticism," a reaction to the upheavals of the previous century with its Civil War and Puritan Commonwealth, the savage reactions of the Restoration period, and the Glorious Revolution of 1688. Hence any sort of zeal, vitality, and concern for souls was disdained and abhorred in the concern to be deemed "moderate." Sadly, both Anglican and Dissenting ministers succumbed to this prevailing mood, part of the general deadness.

EARLY PREACHING

The Wesleys now began preaching "faith alone" as the way of salvation, and also roundly attacked the doctrine of baptismal regeneration, as George Whitefield had been proclaiming already. For all of them, regeneration was a powerful change from darkness to light, from sin to holiness, wrought by the power of God's Holy Spirit. Hence they insisted that if one did not take up the fight against the world, the flesh, and the devil, and pursue the path of holiness then that person was none of Christ's, no matter that he had received a few drops of water on his head in infancy. This robust challenge to the prevailing "orthodoxy" scandalized many, and they soon found pulpits of the Established Church barred against them as the bishops, annoyed at what they saw as novel doctrines, closed ranks.

Although the pulpits of the Church of England were now off limits to them, the Wesleys continued to preach wherever opportunity presented. However, since George Whitefield had already taken to preaching to large crowds in the open air—on common fields at both London and Bristol, he encouraged the Wesleys into the same work, particularly at Kingswood in Bristol and Blackheath and Moorfields in London. It was with great reluctance that they adopted this practice, due to their scruples over Church of England rules, but for them the need of souls took priority. John recorded in his Journal for June 11, 1739:

> "On Scriptural principles, I do not think it hard to justify whatever I do. God in Scripture commands me, according to my power, to instruct the ignorant, reform the wicked, confirm the virtuous. Man forbids me to do this in another's parish . . . I have now no parish of my own, nor probably ever shall. Whom then shall I hear, God or man? . . . Suffer me now to tell you my principles in this matter. I look upon all the world as my parish . . ."[9]

FACING THE MOBS IN DARKEST ENGLAND

Since the Restoration in 1660, social life had become notorious for violence, such that the country at large was unsafe. Travel in particular, was exceedingly dangerous as highwaymen stalked the primitive roads: these men were not normally the romantic figures or lovable rogues of legend, but ruthless robbers and murderers.

The Wesleys, opposed by both the rectors of the parish churches and many of the local gentry, now went boldly to the most violence-prone regions of the country, and preached the love of God to sinners, the Christ of the cross, and of the Judgment throne; but they constantly faced hostile, stone-throwing mobs. All too often these mobs were stirred up by the local parish parsons, who believed that the Wesleys were not only heretics, but Catholics—or even Jesuits—in disguise. One such place was Wednesbury in the Midlands, where both John and Charles faced such hostile mobs.

---

9. JWJ, vol. 1, 109. This is an excerpt from a letter to certain friends in the Moravian congregation in London.

Part I: Introduction to Wesley's Hymns

Both Charles and John preached there, facing the same violence, and Charles for his part consistently proclaimed, "Behold the Lamb of God!"[10] His well-known verse aptly sums up his theme:

> *His only righteousness I show,*
> *His saving grace proclaim;*
> *'Tis all my business here below*
> *To cry: "Behold the Lamb!"*[11]

The same happened also in a visit to Cornwall in 1743 when Charles went on his own. It was with some trepidation that he embarked, and he expressed himself in verse before preaching:

> *Send forth the everlasting word,*
> *The word of reconciling grace,*
> *That all may know their bleeding Lord,*
> *The freely proffered gift embrace,*
> *Hang on the all-atoning Lamb,*
> *And bless the sound of Jesus's name.*
>
> *Teach me to cast my net aright,*
> *The Gospel net of general grace,*
> *So shall I all to Thee invite,*
> *And draw them to their Lord's embrace,*
> *Within Thine arms of love include,*
> *And catch a willing multitude.*[12]

He traveled through Cornwall, then a hotbed of crime and violence, particularly wrecking (i.e., leading ships on to the rocks, then looting the ship and murdering the survivors), and widespread smuggling. When he preached at St. Ives, rebels broke into the building, smashed the furniture,

---

10. See the account in JWJ, February 18, 1744, vol. 1, 425–27, wherein he gives an account of these events which occurred in the previous month. See also Charles Wesley's hymn in response, "For the Brethren at Wednesbury," in Osborn, vol. 5, 251–52. The first verse is:

> *Dear dying Lamb, for whom alone*
> *We suffer pain, and shame, and loss,*
> *Hear Thine afflicted people groan,*
> *Crushed by the burden of Thy cross,*
> *And bear our fainting spirits up,*
> *And bless the bitter, sacred cup.*

11. Osborn, vol. 5, 112.

12. "Hymn before Setting out for Cornwall," in Osborn, vol. 5, 125–26.

and beat up the women and aged. Charles stood firm, but soon the rioters began quarrelling among themselves, and so the meeting proceeded. Charles then preached powerfully the next day, and also on Sunday, before proceeding to Gwennap and other towns where hungry souls received him with joy. The rioters still pursued them, however, until the Mayor of St. Ives threatened them with police action, something Charles disdained. He rather urged his followers to suffer all things for the sake of Christ, and in the end this admonition won over many former opponents. At the end of 1744 Charles left Cornwall, having seen the Gospel door firmly opened. He was to return many times, and at Gwennap the Gospel had wrought such a powerful result that, he recorded:

> "The whole county is sensible of the change; for last Assizes there was a jail-delivery—not one felon to be found in their prisons, which has not been known before in the memory of man."[13]

Probably the worst encounter with determined and extreme violence came at Devizes in Wiltshire, where in February 1747, Charles faced some of the worst violence he faced in his entire career.[14] Here Edward Innes, the local curate, had stirred up the mob such that they stormed a house where they believed Charles was leading a meeting and preaching. After they had succeeded in smashing windows, blocking the door, turning loose his and other horses, spraying water into the rooms from a hand-operated pump, and creating a general riot through the town which the constables made no effort to quell, even one of his supporters pleaded with him to don a disguise and escape. But the rioters blocked the back door, swearing that they would lay hands on Wesley and kill him. However, eventually the prayers of those inside prevailed and "God made bare His arm": the constable came with his posse, and the riot abated, although when Wesley and his fellow clergyman went into the street to depart, the rioters did not know which one was Wesley. They set bulldogs on his companion, who suffered some injury, but they eventually rode away. A work of God had begun, even there, and Charles felt deeply for the persecuted brethren, and composed a lengthy prayer in verse, one verse reading as follows:

> *Let none forsake the fold, and fly,*
> *Let none through fear their Lord deny,*
> *But stand the fiery hour;*

---

13. CWJ, August 4, 1744.
14. Charles Wesley gives a lengthy account of this in his Journal, CWJ, April 27, 1747.

Part I: Introduction to Wesley's Hymns

> *The greatness of Thy mercy prove,*
> *The truth of Thy redeeming love,*
> *And all-sufficient power.*[15]

For all the persecution, John Wesley was able to report twenty-five years later:

> "The furious prejudice which has long reigned in this town is now vanished away, the persecutors, almost to a man, being gone to their account."[16]

Later in 1747, John summoned Charles to Ireland, where in Dublin clashes and murders were frequent. Yet Charles boldly preached in the open air from the text, "Come unto Me all ye that are weary" (Matt 11:27), and after returning several times to the same venue both common folk and soldiers responded. The Catholic audience also responded positively when Charles quoted Thomas à Kempis. In all, God's blessing attended the gatherings, and when Charles returned to Wales in March 1748 the work was now solidly established, and the community transformed: no riots; no drunkards!

John S. Simon, writing in 1907, observed:

> "The incessant assaults of the mob on the Methodist preachers showed they had reached the masses. With a superb courage ... the Methodist preachers went again and again to the places from which they had been driven by violence until their persistence wore down the antagonism of their assailants. Then, out of the once furious crowd, men and women were gathered whose hearts the Lord had touched."[17]

MARRIAGE AND DOMESTIC LIFE

An *affaire de coeur* took Charles to Wales in 1749: Charles had already met and fallen deeply in love with Sally Gwynne, daughter of Marmaduke Gwynne, and they were married on April 8, that same year. Charles later recorded of his wedding day:

> "Not a cloud was to be seen from morning till night. I rose at four, spent three hours and a half in prayer, or singing, with my

---

15. Osborn, vol. 5, 253–54.
16. JWJ, March 3, 1772, vol. 3, 430.
17. Simon, *Revival of Religion*, 259–60.

brother, with Sally, with Beck. And led MY SALLY to church . . .
My brother gave out the following hymn,

Come, Thou everlasting Lord,
By our trembling hearts adored;
Come, Thou heaven-descended Guest,
Bidden to the marriage-feast!
Sweetly in the midst appear,
With Thy chosen followers here;
Grant us the peculiar grace,
Show to all Thy glorious face."[18]

It proved to be a most happy marriage, and seven children issued from their union; but sadly, only three survived infancy: Charles, Sarah, & Samuel. Sally herself was most happy to accompany her husband on his itinerant evangelistic work, riding behind him on his horse; and she suffered with him the trials of the mob violence, but also the joys of seeing hardened sinners come to repentance and faith in the Savior.

In 1756, however, Charles made what for him was a momentous decision: he gave up itinerant preaching to concentrate on family life on one hand, but also to consolidate the work in Bristol and London. However, there was probably a third motive: that to continue itinerant preaching he likely saw as promoting Methodism in a direction he clearly did not want it to go, i.e., towards separation from the Church of England.[19] At first he settled in a house in Bristol, where he remained until 1771, preaching regularly; then he moved to London.

As a father Charles loved his surviving children, although he had difficulty communicating with them on their level. The model of parental training from his mother (quite naturally) became his own, with not entirely happy results: the parental training model of the early 1700s was not necessarily that of the 1760s. However, the music which Sally taught them became entrenched, and the two boys went on to become highly musical like their mother. The young Sarah, also called Sally, was, however, more moved to poetry and prose than music.

As regards his children's faith commitment, we must sadly record that none of them shared their father's faith and love toward Christ. Indeed, Charles's bitterest experience came from his youngest son Samuel (born

18. CWJ, April 8, 1749 (emphasis original); also in Dallimore, *Heart Set Free*, 157.
19. At least this is Dallimore's theory, Dallimore, *Heart Set Free*, 202–3.

1766): around age twenty, a friend influenced him in the direction of Roman Catholicism, and so the young Samuel duly joined that communion, leaving his father heartbroken. While Samuel remained a Roman Catholic while Charles was alive, after his father's death he ran foul of priestly authority over the right of private judgment, and returned to the Anglican fold. However, one interesting footnote is worthy of attention: Charles's grandson through Samuel, Samuel Sebastian Wesley (1810–76), became an outstanding church musician in the Victorian period, who composed an impressive array of anthems and hymn tunes, e.g., such tunes as "Aurelia," and "Wrestling Jacob," the latter to accompany the hymn, *Come, O Thou traveller unknown.*

CHARLES THE POET AND HYMN-WRITER

Charles imbibed a love for and appreciation of poetry from his father, and from university days he was deeply immersed in great poets of the past (e.g., Shakespeare, Dryden, Milton), and this acquaintance helped to develop his own poetic gifts. However, his poetic productions prior to his conversion were few, but as a result of his conversion his soul was so filled with emotion and love for Christ that he could not speak without expressing himself in spontaneous verse, such that sacred verse, lined with Scriptural language, came forth in torrents. The following examples come from his first post-conversion year, 1739:

> *Jesus, the sinner's friend, to Thee,*
> *Lost and undone for aid I flee,*
> *Weary of earth, myself, and sin—*
> *Open Thine arms, and take me in.*[20]

Then in more familiar lines:

> *No condemnation now I dread,*
> *Jesus, and all in Him, is mine.*
> *Alive in Him, my living Head,*
> *And clothed in righteousness Divine.*
> *Bold I approach the eternal throne,*
> *And claim the crown through Christ my own!*[21]

Or again:

20. Osborn, vol. 1, 83.
21. Ibid., 106.

A Short Biography of Charles Wesley

> *Christ the Lord is risen today!*
> *Sons of men and angels say,*
> *Raise your joys and triumphs high!*
> *Sing, ye heavens, now earth reply, Halleujah!*

Indeed, his whole thoroughly Christ-centered life and soul can be summed up in these lines from his paraphrase of Psalm 45 (see full text below, no. 64):

> *My heart is full of Christ and longs*
> *Its glorious matter to declare!*
> *Of Him I'll make my loftier songs,*
> *I cannot from His praise forbear.*
> *My ready tongue makes haste to sing*
> *The glories of my heavenly King.*[22]

Or in these lines, based on Luke 10:39–42:

> *O that I could forever sit*
> *With Mary at the Master's feet!*
> *Be this my happy choice:*
> *My only care, delight, and bliss,*
> *My joy, my heaven of earth be this:*
> *To hear the Bridegroom's voice.*[23]

In a day such as our own when we hear much about the Holy Spirit, we need to know what a Spirit-filled person looks like and sounds like. Since the Spirit was sent to glorify Christ (John 16:14), here in the hymns of Charles Wesley, where we can observe "a heart full of Christ," we can likewise see one who was indeed "filled with the Spirit," as in Ephesians 5:18–19.

He would often conceive of verse during his many travels on horseback, and when he arrived at his destination he would call for quill and ink to write it down before it slipped his mind.

However, there was one significant period in his life when he produced a prodigious output of verse, i.e., the year 1760–61, when he fell ill with gout. While it sidelined him for several months, he was able to redeem the time by reading through the entire Bible and composing verses on a multitude of texts and passages on his way through, from Genesis to Revelation. The entire collection was published in 1762 as *Short Hymns on Select Passages of the Holy Scriptures* (hereafter *Scripture Hymns*, 1762) in two

---

22. Ibid., vol. 8, 102.
23. Ibid., vol. 4, 342.

volumes. Several of his best-loved hymns come from these meditations, notably "O Thou who camest from above" (on Lev 6:12–13), "A charge to keep I have" (on Lev 8:35), and "Thou Shepherd of Israel and mine" (on Song 1:7). In his preface to this collection, Wesley asserts, "Several of the hymns are intended to prove, and several to guard, the doctrine of Christian perfection. I durst not publish one without the other," but as will be suggested below (Part III.A.3) by this time he was having second thoughts about the perfection doctrine, and his some of his lines are at best ambiguous, if not a clear move away from it.[24]

Elsie Houghton gives this overall assessment:

> "It is clear that Charles Wesley has enriched the whole church by his hymns. If the succession of hymn-writers can be compared to a long range of hills, Wesley is like a towering peak among them ... As David was the sweet psalmist of Israel, Charles Wesley is undoubtedly the hymnist of the English-speaking race."[25]

As to that final phrase, we should note that many of Wesley's hymns have been translated into a multitude of languages and are sung around the world.

ENDEAVORING TO KEEP METHODISM WITHIN THE ESTABLISHED CHURCH

As early as 1744 John Wesley faced the issue of separation from the Established Church, but insisted that Methodism was a society within the Church, a position with which Charles concurred. However, over subsequent years John's views changed, particularly on episcopal succession, which he confessed, "I know to be a fable, which no man ever did or can prove."[26] Hence in 1784, with American independence from Britain now an accomplished fact—both politically from Westminster, and ecclesiastically from the Church of England—he sought to ordain men for the work in America. Then, having been rebuffed by the Bishop of London, he went ahead himself and ordained Thomas Coke as "Superintendent" (not

---

24. Maddox, *Scripture Hymns*, vol. 1; The *Scripture Hymns* occupy vols. 9–13 of the Osborn edition.

25. Houghton, *Christian Hymn-Writers*, 103.

26. See Wood, *Inextinguishable Blaze*, 174. The line is from a letter that he wrote in response to a very distressed Charles, as recorded in Fitchett, *Wesley and His Century*, 414. John had for a long time criticized the Anglican bishops as "mitred infidels."

"bishop") of the American work, and also named Francis Asbury (already in America) as his co-superintendent. Asbury in particular would go on to become an outstanding and forceful evangelist.

Charles, a staunch Churchman, was alarmed and angry at his brother's action, and warned, "Ordination is separation." He was so upset that he refused even to speak to his brother for nearly a year, while he expressed his dismay in a strongly worded letter, and in a piece of sardonic doggerel:

> *So easily are Bishops made*
> *By man or woman's whim!*
> *Wesley his hands on Coke has laid—*
> *But who laid hands on him?*[27]

Charles declared that the partnership was dissolved, albeit not the friendship.[28] John ruefully conceded. Further ordinations soon followed, and so in the end Charles's efforts were in vain: his brother John, though remaining within the Established Church himself, had in effect set up all the machinery for his followers to separate as soon as he was dead. In 1787 his chapels were licensed under the Toleration Act. John died in 1791; then in 1795, under the Plan of Pacification, Methodism became officially what it had been in principle since 1787, a Dissenting denomination. In Britain and its now expanding empire, Methodism joined the ranks of Nonconformity; but in America it became an episcopal body under the leadership of Coke and Asbury.

IN DECLINING YEARS

After his move to London in 1771, Charles preached regularly at Wesley's Chapel in City Road, and also kept up his visitation of the prisoners in Newgate—which he continued almost to the end.

Newgate, near the Old Bailey, had always been a hellhole of misery, and a term there was a slow death sentence due to perpetual ill treatment, and the notorious "jail-fever" or typhus. Rebuilt during the 1770s, then damaged by fire in 1780, it was rebuilt yet again, only to continue its old ways. The jailers there had no regard for the welfare of their prisoners; but Charles would enter their cells, read Scripture, pray and give them

---

27. Cited in Baker, *John Wesley and the CoE*, 273.
28. Fitchett, *Wesley and His Century*, 414.

Part I: Introduction to Wesley's Hymns

comforting words, especially to the condemned, and often composed verse for their comfort as they faced execution, as for example in these verses from 1785:

> *O let the prisoners' mournful sighs*
> *Come up before Thy gracious throne,*
> *Mixed with the blood and dying cries*
> *Of Jesus, Thy beloved Son.*
>
> *Father, regard His powerful prayer,*
> *Who, hanging on the shameful tree,*
> *Doth all our sins and sorrows bear,*
> *And look, through Jesus' wounds, on me!*
>
> *On us the outcasts of mankind,*
> *Who judge ourselves not fit to live,*
> *But mercy hope from Thee to find,*
> *Through Him that gasped in death, "Forgive!"*
>
> *Hear Him, our Advocate with Thee,*
> *Him, and the blood of sprinkling hear;*
> *He poured out all that blood for me!*
> *He doth before Thy throne appear!*[29]

Many a miserable convict went to the gallows confident in the Savior's love and mercy as a result of Charles Wesley's consoling, salvation-oriented ministry.

However, by 1785 he was clearly failing fast: the old fire in his sermons had largely gone (people had even begun to complain!), but he kept up his pastoral visitation. Early in 1788 it was evident that the end was approaching. Then shortly before he died, his own hand being too weak, he asked Sally to pen his final verse:

> *In age and feebleness extreme,*
> *Who shall a sinful worm redeem?*
> *Jesus, my only hope Thou art,*
> *Strength of my failing flesh and heart;*
> *Oh, could I catch a smile from Thee,*
> *And drop into eternity!*

---

29. From "Prayers for Condemned Malefactors," 1785, poem 5, in Osborn, vol. 8, 342.

A Short Biography of Charles Wesley

And "drop into eternity" he did! On March 29, 1788, this man of God quietly slipped away—not diseased, but simply weary and worn out. Since his conversion nearly 50 years before, he had, by his sermons and especially his hymns, truly witnessed the Gospel as "the power of God unto salvation" to multitudes of sinners.

The Methodist Conference minutes of 1788 tersely but affectionately recorded his death:

> "Mr Charles Wesley, who after spending fourscore years with much sorrow and pain, quietly retired into Abraham's bosom. He had no disease, but after a gradual decay of some months, 'The weary wheels of life stood still at last.'"[30]

John was then itinerating in the English Midlands, and a letter informing him of his brother's death only reached him the day before the funeral, April 5th. A fortnight later, while preaching at Bolton, he gave out his brother's hymn, "Wrestling Jacob,"[31] but when he came to the lines,

> *My company before is gone,*
> *And I am left alone with Thee,*

he burst into tears in the pulpit, then sat down, face in hands.[32]

John had wished his brother to be buried in the cemetery behind his chapel in City Road, but Charles, the staunch Churchman, had instead insisted on a tomb in his parish churchyard at St. Marylebone. There he

---

30. Quoted in Dallimore, *Heart Set Free*, 251.

31. The opening verse of this hymn of twelve stanzas, based on Gen 32:24–32, is as follows:

> *Come, O Thou traveller unknown,*
> *Whom still I hold, but cannot see!*
> *My company before is gone,*
> *And I am left alone with Thee;*
> *With Thee all night I mean to stay,*
> *And wrestle till the break of day.*

The (almost) full version of twelve stanzas is in the 1933 *MHB*, no. 339, and an abridged version in no. 340. Isaac Watts gave high praise to these twelve verses: "That single poem, 'Wrestling Jacob,' is worth all the verses which I have ever written." See Dallimore, *Heart Set Free*, 216. The original actually has fourteen verses; see Osborn, vol. 2, 173–76. A note there (173) records the estimate of the hymnist James Montgomery, who rated it among Wesley's highest achievements.

32. Heitzenrater, *Wesley and the People*, 300.

lies, his tomb bearing these lines, which he had already composed as his epitaph:

> *With poverty of spirit blest,*
> *Rest, happy saint, in Jesus rest;*
> *A sinner saved, through grace forgiven,*
> *Redeemed from earth to reign in heaven.*

Meanwhile John, who died in 1791, lies behind the Chapel in City Road, Moorgate; and across the road is Bunhill Fields, the Nonconformist burial ground, where his mother Susannah lies. All three await a glorious resurrection when our Lord returns.

EPILOGUE: SARAH WESLEY

Charles Wesley's wife Sarah (known affectionately as "Sally"), nearly 19 years his junior, outlived her husband by 34 years. The Methodist Bookroom granted her an annuity of £50 per year, mostly royalties from the sale of his hymn-books. She also received assistance from the good friend of both Charles and Sarah, viz. Lady Selina, Countess of Huntingdon. Sarah finally died in 1822 at the age of 96, and she lies next to her husband in the Garden of the Old St. Marylebone Parish church. The Charles-and-Sarah union constituted for most Methodists the ideal of a strong marriage and a stable and loving family.

3

Notes on Charles Wesley's Sacred Poetry

For the Wesleys, poetry was the handmaid of piety, as he forthrightly states at the beginning of his Preface to the 1780 *Collection*:

> "For many years I have been importuned (i.e., begged) to publish such a Hymn Book as may be used in all our congregations throughout Great Britain and Ireland."

Then in his conclusion he further insists:

> "When Poetry thus keeps its place, as the handmaid of Piety, it shall attain, not a poor perishable wreath, but a crown that fadeth not away."[1]

He furthermore boasted:

> "In what other publication of the kind have you so distinct and full an account of scriptural Christianity...?" Indeed, "this book is, in effect, a little body of experimental and practical divinity."[2]

This was no empty boast for the time, since Wesley had gone well beyond the fine work of his predecessor Isaac Watts, and the fleeting attempts of various hymnists in the previous century. Indeed, although Bernard Manning compared both the 1904 and 1933 Methodist Hymn Books unfavorably with the earlier collections of the nineteenth century, in its day many

---

1. H&B, 73, 75.
2. Ibid., 74.

Part I: Introduction to Wesley's Hymns

Christians—even non-Methodists—considered the 1933 *Collection* to be the "Rolls Royce" of hymnals.

Moreover, the Wesleys sought to produce the best poetry possible, since it was to be used for the glory of the Triune God. John Wesley also wrote towards the end of his Preface to the 1780 *Collection*:[3]

> "May I be permitted to add a few words with regard to the poetry? Then I will speak to those who are judges thereof, with all freedom and unreserve. To these I may say, without offence:
>
> In these hymns there is no doggerel, no botches, nothing put in to patch up the rhyme, no feeble expletives;*
>
> Here is nothing turgid or bombast(ic) on the one hand, nor low and creeping on the other;
>
> Here are no *cant* expressions, no words without meaning. Those who impute this to us know not what they say. We talk common sense (whether they understand it or not) both in verse and prose, and use no word but in a fixed and determinate sense;
>
> Here are (allow me to say) both the purity, the strength, and the elegance of the English language—and at the same time the utmost simplicity and plainness, suited to every capacity;
>
> Lastly, I desire men of taste to judge—these are the only competent judges—whether there is not in some of the following verses the true spirit of poetry, such as cannot be acquired by art and labour, but must be the gift of nature. By labour a man may become a tolerable imitator of Spenser, Shakespeare, or Milton, and may heap together pretty compound epithets, as 'pale-eyed,' 'meek-eyed,' and the like. But unless he is born a poet he will never attain the genuine *spirit of poetry*." (Emphasis JW's)

*N.B. Expletives did not denote swear-words in the eighteenth century.

On this last point one may wonder why the great evangelist has not allowed for a genuine spiritual gift (*charisma*) as the explanation for Charles's poetic genius, rather than merely "the gift of nature." While he displayed early some talent in this regard, it was only after his conversion in 1738 that his verse came forth like a flood, and from the start it was of the highest quality. I have no hesitation in saying that Charles was possessed of a particular charisma, one that served well the great revival of the eighteenth century.

3. Ibid.

This pre-eminently must be the explanation of his genius. And while it may not be quite true to say that "Methodism was born in song,"[4] it remains true that when Methodists found the grace of God through Christ the Savior they began to sing, and it was Charles Wesley, by the grace of God's Holy Spirit, who put new songs in their mouths, "songs of praise to our God" (Ps 40:3).

As to the other points which John Wesley postulates, we can observe the desire to produce the very best—no doggerel, no trite or hackneyed expressions, nothing of the soppy sonnets of romantic poets, still less of anything banal or trivial, nor of the manifold "vain repetitions" which we so often hear in churches today.

A. METER

Isaac Watts worked with a very limited range of meters: mostly short, common, long (and their doubles), and occasionally 6.6.6.6.8.8. Wesley, however, writes in these, but also in a plethora of other meters: around one hundred in all, from 5.5.5.11. to 10.10.11.11. and also some peculiar meters, with a whole range in between. Many of these are of his own making, e.g., the complex 7.6.7.6.7.7.7.6., as in the following sample, based on Deuteronomy 33:26–29 (from *Hymns and Sacred Poems*, 1742);[5] Tune: Jeshurun:

None is like Jeshurun's God,	
So great, so strong, so high;	
Lo, He spreads His wings abroad,	Ps 18:10; 91:4
He rides upon the sky:	Ps 68:4, 33
Israel is His first-born son;	Exod 4:22; Hos 11:1
God, th'Almighty God, is thine;	Gen 17:1–2
See Him to thy help come down,	Ps 46:1; 115:9
The excellence Divine.	1 Pet 2:9
Blest, O Israel, art thou!	Num 22:12; 23:8
What people is like thee?	Num 23:9
Saved from sin by Jesus, now	1 Thess 1:10
Thou art and still shalt be;	1 Thess 5:23–24

4. As in the Preface to the 1933 *MHB*.
5. Osborn, vol. 2, 305–7.

Part I: Introduction to Wesley's Hymns

Jesus is thy sevenfold shield,	Ps 84:11; Rev 5:6
Jesus is thy flaming sword;	Rev 19:15
Earth, and hell, and sin shall yield	Rev 1:18
To God's almighty Word.	Phil 2:10–11

Other meters will receive comment in the following pages, where they occur.

B. ACCENT

Wesley is also flexible with accent in his meter: at once he can write in *trochaic* meter, where the accent falls on the primary syllable, as in this familiar hymn:

   /   /   /   /   /   /   /   /
Je-su, lov-er of my soul, Let me to Thy bo-som fly

At other times he will use *iambic* meter, where the accent falls on the second syllable, as in these lines from *Rejoice! The Lord is king*:

     /   /   /   /   /   /
Je-sus the Sav-iour reigns, The God of truth and love

     /   /   /   /   /   /
When He had purged our stains, He took His seat above.

At still other times he will combine the two, where e.g., a six-syllable iambic line follows a seven-syllable trochaic line, and thus the stressed final syllable of the first line links with the unstressed syllable of the following line, making for a smooth flow from one line to the next, as in this example:

   / /   /   /
Oft I in my heart have said:

     /   /   /
Who shall ascend on high,

   /   /   /
Mount to Christ, my glorious Head,

   /   /   /
To bring Him from the sky?

Another feature of Wesley's verse is Biblical-style antithetic parallelism, where the matching second line is opposite in meaning to the first, then the following lines parallel these in an overall chiastic or inverted arrangement, i.e., ABB^1A^1—again, a pattern from Biblical verse:

> *Just and holy is Thy name* (A),
>   *I am all unrighteousness* (B),
>   *False and full of sin I am* (B^1),
> *Thou art full of truth and grace* (A^1)

Thus we see first the Savior, and then (in hushed tones) the sinner, and again in a parallel line; but after that we are back again to the Savior—in triumphant tones.

Then he employs the more complex *dactylic* and *anapaestic* meters. The former has a stress on the first syllable, followed by two unstressed syllables; the latter is the reverse case, where the stress follows two unstressed syllables.

An example of *dactylic* meter—at least in part—is the famous "And can it be," sometimes reputed to be Charles's conversion hymn, which was indeed written at the same time. Wesley rarely used fully dactylic lines, and here he begins the line with a dactyl, the remainder being iambic:

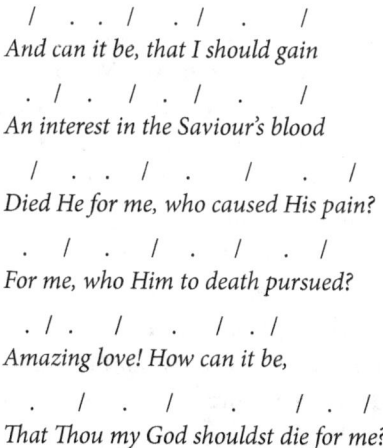

Here the first half of the first and third lines are dactylic, the remainder simple iambic, and the response lines 2 and 4 are likewise iambic, making for a smooth, uninterrupted flow from the first line to the second, and the third to the fourth. Yet for all the mixtures and complexities the lines run fluently from one to the next! As to content, again we have words which beautifully but majestically express the sinner's experience of conversion,

Part I: Introduction to Wesley's Hymns

but at the same time do so in sound theology such that the most Reformed of theologians could not at all object to, but enthusiastically endorse.

The *anapaestic* meter is, as stated, the reverse of dactylic, as in this hymn with overtones of Psalm 23. Meter: 8.8.8.8 D

        /   /   /
Thou Shepherd of Israel and mine,
     /   /   /
The joy and desire of my heart,
      /   /   /
For closer communion I pine,
   /   /   /
I long to reside where Thou art,

The full text of this rich and delightful gem is found in Hymn no. 95 (below).

C. SCRIPTURAL LANGUAGE AND ALLUSIONS

As noted above, Wesley claimed his *Collection* as "a body of experimental and practical divinity," and as such it breathes Scripture in every line. "The heart of Wesley's religion is sound doctrine," remarks Manning—sound doctrine which captures the language of the Gospels, Acts, Epistles, and the Revelation, and all this is enshrined in the hymns of Charles Wesley.[6] Methodism never had an official Creed or Confession, but their hymnbook was their *de facto* confession in verse and song.

Charles Spurgeon once remarked of the Puritan John Bunyan (of *Pilgrim's Progress* fame): "Prick him anywhere and his blood is Bibline: he cannot speak without quoting a text." The same could well be said of Charles Wesley: he cannot speak without breaking into verse; and he cannot compose verse without it being lined with Scripture quotations and allusions. The following two examples highlight this all-pervasive aspect:

"O Thou, who camest from above"

Overall, this hymn is based on Leviticus 6:12–13, as follows:

---

6. Manning, 75–76.

"This is the law for the burnt offering . . . The fire on the altar shall be kept burning on it. It shall not go out, but the priest shall burn wood on it every morning, and he shall lay out the burnt offering on it, and offer up in smoke the fat portions . . . Fire shall be kept burning continually on the altar; it is not to go out."

It is therefore a prayer to the great High Priest to kindle and maintain the fire of His Holy Spirit within him, and so energize him, body and soul, for Christian life and service, until life's end. From *Scripture Hymns*, 1762, vol. 1.[7] Meter: L.M.

Hymn	Scriptural References
O Thou who camest from above	John 3:13, 8:23
The pure, celestial fire to impart,	Matt 3:11
Kindle a flame of sacred love	Acts 2:3; Eph 3:17
On the mean altar of my heart.	Rom 12:1; Ps 131:1
There let it for Thy glory burn	Ezek 1:27–28
With inextinguishable blaze;	Exod 27:20; Jer 20:9
And trembling to its source return,	Ps 2:11; Phil 2:12
In humble prayer and fervent praise.	Rev 5:8; Heb 13:15
Jesus, confirm my heart's desire	Ps 84:2; Rom 10:1
To work, and speak, and think for thee;	Phil 2:12–13; Rom 12:1–2
Still let me guard the holy fire,	Lev 6:9–10; Rom 15:16
And still stir up Thy gift in me.	2 Tim 1:6; 1 Cor 12:7–8
Ready for all Thy perfect will,	Rom 12:2; Eph 5:10
My acts of faith and love repeat,	Gal 5:6; 1 Tim 1:14
Till death Thy endless mercies seal,	Ps 116:15; Eph 4:30
And make the sacrifice complete.	2 Tim 4:6, 8; Phil 1:23

Note that "the flame of faith can be lit from outside and above—it is the gift of the Holy Spirit."[8] Tradition has it that when the aging John Wesley was asked about his own state of sanctification, he summed it up in verses 3 & 4 of this hymn. Also, the stirring up of the Divine gift (2 Tim 1:6) was

---

7. Osborn, vol. 9, 58–59.

8. H&B, 474—notes to Hymn 318.

one of Wesley's key texts, and it became one of the standard questions for ordinands into the Methodist ministry.[9]

"Happy the man that finds the grace"

This comes from *Hymns for those that Seek, and those that Have Redemption in the Blood of Jesus*, 1747.[10] This hymn is basically a paraphrase of the "Praise of Wisdom" passage in Proverbs 3:13–18, "Blessed is the man who finds wisdom, and the man who gains understanding." However, there are many other texts and allusions woven into its lines, particularly from the New Testament. Wesley sees in this passage Christ as the supreme Wisdom, and the Source of all riches and blessing for the believer. Meter: L.M.

Happy the man that finds the grace,	Matt 7:7, 13:44
The blessing of God's chosen race,	Isa 44:3, 65:23; 1 Pet 2:9
The wisdom coming from above,	Jas 3:17
The faith that sweetly works by love.	Gal 5:6; Col 1:4
Happy beyond description he,	Matt 13:16–17
Who knows, the Saviour died for me,	Gal 2:20
The gift unspeakable obtains,	2 Cor 9:15; 1 Pet 1:8
And heavenly understanding gains.	Prov 2:6; 1 John 5:20
Wisdom divine! Who tells the price	Matt 13:45–46
Of wisdom's costly merchandise?	Prov 2:4
Wisdom to silver we prefer,	Prov 8:10–11; Matt 13:44
And gold is dross compared to her.	Prov 8:19; Ps 19:10, 119:72
Her hands are filled with length of days,	Ps 34:11–15;
True riches, and immortal praise:	Luke 16:11;
Riches of Christ on all bestowed,	Eph 1:7–8, 3:8
And honour, that descends from God.	1 Kgs 3:11–13; Rom 2:7; Heb 2:7

---

9. Ibid. See also Kimbrough, *Lyrical Theology*, 82, who makes a similar report in regard to this hymn as summing up Wesley's spiritual experience.

10. Osborn, vol. 4, 234–35. The original has a total of nine verses; nos. 4, 5, 8 are omitted here.

To purest joys she all invites,	John 16:24; Rom 14:17
Chaste, holy, spiritual delights;	Ps 37:4, 119:143
Her ways are ways of pleasantness,	Jer 6:16; Heb 10:20
And all her flowery paths are peace.	Luke 1:79
Happy the man who wisdom gains;	Jas 1:5
Thrice happy who his guest retains;	Rev 3:20
He owns, and shall forever own,	Dan 7:18
Wisdom, and Christ, and heaven are one.	Luke 2:40; 1 Cor 1:30; Col 2:3

Accordingly, all the hymns in this collection have Scripture references attached—not to every line, but at least two or three references (sometimes four, five, or six, depending on the number of lines) to each verse. These are intended in particular as an aid to Bible study, but readers can feel free to add to this list. More broadly, the Scripture references are added to serve the cause of Christian truth: poetry set to music is intended to convey the truths which are held among us (cf. Luke 1:1), of which we see an outstanding example in 1 Timothy 3:16, as follows:

> *God[11] was revealed in the flesh,*
> *Was vindicated in the Spirit,*
> *Seen by angels,*
> *Proclaimed among the nations,*
> *Believed on in the world,*
> *Taken up in glory.*

In this short verse (in the Greek manifesting a metrical and rhythmic structure) we have statements on the Incarnation, Christ's proclamation as Son of God by the Spirit (cf. Rom 1:4), Gospel proclamation, faith unto salvation, and the Ascension. This is the sort of thing Christian verse should be, and the many Scripture references above demonstrate how Wesley shows the way in this regard.

---

11 It has become fashionable to read "He who . . ." at this point, following Codex Alexandrinus (A) and certain other early manuscripts. However, Codex A, one of the earliest and best witnesses for the Pastoral Epistles, on closer examination with the aid of high-resolution photography, actually does read "God" here (ΘΣ, with the *nominum sacrum* overline), in line with early correctors of the other uncial manuscripts. See the British Library on-line reproduction at
  http://www.bl.uk/manuscripts/Viewer.aspx?ref=royal_ms_1_d_viii_fs001r#
  p.120, first column, eighth line from top.

4

Music for the Hymns[1]

CHARLES WESLEY WAS HIGHLY musical himself; likewise his wife Sally, and they inspired the same love through the family. Just as he sought to compose sublime, Christ-honoring verse, Charles also sought to have correspondingly good music for his hymns, yet music which at the same time the common people could sing.

However, there is a persistent and popular myth that Wesley set his hymns to the "honkytonk" tunes from the tavern and the burlesque theatre as a means of evangelism and to relate Gospel truths to the masses. This idea has been repeated and quoted time and again *ad nauseam*—especially when allied with the rhetorical canard, "Why should the devil have all the best tunes?"—until nobody knows from where the notion originated, or how it came to be so pervasive. But mythical it is! As Bready forcefully remarks in this connection regarding the music of Wesley's hymns:

> "The popular hymns and choruses of the Revival contained no trace of ranting jingo or syncopated clamour: they bore no kinship to the uproar and fury of modern jazz, to the stupid insipidity of radio 'crooning' ... On the contrary, this new hymnody, born of a new and vital experience, was expressive of noble aspirations: it strove to penetrate the purpose, the meaning and end of life ..."[2]

---

1. Much (though by no means all) of the material in this section has been obtained from H&B, Appendix J.

2. Bready, *England before and after Wesley*, 273.

Indeed, for Wesley the glory of God was paramount; hence just as poetry for him was the handmaid of piety, so also was quality music—and nothing but the best would do.

At first the tunes from the Scottish Metrical Psalter were adopted for the hymns, but as Wesley ventured from the common meter and long meter of most of these compositions, and into more varied and complex meters, the Scottish metrical tunes proved inadequate. The Wesleys then turned to and adopted tunes from Luther and the Reformation musicians, notably the tune "Kingswood," from the *French Psalter* of 1561, and "Leeds," a chorale dating back to 1554. Another prime source was the music which the Moravians sang in their meetings, derived in large part from the growing German chorale tradition (some of which traced back to Luther), notably such tunes as "Amsterdam," "Fetter Lane," "Love-Feast," "Old German," et al.[3] John Wesley picked up some of these tunes when he visited the Moravian community at Herrnhut in 1738, and through continuing contacts in England. These German tunes constitute a solid contribution to Wesley's *Sacred Harmony* of 1780 (see below).

One of Wesley's early converts, a Mrs. Priscilla Rich, introduced him to a man also converted under Wesley's preaching, viz. the Saxony-born John Frederick Lampe (1703?–51), a talented musician whose wife Isabella was related by marriage to the composer Thomas Arne, and who associated with Arne in many concert performances. However, after his conversion Lampe composed many tunes for Charles Wesley's hymns, some of which then passed into the standard repertoire of Methodist hymnody. His first publication of tunes was a set entitled *Hymns on the Great Festivals*, 1746, to accompany Charles Wesley's collection of the same year on this same theme. Although Lampe died in 1751, his tunes still exerted a powerful influence on the Methodist movement as a whole, and around twenty tunes in *Sacred Harmony* come from Lampe. The 1933 *MHB* still retained two of Lampe's tunes: the simple long meter tune, "Invitation" (no. 496, otherwise known as "Kent" or "Devonshire"), and the more complex tune, "Dying Stephen" (7.7.4.4.7 D; no. 411).

Wesley also turned to the great composers of the previous century: Sir Henry Purcell and Jeremiah Clarke, and likewise to the great church musicians of former periods. Among the latter were Thomas Tallis (1505–85),

---

3. Catherine Winkworth (1827–78) in the nineteenth century imported more of this tradition into Britain as a result of her residence in Dresden, Germany and contacts with German Christians. See Julian, vol. 2, 1287.

Part I: Introduction to Wesley's Hymns

and Orlando Gibbons (1583–1625)—church musicians of the Elizabethan and Jacobean periods respectively. Closer to his own time there were first the popular composer Thomas Arne (1710–78), and the German Andreas Roner, a music master and associate of Handel, who had produced in 1721 *A Collection of Psalms and Hymns by Mr Addison and Sir John Denham, Set to Music in a New Method*. Martin Madan, an Anglican clergyman, also composed some tunes for Wesley's *Sacred Harmony*, but by far the largest contributors were those of Lampe, the Scottish psalm tunes, and the German tunes, as can be seen below.

One composer, however, deserves particular mention: viz. the great musician of the age, the famous German immigrant Georg Friedrich Händel. In the aftermath of his serious illness in 1741 (when he composed *The Messiah*), he became a much more devout Christian, and likewise became very interested in Wesley's hymns, now coming to public notice. In all he composed about 40 tunes specifically for them, one notable example being the tune "Gopsal," to the hymn "Rejoice the Lord is King" (see below). Some tunes in *Sacred Harmony* also seem to derive from Handel's early operas (prior to 1742), although the attributions are uncertain. Charles Wesley, as a musical person himself, was a great admirer of Händel, and it is possible the two met at the home of Mr. and Mrs. Rich, but this too is uncertain.[4] Whatever, both Wesleys were greatly moved by the arias of *The Messiah*, and later editions of Wesley's 1780 *Collection* included some of Händel's tunes, something Charles would have thoroughly endorsed. A notable example in this respect is "Bradford," adapted from the aria from *The Messiah*, "I know that my Redeemer liveth" (below).

In addition, Thomas Butts, Wesley's book-keeper, figures in the development of the musical side of Wesley's hymn-books: he almost certainly worked with Lampe's tunes in the compilation and setting of the music for Wesley's *Sacred Harmony*. Butts established his own music publishing operation in the 1750s; and his *Harmonia Sacra* of 1754, intended as an accompaniment for Wesley's *Hymns and Spiritual Songs* of 1753, proved popular and useful, and went through further editions in 1765 and 1770.

In all, only two tunes in Wesley's *Sacred Harmony* of 1780 could be described as from the popular idiom of the day, and even those came from recognized composers of the age: (i) "Händel's March," from Händel's opera *Ricardo Primo* (1719); and (ii) "Judgment," adapted from an air by

---

4. See Van Til, *George Frideric Handel*, 223–25.

the popular composer Henry Carey, in turn composed for a naval hero, Admiral Vernon.

In brief, the time-line of Wesley's tune publications is as follows:

1742: The initial publication, *A Collection of Tunes, set to Music, as they are commonly sung at the Foundery*. (Hereafter *The Foundery Collection*. The Foundery was the original meeting place for the Methodists in London.)

1753: A collection of tunes accompanied with John Wesley's *Hymns and Spiritual Songs for the use of Real Christians of all Denominations*.

1761: *Sacred Melody, or a Choice Collection of Psalm and Hymn Tunes*, intended as a companion to *Select Hymns with Tunes Annext*. This contained 102 tunes, and included in this publication were both directions for congregational singing, and introductory lessons ("The Gamut") outlining the principles of music for the musically illiterate: the basic musical scales, timing and rhythm (2:4, 3:4, 4:4, etc.), the basics of musical notation (quavers, crotchets, and minims, etc.), and guidelines for singing.[5] Wesley insists, "I want the people called Methodists to sing true the tunes which are in common use among them."[6]

In his *Directions for Singing*, Wesley *inter alia* urges:

> "Sing *lustily* . . . lift up your voice with strength; Sing *modestly*. Do not bawl, so as to be heard above . . . the rest of the congregation; Sing *in time* . . . Do not run before nor stay behind it; Above all, sing *spiritually*. Have an eye to God in every word you sing." (Emphases his)[7]

Hence Wesley's approach was not to accommodate his congregations downwards to a "lowest common denominator" of popular jingles, but to raise them to a higher level through musical education, so that they all could sing tunefully and intelligently to the glory of God.

1780: *Sacred Harmony: A choice Collection of Psalms and Hymns set to Music in two or three parts for the Voice, Harpsichord and Organ*, a companion volume to the *Collection of Hymns for the use of the People*

---

5. H&B, Appendix F, 739–64.
6. Ibid., Appendix E, 738.
7. Ibid., Appendix H, 765.

called *Methodists* of the same year. The collection contains 104 tunes in 31 different meters, but some are used several times.[8]

While not an exhaustive analysis, the following list gives a fair indication of the main sources and authorship of the majority of the tunes in *Sacred Harmony*:

John F. Lampe: 19 (of which four are uncertain but probable)

Moravian and German chorales: 16 (two uncertain)

Georg F. Handel: 4 (two uncertain)

Thomas A. Arne: 4 (one uncertain. Three are included in the 1933 *MHB*)

Jeremiah Clarke: 2 (one uncertain)

Reformation and Elizabethan periods: 6

Andreas Roner: 2

Sir Henry Purcell: 1

As to the remainder of the tunes, apart from the many Scottish Psalm tunes, these are folk melodies from the various regions where the Wesleys traveled: Cornwall, Wales, Ireland, and the English Midlands. Then Lampe, and in turn Butts, apparently adapted and uprated these tunes for sacred use.

However, the tunes in *Sacred Harmony* do not tell the whole story. On one occasion before he began preaching, John Wesley started to sing a hymn to the tune of the Hero's March from Handel's oratorio *Judas Maccabaeus*,[9] a tune which went on to obtain a settled place in Methodist hymn-books, and one which is today regularly used for Edmond Budry's hymn, "Thine be the glory."

A final point in this connection: in the year prior to the 1780 *Collection*, John Wesley published "Thoughts on the Power of Music," wherein he gave his opinion that of all the components of music, i.e., melody, harmony, and rhythm, melody should be primary, as that alone could "move the passions." "Modern music" (i.e., of the 1770s), he complained, stresses harmony and counterpoint rather than melody, and consequently fails to excite passion.[10] One may wonder whether, if Wesley were here today, he would make the same observation, i.e., that guitarists who strum chords

---

8. Ibid., 772.

9. JWJ, entry for March 29, 1774, vol. 4, 9. The tune in question is the chorus, "See the conquering hero comes," celebrating the arrival of Judas Maccabaeus at Jerusalem.

10. H&B, Appendix I, 766–67.

but show little knowledge of horizontal melody, "the due arrangement of notes" as Wesley put it, likewise fail to move the emotions. They may indeed move hearers to *carnal* passions (sensuous gyrations and arm-waving), but whether to *holy* responses of the soul, and wholesome desires is to be doubted. Put another way, both sanctity and beauty have disappeared from the heavily syncopated music of our present times—and some of that is due to the lack of tuneful melody (and also to appreciation of Christian truths); and while Wesley may have been one-sided in his dismissive comments about harmony and counterpoint, there is little of that either in much of the modern genre of music.

Here are two tunes for Wesley's hymns either by or adapted from Handel:

BRADFORD, CM

Arranged from George F. Handel, 1741

Public Domain
Courtesy of the Cyber Hymnal™

Part I: Introduction to Wesley's Hymns

GOPSAL

G. F. Handel

(public domain)

MUSIC FOR THE HYMNS

Here also is one of Lampe's tunes, "Dying Stephen"

DYING STEPHEN, 77.87D

John Frederick Lampe, 1746

Public Domain
Courtesy of the Cyber Hymnal™

PART II

Psalms and Hymns arranged according to the Christian Year

Psalms and Hymns with Introductory Notes

A. Morning and Evening

We begin with two psalms for each day, one each for morning and evening.

1. Psalm 30:1–5

A morning Psalm. From *The Arminian Magazine*, 1797. Meter: 7.7.7.7.D. Tunes: Hollingside; Love Feast; St. George's Windsor.

1. Lord, I will exalt thy grace,	Eph 1:6–7
Grace which hath exalted me;	
Me Thou hast vouchsafed to raise,	Eph 2:6
Sunk in sin and misery;	
But Thine own Thou wouldst not leave,	Heb 13:5
Wouldst not let my foes prevail,	
Me Thou dost the victory give,	1 Cor 15:57
Victory over earth and hell.	
2. Sick of sin, to Thee I cried,	Ps 130:1–3
Thee, my loving Lord and God!	
Thou the medicine hast applied,	Isa 1:18
Healed me by Thy balmy blood.	Jer 8:22
Thou, omnipotent to save,	
Hast redeemed my soul from death,	Ps 103:4

Part II: Psalms and Hymns arranged according to the Christian Year

> Snatched it from the infernal grave,   Zech 3:2
> Kept it from the gulf beneath.

> 3. Sing, ye saints, unto the Lord,
> Thank the Lord our Righteousness;   Jer 23:6
> All His faithfulness record,
> All His power and pardoning grace: Mic 7:18
> Quickly is His anger past,   Ps 103:9
> Never doth His grace remove;
> Long as life His love shall last,   Rom 8:38–39
> Life eternal is His love.

> 4. If He seem awhile to chide,   Isa 57:16
> Leave us a whole night to mourn,
> Yet the veil is cast aside,   2 Cor 3:16
> Yet He hastens to return.   Ps 6:4
> Sure as the return of day
> Chases all the shades of night,   Job 20:8
> Sorrow doth to joy give way,   John 16:20
> Darkness to the Gospel light.   2 Cor 4:4, 6

2. Psalm 63

A Psalm for the Evening. From *The Arminian Magazine*, 1798. Meter: 8.8.6.D. Tunes: Pembroke; Grosvenor; St. Justin.

> 1. O God, Thou art in Jesus mine!   Phil 3:12
> For Thee I sigh, for Thee I pine,
> And pant Thy power to prove.
> My longing soul implores Thy grace,   Ps 119:174
> In a dry, barren wilderness,   Isa 32:2
> Unwatered by Thy love.

> 2. Thee, Thee my restless heart requires,
> And still I am, with strong desires

Psalms and Hymns with Introductory Notes

Thy glorious power to see: Heb 2:9
To see Thee, as I once beheld,
My pardoning God in Christ revealed,   Exod 34:6–7
My Lord, who died for me!   Gal 2:20

3. Thy love doth all delights exceed!
Thy precious love is life indeed;   John 6:54–55
My lips shall sing Thy praise;
My hands I lift in Jesu's name;
My life and strength, and all I am,   Ps 27:1
Shall glorify Thy grace.

4. Thee Lord, my latest breath shall bless;   Luke 2:28–29
My joyful lips shall never cease
To glory in Thy love: Gal 6:14
My soul shall feast on heavenly meat,   John 6:50–51
With sacred joy Thy praise repeat,
Nor envy those above.

5. On Thee I muse with pure delight;   Ps 4:4
Through all the happy hours of night
I lean as on Thy breast: John 13:23–25
Beneath the shadow of Thy wing,   Ps 17:8
Jesus, my Peace, my Joy, I sing,   Eph 2:14
My everlasting rest.   2 Sam 7:1; Matt 11:29

6. My soul pursues and hangs on Thee;
Thy hand upholds and strengthens me;   Ps 145:14
And me Thou still wilt save
From all who seek my soul to slay: Ps 38:12
My foes shall fall by beasts of prey,
Or sink into the grave.   Ps 7:15

7. Who deal in lies and perjury,
Forever stopped their mouths shall be: Rom 3:19

Part II: Psalms and Hymns arranged according to the Christian Year

But who their God revere,
With Jesus kings shall lift their voice,   Isa 49:7
With Jesus confessors rejoice,
And reign triumphant there.   2 Tim 2:12

MORNING AND EVENING HYMNS

3. "Christ, whose glory fills the skies"

The following selection first appeared in *Hymns and Sacred Poems*, 1739, being designated as a morning hymn, which converts would sing before they embarked on the day's activities; and for that matter it is eminently suited for the beginning of the Lord's Day. Meter: 7.7.7.7.7.7. Tunes: Heathlands; Ratisbon; Spanish Chant.

1. *Christ, whose glory fills the skies,*   Isa 6:3
Christ, the true, the only Light,   John 8:12
Sun of Righteousness, arise,   Mal 4:2
Triumph o'er the shades of night;
Day-spring from on high, be near;   2 Pet 1:19
Day-star, in my heart appear.

2. *Dark and cheerless is the morn*   Ps 5:3
Unaccompanied by Thee:
Joyless is the day's return,   John 9:4–5
Till Thy mercy's beams I see,
Till Thou inward light impart,   2 Cor 4:16
Glad my eyes, and warm my heart.

3. *Visit then this soul of mine;*   Luke 1:78
Pierce the gloom of sin and grief;
Fill me, Radiancy Divine;   Heb 1:3
Scatter all my unbelief;
More and more Thyself display,   2 Cor 3:18
Shining to the perfect day.   Prov 4:18

4. "Jesus, the all-atoning Lamb"

This hymn first appeared in *Hymns and Sacred Poems*, 1740, designated as "An Evening Hymn." Meter: C.M. Tunes: Horsley; Kilmarnock; St. Peter.

1. *Jesus, the all-atoning Lamb,*	Heb 9:12
Lover of lost mankind,	
Salvation in whose only name	Acts 4:12
A sinful world can find.	
2. *I ask Thy grace to make me clean;*	1 John 1:7
I come to Thee, my God:	
Open, O Lord, for this day's sin,	
The fountain of Thy blood.	Zech 13:1
3. *Hither my spotted soul be brought,*	Rom 7:18
And every idle word,	
And every word, and every thought	Matt 12:36
That hath not pleased my Lord.	
4. *Hither my actions righteous deemed*	
By man, and counted good;	Isa 5:20–21
As filthy rags by God esteemed,	Isa 64:6
Till sprinkled with Thy blood.	
5. *No! my best actions cannot save,*	Titus 3:5
But Thou must purge e'en them:	
And (if in Thee I do believe)	
My worst cannot condemn.	Rom 8:1
6. *To Thee, then, O vouchsafe me power*	Phil 3:10
For pardon still to flee,	
And every day, and every hour,	
To wash myself in Thee.	Isa 1:16, 18

Part II: Psalms and Hymns arranged according to the Christian Year

5. "Omnipresent God! Whose aid"

Another evening hymn, expressing Wesley's characteristic longing for holiness. From *Hymns and Sacred Poems*, 1749, Part I. Meter: 7.7.7.7.D. Tunes: Benevento; Aberystwyth; Tichfield.

1. *Omnipresent God! Whose aid*	Ps 139:7–12
No-one ever asked in vain,	
Be this night about my bed,	Ps 63:6
Every evil thought restrain;	Mark 7:21–23
Lay Thy hand upon my soul,	Ps 32:4
God of my unguarded hours;	
All my enemies control,	
Hell, and earth, and nature's powers.	Eph 6:12

(two verses omitted)

#4. *O Thou jealous God! Come down,*	Deut 4:24
God of spotless purity,	Hab 1:13
Claim, and seize me for Thy own,	
Consecrate my heart to Thee!	
Under Thy protection take,	Isa 4:6
Songs in the night season give;	Job 35:10
Let me sleep to Thee, and wake,	Ps 3:4–5
Let me die to Thee, and live.	

(one verse omitted)

6. *Loose me from the chains of sense,*	Col 3:5
Set me from the body free,	
Draw with stronger influence	
My unfettered soul to Thee;	John 6:44–45
In me, Lord, Thyself reveal,	Gal 4:19
Fill me with a sweet surprise;	
Let me Thee when waking feel,	
Let me in Thy image rise.	Col 3:10

7. *Let me of Thy life partake,*	
Thy own holiness impart,	Heb 12:10

O that I might sweetly wake
With my Saviour in my heart!   Rom 8:10
O that I might know Thee mine!
O that I might Thee receive!   John 1:12
Only live the life divine,
Only to Thy glory live.   2 Cor 5:15

8. Or if Thou my soul require   Luke 12:20
Ere I see the morning light,
Grant me, Lord, my heart's desire,
Perfect me in love tonight;   1 John 2:5
Finish Thy great work of love,   1 John 4:12
Cut it short in righteousness,
Fit me for the realms above,   Heb 12:23
Change, and bid me die in peace.

Part II: Psalms and Hymns arranged according to the Christian Year

B. On the Importance of Studying Scripture

Daily study of Scripture and prayer was vitally important in the Wesley home, with his mother Susannah supervising, and throughout their lives the Wesley brothers studied Scripture, and prayed earnestly for the work of God's Spirit in their own lives, and in the lives of their hearers. We begin with two psalm selections on this theme, and then three hymns.

6. Psalm 19:7–11

From *The Arminian Magazine*, 1800. Meter: 8.8.8.8.8.8. Tunes: Melita, Stella; Arne's; Mount Sion.

1. The book of covenanted grace	Exod 24:7
Its heavenly origin displays;	
Strong characters of love Divine	
Throughout the sacred volume shine;	Ps 1:2
Jehovah, by His word, is showed	
The glorious legislative* God.	Deut 31:8–9
2. Jehovah's Law all perfect is,	Ps 119:160
Nor can it e'er receive increase;	
Nor can it e'er diminished be—	Deut 4:2
From error and corruption free.	Ps 12:6
It turns the soul which turns to it,	
And makes the man of God complete.	2 Tim 3:17
3. The testimony of the Lord,	
Delivered in His written word,	Isa 8:20
Is sure, inviolably sure,	
And shall from age to age endure;	Ps 119:89–90
The simple with it grace supplies,	
And makes them to salvation wise.	2 Tim 3:15
4. The statutes of the Lord are right;	Ps 119:128
His laws and equity unite;	
Reason Divine in all is showed,	Eccl 12:10–11

Psalms and Hymns with Introductory Notes

Adjusted to His creatures' good;   Rom 7:12
They bring us peace, and power impart,
When written on the obedient heart.   Jer 31:33

5. The Lord's command is plain, and free
From darkness and impurity;   Prov 6:23
It purges and restores the sight,
Guides, by a clear, unerring light,
The sinner in the paths of peace,   Luke 1:79
Convinced of sin and righteousness.   John 16:8

6. The fear of God restrains from sin,   Prov 8:13, 16:6
Is clean, and makes the sinner clean:
The strict, unalterable law,
Which keeps the faithful soul in awe,
Can never lose its binding power,   Matt 5:17–18
But lives and reigns forevermore.   Matt 24:35

7. The judgments of the Lord are true,   Isa 26:9
And all His faithfulness they show:
His perfect equity decrees,   Isa 11:4
To all, rewards or penalties;   Gen 18:25
And soon the righteous Judge shall seal
Their endless doom—in heaven or hell.   Matt 25:46

8. How precious all Thy sayings are!   Ps 139:17
No treasure can with these compare: 2 Pet 1:4
Thy sayings are the soul's repast,
Sweeter than honey to the taste;
They drop like manna from above,   John 6:50–51
Or flow in streams of joy and love.

9. Thy words are my delight and guide,   Ps 1:2
And warn me, lest I start aside:
Thrice happy are Thy servants, Lord;   1 Kgs 10:8
Obedience is our great reward;   Isa 55:6; Heb 11:6

Part II: Psalms and Hymns arranged according to the Christian Year

> *We own, to whom the grace is given,*
> *To do Thy will on earth—is heaven.*   Matt 6:10
> (three more verses omitted)

*While "legislative" today has overtones of "laying down the law" with strident and dispassionate authority(usually of the State), Wesley's use is of Divinely revealed guidance and care for our benefit and well-being—in line with the true meaning of the Hebrew "*torah*"—as the rest of this piece makes clear.

7. Psalm 119:105–112 (Part Nun)

From *The Arminian Magazine*, 1799. Meter: 7.7.7.7.D. Tunes: St. George's Windsor; Maidstone; Syria.

1. LORD, Thy word's unerring light	Prov 6:23
As a lamp my path doth show,	
Guides my steady feet aright;	Luke 1:79
Every one that doth shall know.	
I have sworn to do Thy will;	Neh 10:29
Through Thine all-sufficient grace,	
I shall all my vows fulfil,	Ps 116:14
Shall fulfil all righteousness.	
2. Troubled and distressed I am;	Jas 5:10–11
O be mindful of Thy word!	
Grant the promised help I claim,	
Speak me now to life restored.	Jer 17:14
Thanks for all Thy former grace	
From a willing heart receive;	Prov 10:8
Still instruct me in Thy ways,	
Bid me to Thy glory live.	Jer 9:23–24
3. Lord, my life is in Thy hand,	Ps 31:15
Ever sinking into hell;	
Yet I in thy precepts stand,	
In the paths of duty dwell.	

Me the world hath sought to ensnare,	Ps 140:4–5
Joining with my treacherous heart;	
Yet from Thee I did not err,	Heb 3:14
Would not from Thy statutes start.	

4. I have Thy commandments took	
For my heritage below;	Ps 16:6
From the volume of Thy book	Heb 10:7
All my joys and comforts flow.	John 16:24
In obedience to Thy will	Isa 1:19
I have longed my life to spend,	
All Thy statutes to fulfil,	
Serve and love Thee to the end.	Matt 24:13

HYMNS ON SCRIPTURE STUDY

8. "Spirit of Truth, essential God"

The inspiration or God-breathed character of Scripture is in turn based on the Triune nature of God, since it is the Third Person of the Godhead who gave us the Scripture in the first place, and whose ongoing ministry is essential to its true interpretation. Wesley has grasped this truth beautifully in the following lines. From *Hymns on the Trinity*, 1767, Hymn LXIV, a meditation on 2 Timothy 3:16 and 2 Peter 1:21. Meter: 8.8.8.8.8.8. Tunes: Mozart; Pater Omnium.

1. Spirit of Truth, essential God,	
Who didst Thine ancient saints inspire,	2 Pet 1:21
Shed in their hearts Thy love abroad,	
And touch their hallowed lips with fire;	Isa 6:6–7
Our God from all eternity,	
World without end we worship Thee.	Ps 90:2

2. Still we believe, almighty Lord,	
Whose presence fills both earth and heaven,	Jer 23:24
The meaning of the written word	

Part II: Psalms and Hymns arranged according to the Christian Year

Is by Thy* inspiration given;   2 Pet 1:20–21
Thou only dost Thyself explain
The secret mind of God to man.   1 Cor 2:11–12

3. Come then, Divine Interpreter,
The scriptures to our hearts apply;   John 16:13–14
And, taught by Thee, we God revere,   1 Cor 2:12–13
Him in Three Persons magnify;
In each the Triune God adore,
Who was, and is, forever more.   Rev 1:4, 8

*Wesley's original has, "Is still by inspiration . . ."

9. "Doctrines, experiences to try"

On the sufficiency and sole authority of Scripture Wesley is abundantly clear, as in his meditation here on Isaiah 8:20. There is here no joy for either modern liberalism with its denials of Scripture, or for the modern charismatic movement with its dependence on new revelations of the Spirit (From *Scripture Hymns*, Vol. 1, 1762). Meter: L.M.D. Tunes: Kettering (repeat last line); Stanley.

1. Doctrines, experiences to try,
We to the sacred standard fly,   2 Tim 3:16
Assured the Spirit of our Lord
Can never contradict His word: John 15:26; 16:14
Whate'er His Spirit speaks in me,   1 Cor 2:9–10
Must with the written word agree;   Luke 24:45
If not—I cast it all aside,
As Satan's voice, or nature's pride.

2. The test of truth and righteousness,
O God, Thy records we confess,   Luke 10:25–26
And who Thine oracles gainsay
Have missed the right celestial way: Luke 16:31
Their pardon sure they vainly boast,
In nature sunk, in darkness lost;

Or if they of perfection dream,	Ps 119:96
The light of grace is not in them.	1 Cor 2:14

10. "When quiet in my house I sit"

Here in a more devotional, personal strain, Wesley writes of personal Bible study, a series of four verse meditations on Deuteronomy 6:7. It was included in the 1780 *Collection* (no. 319), in the 1904 *MHB* (no. 264), and also included in the 1933 *MHB* (no. 310). From *Scripture Hymns*, 1762. Meter: 8.8.8.8.8.8. Tunes: Companion; Marienlyst.

1. *When quiet in my house I sit,*	Ps 1:2
Thy Book be my companion still,	
My joy Thy sayings to repeat,	Neh 8:8, 10
Talk o'er the records of Thy will,	
And search the oracles Divine,	John 5:39
Till every heartfelt word be mine.	Ezek 3:2–3
2. *O may the gracious words Divine*	
Subject of all my converse be!	Deut 6:6–7
So will the Lord His follower join,	Rev 14:4
And walk and talk Himself with me;	Gen 5:24
So shall my heart His presence prove,	
And burn with everlasting love.	2 Cor 5:14
3. *Oft as I lay me down to rest,*	Ps 4:8
O may the reconciling word	
Sweetly compose my weary breast!	
While on the bosom of my Lord,	John 21:20
I sink in blissful dreams away,	
And visions of eternal day.	Isa 60:19
4. *Rising to sing my Saviour's praise,*	Ps 145:2
Thee may I publish all day long;	
And let Thy precious word of grace	John 1:16–17
Flow from my heart, and fill my tongue;	

Part II: Psalms and Hymns arranged according to the Christian Year

Fill all my life with purest love,   1 Cor 13:4–7
And join me to the Church above.   Heb 12:23

C. Prayer

John Wesley wrote of his practice of prayer, "I resolve to devote an hour morning and evening to private prayer: no pretense, no excuse whatsoever."[1] He furthermore insists that neglect of prayer is a "grand hindrance of holiness."[2]

11. "Pray without ceasing"

Although the first line recalls 1 Thessalonians 5:17, this is an excerpt from Wesley's paraphrase of Ephesians 6:13ff., entitled "The Whole Armour of God," from *Hymns and Sacred Poems*, 1749. The opening verses of this lengthy paraphrase are the famous hymn "Soldiers of Christ, arise," but the verses 12, 13, 15, 16 are reproduced here. One will notice here a degree of repetition in places, but for all that his words are not wasted, but rather, climactic, as in the last two lines of verse 1. Meter: D.S.M. Tunes: Diademata; Nearer Home.

1. *Pray, without ceasing, pray,*   1 Thess 5:17
Your Captain gives the word;
His summons cheerfully obey,   Mark 14:38
And call upon the Lord:
To God your every want   John 15:7
In instant prayer display;   Phil 4:6
Pray always; pray and never faint;   Luke 18:1
Pray, without ceasing, pray!

2. *In fellowship, alone,*
To God with faith draw near,   Jas 1:5–6
Approach His courts, besiege His throne   Ps 100:4
With all the powers of prayer;
Go to His temple, go,   2 Kgs 19:14
Nor from His altar move;
Let every house His worship know,   Acts 2:46
And every heart His love.

---

1. Cited in Feucht, *Practice of Prayer*, 24.
2. Wesley, *Sermons on Several Occasions*, "Sermon on the Mount," Discourse X.19.

Part II: Psalms and Hymns arranged according to the Christian Year

3. Pour out your souls to God,	Ps 42:4
And bow them with your knees,	
And spread your hearts and hands abroad,	Ezra 9:5
And pray for Zion's peace;	Ps 122:6–7
Your guides and brethren bear	
Forever on your mind;	Ps 122:8
Extend the arms of mighty prayer,	
In grasping all mankind.	
4. From strength to strength go on,	Ps 84:7
Wrestle, and fight, and pray,	Gen 32:24, 28
Tread all the powers of darkness down,	1 Pet 5:8–9
And win the well fought day;	
Still let the Spirit cry	
In all His soldiers: Come!	Rev 22:17
Till Christ the Lord descend from high,	1 Thess 4:16
And takes the conquerors home.	

12. "Jesu, my strength, my hope"

From *Hymns and Sacred Poems*, titled "A Poor Sinner," 1742. Meter: S.M.D. Tunes: Leominster; Fairfield.

1. Jesu, my strength, my hope,	Phil 4:13
On Thee I cast my care,	1 Pet 5:7
With humble confidence look up,	
And know Thou hear'st my prayer.	1 John 5:14
Give me on Thee to wait,	
Till I can all things do,	Isa 40:31
On Thee, almighty to create,	2 Cor 4:6
Almighty to renew.	2 Cor 4:16
2. I rest upon Thy word;	Ps 119:42
The promise is for me;	

Psalms and Hymns with Introductory Notes

My succour and salvation, Lord,	Heb 2:18
Shall surely come from Thee:	Isa 12:2–3
But let me still abide,	
Nor from my Hope remove,	Heb 6:18–19
Till Thou my patient spirit guide	
Into Thy perfect love.	Rom 5:5
#3. I want a sober mind,	1 Pet 1:13
A self-renouncing will,	Matt 16:24–25
That tramples down and casts behind	
The baits of pleasing ill;	1 John 2:15
A soul inured to pain,	
To hardship, grief, and loss;	2 Cor 4:8–10
Bold to take up, firm to sustain,	
The consecrated cross.	Matt 10:38
4. I want a godly fear,	2 Cor 7:1
A quick-discerning eye,	Heb 5:14
That looks to Thee when sin is near,	
And sees the tempter fly:	1 Pet 5:8
A spirit still prepared,	
And armed with jealous care,	Eph 6:18
Forever standing on its guard	
And watching unto prayer.	Matt 26:41
5. I want an heart to pray,	Luke 11:1
To pray and never cease;	Luke 11:5–8
Never to murmur at Thy stay,	1 Cor 10:10
Or wish my sufferings less.	
This blessing above all,	
Always to pray, I want,	Matt 7:7
Out of the deep on Thee to call,	Ps 130:1
And never, never faint.	Luke 18:1
6. I want a true regard,	
A single, steady aim,	

Part II: Psalms and Hymns arranged according to the Christian Year

Unmoved by threatening or reward,	1 John 4:10, 19
To Thee and Thy great name;	Ps 138:2
A jealous, just concern	
For Thine immortal praise:	
A pure desire that all may learn	Ps 51:13
And glorify Thy grace.	Eph 1:6, 12
(one verse omitted)	

D. The Lord's Day

Regular Sunday worship for the Wesleys was supremely important, and Methodist Society meetings were never allowed to clash with Anglican parish services. However, it was not only stated services on Sunday which the Wesleys enjoined, but the entire day. They adopted the Puritan Sunday as their own and taught as much, whereby the Fourth Commandment abides under a change of day, from the seventh day of the week to the first. No less than Christ's resurrection on that day authorizes the change, as is clearly set out in the following selections.

13. Psalm 118:22–29

This version of Psalm 118 sets the tone for Wesley's understanding of the Divine appointment of the Lord's Day. From *Psalms and Hymns*, 1743. Meter: 8.8.8.8.8.8. Tunes: St. Catherine; Aldersgate Street; Madrid.

1. *Jesus is lifted up on high;*	John 12:32–33
Whom man refused and doomed to die,	Luke 23:18, 21
He is become the corner-stone;	Matt 21:42
Head of His church He lives and reigns,	Eph 1:22–23
His kingdom over all maintains,	
High on His everlasting throne.	Heb 1:4, 8:1
2. *The Lord the amazing work hath wrought,*	
Hath from the dead our Shepherd brought,	Heb 13:20
Revived on the third glorious day;	1 Cor 15:4
This is the day our God hath made,	Mark 2:27
The day for sinners to be glad	
In Him, who bears their sins away.	Isa 53:12
3. *Thee, Lord, with joyful lips we praise:*	Ps 63:5
O send us now Thy saving grace;	
Make this the acceptable hour;	2 Cor 6:2
Our hearts would now receive Thee in;	
Enter, and make an end of sin,	Dan 9:24
And bless us with the perfect power.	Eph 1:19

4. Bless us, that we may call Thee blest;	
Sent down from heaven to give us rest,	Luke 24:49
Thy gracious Father to proclaim;	John 15:26
His sinless nature to impart,	Ps 5:4
In every new, believing heart	
To manifest His glorious name.	John 17:6
5. God is the Lord that shows us light;	Ps 36:9
Then let us render Him His right,	
The offering of a thankful mind:	Heb 13:15
Present our living sacrifice;	Rom 12:1
And to His cross, in closest ties,	
With cords of love our spirit bind.	Hos 11:4
6. Thou art my God, and Thee I praise;	Ps 63:1
Thou art my God, I sing Thy grace,	
And call mankind to extol Thy name:	Ps 96:1–3
All glory to our gracious Lord!	Rom 16:27
His name be praised, His love adored,	
Through all eternity the same!	Ps 72:17

HYMNS ON THE LORD'S DAY

14. "Come, let us with our Lord arise"

This admirably lays out Wesley's understanding of the theology of the Lord's Day as having Christ's stamp of authority upon it by virtue of His resurrection. In the final verse Wesley outlines our Christian duties which attach to it. This hymn first appeared in *A Collection of Hymns for Children*, 1763. Meter: 8.8.8.8.8.8. Tunes: Plymouth Dock; St. Catherine; St. Petersburg.

1. Come, let us with our Lord arise,	
Our Lord, who made both earth and skies;	Col 1:16
Who died to save the world He made,	1 John 2:2
And rose triumphant from the dead;	Rom 1:4

Psalms and Hymns with Introductory Notes

He rose, the Prince of life and peace,	Acts 3:15
And stamped the day forever His.	Rev 1:10

2. This is the day the Lord has made,	Ps 118:24
That all may see His love displayed,	
May feel His resurrection's power,	Phil 3:10
And rise again to fall no more;	
In perfect righteousness renewed,	Phil 3:9
And filled with all the life of God.	Eph 3:19

3. Then let us render Him His own,	Ps 116:12–13
With solemn prayer approach the throne,	Heb 4:16
With meekness hear the Gospel word,	Rev 14:6–7
With thanks His dying love record;	
Our joyful hearts and voices raise,	
And fill His courts with songs of praise.	Ps 96:8

4. Honour and praise to Jesus pay	Rev 5:12
Throughout His consecrated day;	Ps 92:2
Be all in Jesu's praise employed,	Acts 2:1, 22–24
Nor leave a single moment void;	
With utmost care the time improve,	
And only breathe His praise and love.	Eph 6:23–24

Amen.

15. "Come, let us join with one accord"

This next selection comes immediately after the previous hymn in the same *Collection of Hymns for Children*, 1763, again for the Lord's Day. Meter: C.M. Tunes: Irish; Nativity; Jackson.

1. Come, let us join with one accord	
In hymns around the throne;	Rev 5:13
This is the day our rising Lord	Luke 24:1, 6
Hath made and called His own.	Isa 58:13

2. This is the day which God hath blessed,
The brightest of the seven;　　　　　　　John 20:19
Type of that everlasting rest　　　　　　　Heb 4:9–11
The saints enjoy in heaven.

3. Then let us in His name sing on,
And hasten to that day,　　　　　　　　2 Pet 3:12
When our Redeemer shall come down,　　Acts 1:11
And shadows pass away.

4. Not one, but all our days below,
Let us in hymns employ;　　　　　　　Eph 5:19–20
And in our Lord rejoicing, go
To His eternal joy.　　　　　　　　　Isa 51:11

16. "Saviour, this sacred day"

This hymn clearly expresses the change of day from the Jewish Sabbath to the Christian Lord's Day. This first appears in *Scripture Hymns*, 1762, where Wesley comments on Matt 12:8. Meter: 6.6.7.7.7.7. Tunes: Irene; Devotion.

1. Saviour, Thy sacred day　　　　　　Rev 1:10
Is subject to Thy sway,
Made Thy pleasure to fulfil;　　　　　　Isa 58:13
Thou, the Son of Man, alone　　　　　　Mark 2:28
Canst, according to Thy will,
Abrogate, or change Thine own.　　　　Gen 2:3

2. Thy love the day designed
A blessing to mankind;　　　　　　　Mark 2:27
But Thy more abundant grace,
Gospel grace unsearchable,　　　　　　1 Cor 15:1–2
Bade the Jewish feast give place,
Fixed the Christian festival.　　　　　　Luke 23:56—24:1

3. Lord of the hallowed day,
Once more Thy power display;   Acts 10:38, 44
Now returning from above,
Change it to that heavenly feast,   Rev 19:7–9
Sabbath of celestial love,
Sabbath of eternal rest.   Heb 4:7–9

Part II: Psalms and Hymns arranged according to the Christian Year

E. Christmas

Christmas comes as the climax of the Advent season, and celebrates the Incarnation, when "the Word became flesh" (John 1:14). Since Christ was born as God incarnate, He was born to be King of kings. Therefore, Psalm 45 is an appropriate psalm for considering the Deity of Christ, His Incarnation, and His future kingdom.

17. Psalm 45:8–17

This first appeared in *Psalms and Hymns*, 1743. These verses, being Wesley's version of Psalm 45, begin at verse 8 in our Bibles. The opening verses will be found below, in the section "Between Trinity and Advent." Wesley here sees Christ as having come for His Church, and bestowing on it all His heavenly blessings. Meter: 8.8.8.8.8.8. Tunes: Giessen; Colchester; Crucifixion.

11. *Sweet is the odour of Thy name,*	2 Cor 2:15–16
Through all the means a fragrance comes;	
Thy garments hide the sinner's shame,	Isa 61:10
Thy garments shed Divine perfumes,	Song 1:12
That through the ivory palace flow,	
The church, in which Thou reign'st below.	Eph 1:21–22
12. *Thy heavenly charms the virgins move,*	2 Cor 11:2
And bow them to Thy pleasing sway;	
They triumph in thy princely love,	2 Cor 2:14
Thy will with all their hearts obey;	Ps 143:10
Revere Thine honourable word,	
The glorious handmaids of the Lord.	Joel 2:29
13. *High above all, at Thy right hand,*	Dan 7:27
Adorned with each diviner grace,	Rev 19:8
Thy favourite queen exults to stand,	
Thy church He heavenly charms displays,	Rev 21:9–11
Clothed with the sun, for glory meet,	Rev 12:1
She sees the moon beneath her feet.	

14. *Daughter of Heaven, though born on earth,*   1 Pet 1:3
Incline thy willing heart and ear;   Ps 119:36
Forget thy first ignoble birth,
Thy people, and thy kinsfolk here;   Gen 12:1
So shall the King delight to see   Isa 33:17
His beauties copied out on thee.

15. *He only is thy God and Lord;*   John 20:28
Worship divine to Him be given,
By all the host of heaven adored,   Luke 2:14
By every creature under heaven;
And all the Gentile world shall know,   Isa 11:10
And freely to His service flow.   Rom 15:9ff.

16. *The rich shall lay their riches down,*   Isa 60:6
And poor become, for Jesu's sake;
Kings at His feet shall cast their crown,   Rev 4:10
And humble suit for mercy make,   Isa 49:23
(Mercy alike on all bestowed)
And languish to be great in God.

17. *Are not His servants kings? And rule*
They not o'er hell, and earth, and sin?   Rev 3:21
His daughter is divinely full   Eph 3:19
Of Christ, and "glorious all within";
All glorious inwardly she reigns,
And not one spot of sin remains.   Eph 5:27

18. *Clothed with humility and love,*   1 Pet 5:5
With every dazzling virtue bright,   Rev 21:9–11
With faith which God vouchsafes to approve,
Precious in her great Father's sight,   1 Pet 1:7
The royal maid with joy shall come,
Triumphant, to her heavenly home.   Isa 35:8–10

Part II: Psalms and Hymns arranged according to the Christian Year

19. *Brought by His sweet attracting grace,*	John 6:44
She first shall in His sight appear	
In holiness before His face,	Eph 1:4
Made perfect with her fellows here:	
Spotless and pure, a virgin train,	
They all shall in His palace reign.	2 Tim 2:12

20. *In lieu of seers and patriarchs old,*	Luke 10:24
Of whom she once did make her boast,	
The virgin-mother shall behold	
Her numerous sons a princely host,	Heb 2:10
Installed o'er all the earth abroad,	
Anointed kings and priests to God.	Isa 61:6; Rev 1:6

21. *Thee, Jesus, King of kings, and Lord*	Rev 19:16
Of lords, I glory to proclaim;	
From age to age Thy praise record,	Ps 89:1
That all the world may learn Thy name:	
And all shall soon thy grace adore,	
When time and sin shall be no more.	Rev 21:4

18. "Rejoice in Jesu's birth"

Christmas verses would not be complete without a rendering of *Isaiah 9:6–7*. Here is Wesley's paraphrase of this passage, from *Scripture Hymns*, 1762. Meter: S.M.D. Tunes: Ascension; Ishmael; Ridge.

1. *Rejoice in Jesu's birth*	Luke 2:14
To us a Son is given,	
To us a Child is born on earth,	
Who made both earth and heaven!	John 1:3
His shoulder props the sky,*	
This universe sustains!	Heb 1:3
The God supreme, the Lord most high,	
The King Messiah reigns!	Rev 11:15

2. His name, His nature soars
Beyond the creature's ken: Phil 2:9–10
Yet whom the angelic host adores, Ps 103:20–21
He pleads the cause of men. Heb 7:25
Our Counsellor we praise,
Our Advocate above, 1 John 2:1
Who daily in His church displays Acts 5:12
His miracles of love. John 14:12

3. The Almighty God is He Rom 9:5
Author of heavenly bliss,
The Father of eternity, Isa 57:15
The glorious Prince of Peace! Zech 9:10
Wider and wider still
He doth His sway extend, Ps 72:8
With peace Divine His people fill,
And joys that never end: Isa 35:10

4. His government shall grow, Luke 1:33
From strength to strength proceed,
His righteousness the church o'erflow, Isa 45:25
And all the earth o'erspread; Zech 9:9, 10
His presence shall increase
The happiness above, Rev 7:16–17
The full, progressive happiness
Of everlasting love. Ps 103:17

*To be taken metaphorically, of course!

HYMNS ON THE INCARNATION

19. "Let Earth and Heaven Combine"

A greater hymn on the mystery of the Incarnation has never been written, although there have been many good ones, both ancient and more recent. Christ is here on one hand "our God contracted to a span," but that resultant combination of Divine and human is an incomprehensible mystery.

Part II: Psalms and Hymns arranged according to the Christian Year

The hymn first appears in *Hymns for the Nativity of Our Lord*, 1746, but was omitted from the 1780 *Collection,* and had to wait until the nineteenth century for inclusion in Methodist hymnals. Meanwhile verse 5, with its lines about bringing our vileness near, and making us all divine, reflects to a degree the Incarnational theology of the Eastern Church (see below, Part III.A.1), in turn possibly due to the mystical, Non-juror influences from his mother Susannah. As it stands it reflects simply the teaching of 2 Peter 1:4, whereby we become "partakers of the Divine nature." Meter: 6.6.6.6.8.8. Tune: Adoration (St. John's); Darwall.

1. *Let earth and heaven combine,*	
Angels and men agree,	Luke 2:13, 20
To praise in songs Divine	
The incarnate Deity,	John 1:14
Our God contracted to a span,	
Incomprehensibly made man.	Luke 1:34–35
2. *He laid His glory by,*	Phil 2:7
He wrapped Him in our clay,	
Unmarked by human eye	2 Cor 5:16
The latent Godhead lay;	John 1:33
Infant of days He here became,	
And bore the mild Immanuel's name.	Isa 7:14; Matt 1:23
#3. *See in that Infant's face*	
The depths of Deity,	Luke 2:28–32
And labour while ye gaze	
To sound that mystery:	Job 11:7–8
In vain, ye angels, gaze no more,	
But fall, and silently adore.	Matt 2:11, 14:33
4. *Unsearchable the love*	
That hath the Saviour brought,	John 3:16
The grace is far above	
Or man or angel's thought;	1 Pet 1:12
Suffice for us, that God we know,	
Our God is manifest below.	1 Tim 3:16

5. He deigns in flesh to appear,	Heb 2:14
Widest extremes to join,	
To bring our vileness near,	Isa 32:4–5
And make us all divine;	2 Pet 1:4
And we the life of God shall know,	John 10:10
For God is manifest below.	

6. Made perfect first in love,	
And sanctified by grace,	1 Thess 5:23–24
We shall from earth remove,	Phil 1:23
And see His glorious face;	Rev 22:4
His love shall then be fully showed	
And man shall then be lost in God.	1 Cor 15:28

20. "All glory to God"

This also first appeared in *Hymns for the Nativity of Our Lord*, 1746. Meter: 10.10.11.11. Tunes: Montgomery; Laudate Dominum.

1. All glory to God, And peace upon earth,	Luke 2:14
Be published abroad At Jesus's birth;	
The forfeited favour Of heaven we find	John 3:17
Restored in the Saviour And Friend of mankind.	1 Tim 1:15

2. Then let us behold Messiah the Lord,	Luke 2:11
By prophets foretold, By angels adored;	Luke 1:69–70
Our God's incarnation With angels proclaim,	
And publish salvation In Jesus's name.	Isa 49:6

3. Our newly born King By faith we have seen,	Matt 2:2
And joyfully sing His goodness to men,	
That all men may wonder At what we impart,	Luke 2:18
And thankfully ponder His love in their heart.	Luke 2:19

Part II: Psalms and Hymns arranged according to the Christian Year

4. What moved the Most High So greatly to stoop?	Phil 2:6–8
He comes from the sky Our souls to lift up;	Luke 19:10
That sinners forgiven Might sinless return	Titus 2:14
To God and to heaven; Their Maker is born.	

5. Immanuel's love Let sinners confess,	Rev 1:5
Who comes from above, To bring us His peace:	John 14:27
Let every believer His mercy adore,	
And praise Him forever, When time is no more.	Rev 19:6–7

21. "Hark! the herald angels sing"

The first two verses differ from the version normally sung today. See discussion below. Meter: 7.7.7.7. Tune: Ephraim; or in 7.7.7.7.D. Tune: Mendelssohn (combining four-line verses into eight-line).

1. Hark how all the welkin rings,	
"Glory to the King of kings,	1 Tim 6:14–15
Peace on earth, and mercy mild,	
God and sinners reconciled!"	Rom 5:9–10

2. Joyful, all ye nations, rise,	Ps 117:1
Join the triumph of the skies;	Rev 7:10–12
Universal Nature, say,	
"Christ the Lord is born today!"	Luke 2:11

3. Christ, by highest heaven adored,	Rev 5:13
Christ the everlasting Lord,	
Late in time behold Him come,	Gal 4:4
Offspring of a virgin's womb.	Matt 1:18

4. Veiled in flesh, the Godhead see,	1 John 4:2
Hail the Incarnate Deity!	
Pleased as man with men to appear	
Jesus our Immanuel here!	Matt 1:21, 23

Psalms and Hymns with Introductory Notes

5. Hail the heavenly Prince of Peace!   Isa 9:6
Hail the Sun of Righteousness!   Mal 4:2
Light and life to all He brings,   John 1:4
Risen with healing in His wings.

6. Mild He lays His glory by,   Heb 2:9
Born, that man no more may die,
Born, to raise the sons of earth,   1 Cor 15:47, 49
Born, to give them second birth.   1 Pet 1:3

#7. Come, Desire of nations, come,   Hag 2:7
Fix in us Thy humble home;
Rise, the woman's conquering Seed,   Gen 3:15
Bruise in us the serpent's head.

#8. Now display Thy saving power,   2 Cor 4:7
Ruined nature now restore;
Now in mystic union join
Thine to ours, and ours to Thine.   John 17:22–23

#9. Adam's likeness, Lord efface,
Stamp Thine image in its place;   Eph 4:24
Second Adam from above,   1 Cor 15:45
Reinstate us in Thy love.

#10. Let us Thee, though lost, regain,
Thee, the Life, the inner man: 2 Cor 4:16
O! to all Thyself impart,
Formed in each believing heart.   Gal 4:19

This hymn originally appeared in *Hymns and Sacred Poems*, Part II, 1739, as "A Hymn for Christmas Day," and readers will immediately note a difference in the opening two verses from the version now commonly sung—usually at Christmas time. The word "welkin" is an old word meaning "vault of heaven," and tradition has it that it was the evangelist George Whitefield who changed the lines to the more familiar version, but that Charles Wesley never approved this change. Certainly in Whitefield's *Collection* of 1753 the change in the opening lines is evident; then in 1760, Martin Madan altered the latter two lines of verse 2 to the familiar "*With the angelic host proclaim . . .*," while in 1807 the Anglican *New Version* added the refrain.[3] We can therefore be grateful that both the opening two lines and lines three and four of the second verse are delivered from their archaic cast to what we sing today.

The original tune setting in the 1780 *Collection* was that of the Easter hymn "Jesus Christ is risen today." The version we now sing was modified by William Cummings in 1856, whereby the four-line verses were combined to the eight-line ones we now sing, and attached to a tune adapted from the composer Felix Mendelssohn:

> Hark! the herald angels sing
> Glory to the new-born King,
> Peace on earth, and mercy mild,
> God and sinners reconciled.
> Joyful, all ye nations rise,
> Join the triumph of the skies;
> With th'angelic hosts proclaim,
> Christ is born in Bethlehem.
>
> Then the refrain:
> *Hark! the herald angels sing*
> *Glory to the new-born King.*

22. "My soul extols the mighty Lord"

Here is Wesley's version of the Magnificat, Luke 1:46–55. This first appears in the original collection of *Hymns and Sacred Poems*, 1739. Meter: L.M. Tunes: Herongate; Maryton; Williams.

1. *My soul extols the mighty Lord,*	1 Sam 2:1
In God the Saviour joys my heart:	
Thou hast not my low (e)state abhorred;	Ps 138:6
Now know I, Thou my Saviour art.	Isa 43:3
2. *Sorrow and sighs are fled away,*	Isa 35:10

---

3. Masters, *Worship in the Melting Pot*, 108. This important book repays careful reflection as a critique of what passes for worship in the modern evangelical church.

Peace now I feel, and joy and rest: John 16:33
Renewed, I hail the festal day,   Ps 122:1–2
Henceforth by endless ages blest.

3. Great are the things which Thou hast done;
How holy is Thy name. O Lord!   1 Sam 2:2; Isa 6:3
How wondrous is Thy mercy shown   Ps 103:17
To all that tremble at Thy Word!   Isa 66:2

4. Thy conquering arm with terror crowned
Appeared the humble to sustain;   Ps 113:7
And all the sons of pride have found
Their boasted wisdom void and vain.   1 Cor 1:19

5. The mighty, from their native sky
Cast down, Thou hast in darkness bound;   Dan 4:31–32
And raised the worms of earth on high   Job 19:26
With majesty and glory crowned.

6. The rich have pined amidst their store,
Nor e'er the way of peace have trod;   Isa 59:8
Meanwhile the hungry souls Thy power
Filled with the fullness of their God.   Eph 3:19

7. Come, Saviour, come, of old decreed!   1 Pet 1:20
Faithful and true be Thou confessed;   Rev 19:11
By all earth's tribes in Abraham's Seed   Rom 4:13
Henceforth through endless ages blest.

Part II: Psalms and Hymns arranged according to the Christian Year

F. Epiphany

In the Western Calendar, Epiphany (January 6th) denotes Christ's manifestation to Israel through His presentation at the Temple. It also marks the visit of the Magi, as recorded in Matthew 2:1–12. In the Eastern Calendar it denotes the Orthodox Christmas.

The incident of the visit of the Magi heralds the universality of God's redeeming plan for the nations; hence the following two psalms are appropriate for the occasion.

23. Psalm 67

First published in 1854, by Rev. H. Fish, from a manuscript in his own personal possession. Meter: 7.6.7.6.7.7.7.6. Tunes: Leamington; Jeshurun.

1. God on us His grace bestow,	
His freely pardoning grace;	Isa 43:25
Bless us from our sins, and show	
The brightness of His face!	Ps 80:3
Let Thy way on earth be shown;	Titus 2:11
Thee let every sinner find,	Luke 18:10
Make Thy great salvation known	Luke 2:30–31
To us, and all mankind.	
2. Let the people praise Thee, Lord,	
The God of truth and grace;	Gen 24:27
Thee, the everlasting Word,	John 1:1
Let all the peoples praise!	Ps 66:8
O give thanks, rejoice, and sing,	
Every creature under heaven;	Col 1:23
Let them triumph in their King,	
And shout their sins forgiven.	Isa 44:22–23
3. Thou shalt judge the nations right,	Rom 2:6–8
Thy equal sway maintain;	Ps 98:9
Rule them by Thy mercy's might,	Isa 40:10
And bless them by Thy reign.	

Let the people praise Thee, Lord,	Isa 42:10, 12
Thee, the God of truth and grace!	
Thee, the everlasting Word,	
Let all the nations praise!	Ps 47:6–7

4. Then to perfect holiness	
The earth her fruit shall have;	Ps 85:12–13
God, our God, His saints shall bless,	
And to the utmost save.	Heb 7:25
God shall perfect us in one;	John 17:23; Eph 4:13
Then the world their Lord shall see,	
Thee the nations all shall own,	
And give their hearts to Thee.	Ps 72:17

24. Psalm 117

From the first collection of *Hymns and Sacred Poems*, 1739. Meter: 8.8.8.8.8.8. Tunes: Worsley; Adam; Dura.

1. Ye nations, who the globe divide,	Isa 66:18–19
Ye numerous nations scattered wide,	
To God your grateful voices raise:	Deut 32:43
To all His boundless mercy shown,	
His truth to endless ages known,	Ps 146:6
Require our endless love and praise.	Ps 146:2

2. To Him who reigns enthroned on high,	Ps 113:5
To His dear Son who deigned to die	John 10:17
Our guilt and errors to remove;	Acts 13:38–39
To that blest Spirit who grace imparts,	John 6:63
Who rules in all believing hearts,	Rom 8:14
Be ceaseless glory, praise, and love!	

Part II: Psalms and Hymns arranged according to the Christian Year

EPIPHANY HYMNS

25. "Sons of men, behold from far"

The following hymn first appeared in 1739, in the first collection of *Hymns and Sacred Poems*, as a Hymn for Epiphany. Meter: 7.7.7.7. Tunes: Savannah; Consecration.

1. *Sons of men, behold from far,*	Isa 11:11–12
Hail, the long-expected Star!	Num 24:17
Jacob's star that gilds the night,	Matt 2:9
Guides bewildered nature right.	
2. *Fear not hence that ill should flow,*	
Wars or pestilence below:	Matt 24:6
Wars it bids and tumults cease,	Ps 46:9
Ushering in the Prince of Peace.	Isa 9:6
3. *Mild He shines on all beneath,*	
Piercing through the shades of death,	Ps 23:4
Scattering error's wide-spread night,	Isa 9:2
Kindling darkness into light.	John 1:5
4. *Nations all, far off and near,*	Isa 57:19
Haste to see your God appear!	Eph 3:8
Haste, for Him your hearts prepare,	
Meet Him manifested there.	Isa 33:17
5. *There behold the Dayspring rise,*	Luke 1:78
Pouring eye-sight on your eyes;	Isa 32:3
God in His own light survey,	
Shining to the perfect day.	Prov 4:18
6. *Sing, ye morning stars, again!*	Job 38:7
God descends on earth to reign,	Luke 1:33–34
Deigns for man His life to employ;	

Shout, ye sons of God, for joy!   Ps 89:5–6

26. "Drawn by Thy grace the sons of night"

Appropriate also is Wesley's rendering of verses from *Isaiah 60*; here verses 3, 4, 5, 6, *and* 9, where the prophet foresees nations and their kings bringing their wealth to worship Israel's God and His Christ. Wesley sees Zion here as the New Testament church, hence the pronouns "thee" and "thy" (small "t"). From *Scripture Hymns*, 1762. Meter: L.M.D. Tunes: L.M.D. Firmament; L.M. Truro.

1. *Drawn by Thy grace the sons of night,*	John 6:44
The Gentile world shall come to thee,	Isa 2:2–3
And kings o'erpowered with heavenly light	
Admire thy dazzling purity;	Isa 52:15
Soon as to thee their face they turn,	
They shall their royal state forget,	
On earth look down with holy scorn	
And lay their crowns at Jesu's feet.	Isa 49:7
2. *Zion, look round with joyful eyes,*	Isa 62:1
On all those gathering nations gaze,	
Behold, with one consent they rise,	
And flock, and flow to thy embrace!	Isa 56:7
Thy countless sons and daughters see;	
They come from far with duteous speed,	
Come to be nursed, and fed by thee,	Isa 66:12
With milk sincere, and living bread.	1 Pet 2:2
3. *Afraid to think the vision true,*	
Thy heart with dubious joy shall beat,	
Thy heart enlarged shall pant anew,	Ps 119:32
When forced the real bliss to admit,	
When hosts and fleets to thee resign	
The fullness of the lands and floods,	Mic 4:13

Part II: Psalms and Hymns arranged according to the Christian Year

And earth, and sea, and all is thine,	Ps 98:7–8
And thou art Christ's, and Christ's is God's.	1 Cor 3:23

4. Their wealth the children of the East	
Shall first into thy treasury bring,	Matt 2:11
Devote their most beloved and best,	
As holiness to Zion's King;	Rev 21:24
Incense they shall with gold bestow,	
Joined to thy faithful wrestling race,	
And fill Jehovah's courts below	Ps 116:19
With sweet perfumes of prayer and praise.	Rev 8:4

5. Surely for Christ the isles shall wait,	Isa 42:4
And ships to bring their sons from far:	
They come from their dispersed estate,	Jer 23:7–8
With all they have, and all they are:	
Jesus, thy Lord, the Holy One	Isa 9:6
Of Israel for their God they claim,	Isa 10:20–21
Who makes in thee His nature known,	
His image, and His glorious name.	Col 1:15

G. Good Friday

As we contemplate the cross in Wesley's thought and verse, this comment of Bernard Lord Manning cannot be bettered, where he compares Wesley with Isaac Watts:

> "(Watts) surveys the whole realm of Nature, as in an immortal phrase he has described it,† and at the centre he always sees the dying and crucified Creator." Wesley, however, "is obsessed with one theme: God and the soul; for the stage in space and time on which that drama is set he has little concern. He is always at Calvary; no other place in the universe matters, and for him the course of historic time is lost in the eternal NOW."[4]

†He refers here to the line "Were the whole realm of Nature mine," in the hymn "When I survey the Wondrous Cross."

27. Psalm 22

This first appeared in *The Arminian Magazine*, 1799. Meter: 8.8.6.D. Tunes: Pembroke; Purleigh.

Part I

1. *My God, my God! I cry to Thee!*   Mark 15:34
Ah! Why hast Thou forsaken me,
Who still lament and groan!
Far from my passionate complaint,
Why hast Thou suffered me to faint,   Lam 1:13
And seemed forever gone?

2. *To Thee by day and night, I cry,*   Ps 88:1
Incessant pray; but no reply
To soothe my endless care!
O Thou, that answerest not a word,
O Thou, by Israel's tribes adored,   Deut 10:21
Regard my dying prayer!

---

4. Manning, 43.

Part II: Psalms and Hymns arranged according to the Christian Year

3. Our fathers trusted in Thy aid,	Ps 33:20–22
To Thee in all their troubles prayed,	
And Thou didst hear their cry.	
Our fathers were not put to shame,	Ps 78:53
But oft, as they invoked Thy name,	
They found deliverance nigh.	

4. But I, a slighted worm, in vain   Job 25:6
For help unto my God complain;
The help I cannot find;   Ps 88:9
Cut off, alas! From all relief,
A wretched man of hopeless grief,   Ps 88:13–14
The outcast of mankind!

5. All those that see me bruised and torn,
Rejoice and laughed my soul to scorn,   Matt 27:39–40
And aggravate my load;
They glory in their cruel deed,   Mark 15:31–32
Shoot out the lip, and shake their head,
And mock my trust in God.

6. "He trusted in the Lord," they cry,
"That He would save him from on high;   Matt 27:43
Let Him His own receive;
If God in Him doth take delight,   Luke 23:35–37
He now may claim His lawful right,
And bid His favourite live!"

Part II

(two verses omitted)

9. My blood poured out like water is,   John 19:34
Sharp pangs my soul and body seize,
Disjointing all my bones;
My heart like wax before the fire   Ps 68:2

Psalms and Hymns with Introductory Notes

Dissolves; my life doth all expire
In agonizing groans!

10. *Thy wrath doth on my soul abide;*   Ps 75:8; Luke 22:42f.

My strength is as a potsherd dried;
And, blasted by Thy breath,
My tongue cleaves to my gums: Thy frown   John 19:28
Hath broke my heart, and brought me down
Into the dust of death!   Job 7:21

11. *Encompassed by the dogs of hell,*
The rage of fiends and men I feel.   Luke 23:35–36
They pierced my hands and feet;   John 19:18, 20:25
My starting bones may all be told;
With joy my sufferings they behold,   Mark 15:29
And all my pangs repeat!

12. *My clothes they equally divide,*
My vesture they by lot decide: John 19:23–24
But Thou, O Lord, be nigh;
Make haste to appear, my Strength, my Lord,   Jer 16:19
My soul deliver from the sword,
Revive me when I die!

13. *Redeem my life from Satan's power;*   Ps 49:15
Nor let the lion's mouth devour,   Dan 6:22
The unicorn's destroy:
Thou hast from all their fury freed,
And raised Thy Shepherd from the dead,   Heb 13:20
And filled with endless joy.   Luke 24:41–43

Part II: Psalms and Hymns arranged according to the Christian Year

HYMNS ON THE ATONEMENT

It may be said categorically that Wesley "pitched his tent on Calvary's hill, at the foot of the cross." In his verse he always tried to grasp the love of God displayed therein, and the salvation which flowed from it, but the height and depth of "Love Divine" quite overwhelmed him. Consequently his hymns constantly take us to the Cross, and to the justification received by faith alone. Consider the following selections:

28. "O love divine, what hast Thou done?"

This first appeared in *Hymns and Sacred Poems*, 1742. Meter: 8.8.8.8.8.8. Tunes: St. Chrysostom; Euphony (repeat last line).

1. O Love Divine, what hast Thou done?	1 John 4:10
The immortal God hath died for me!	
The Father's co-eternal Son	Heb 1:10, 12
Bore all my sins upon the tree;	1 Pet 2:24
The immortal God for me hath died!	
My Lord, my Love is crucified.	Phil 3:8
2. Behold Him, all ye that pass by,	Lam 1:12; Luke 23:35
The bleeding Prince of life and peace!	Acts 3:15
Come, sinners, see your Maker die,*	Jer 33:2
And say, was ever grief like His?	
Come, feel with me His blood applied:	1 Pet 1:2
My Lord, my Love is crucified:	
3. Is crucified for me and you,	Gal 1:4
To bring us rebels back to God:	Rom 5:8, 10
Believe, believe the record true,	
Ye all are bought with Jesu's blood,	
Pardon for all flows from His side:	Rom 3:24–26
My Lord, my Love is crucified!	
4. Then let us sit beneath His cross,	Heb 12:2

Psalms and Hymns with Introductory Notes

And gladly catch the healing stream,	Isa 66:12
All things for Him account but loss,	Phil 3:7–8
And give up all our hearts to Him;	Phil 3:14
Of nothing think or speak beside:	
My Lord, my Love is crucified.	

*Wesley's original line reads here, "Come see, ye worms, your Maker die." In the 1904 *MHB* and 1933 *MHB* the line reads as above.

29. "All ye that pass by, to Jesus draw nigh"

From *Hymns and Sacred Poems*, 1759. Meter: 5.5.11.D. Tunes: Wareham; Harwich.

1. *All ye that pass by,*	
To Jesus draw nigh:	Heb 7:19
To you is it nothing that Jesus should die?	Lam 1:12
Your ransom and peace,	1 Tim 2:6; Eph 2:14
Your surety He is:	Heb 7:22
Come, see if there ever was sorrow like His.	

#2. *For what you have done*	
His blood must atone:	Heb 9:22
The Father hath punished for you His dear Son.	Rom 8:32
The Lord in the day	
Of His anger did lay	
Your sins on the Lamb; and He bore them away.	Isa 53:6

#3. *He answered for all,*	2 Cor 5:14
O come at His call,	2 Cor 5:20
And low at His cross with astonishment fall.	
But lift up your eyes	
At Jesus's cries:	Matt 27:46
Impassive He suffers, immortal He dies.	

4. *He dies to atone*

Part II: Psalms and Hymns arranged according to the Christian Year

> For sins not His own;   2 Cor 5:21
> Your debt He hath paid, and your work He hath done.   Gal 3:13
> Ye all may receive
> The peace He did leave,   John 14:27
> Who made intercession: "My Father, forgive!"   Luke 23:34
>
> 5. For you and for me
> He prayed on the tree: John 17:9, 19–20
> The prayer is accepted, the sinner is free.
> That sinner am I,
> Who on Jesus rely,   1 Tim 1:16
> And come for the pardon God cannot deny.   1 John 1:9
>
> 6. My pardon I claim;
> For a sinner I am,
> A sinner believing in Jesus's name,   Acts 3:18–19
> He purchased the grace,   Rom 8:32
> Which now I embrace:
> O Father, Thou knowest He hath died in my place.   Gal 2:20
>
> #7. His death is my plea,
> My Advocate see,   1 John 2:1
> And hear the blood speak that hath answered for me.   Heb 12:24
> Acquitted I was,   Heb 9:15
> When He bled on the cross,   Heb 10:14
> And by losing His life He hath carried my cause.

30. The Fifty-third Chapter of Isaiah

This passage has been central to the understanding of Christ's atoning death throughout Christian history, being quoted or alluded to many times in the New Testament (e.g., Acts 8:32–35; 1 Pet 2:22–25), and by our Lord Himself (Luke 22:37). Hence Wesley's paraphrase of Isaiah 53 in its entirety is appropriate here. This first appeared in the original collection of *Hymns*

Psalms and Hymns with Introductory Notes

and Sacred Poems, 1739. Meter: L.M.D. Tune: Kettering; Tunes L.M. Doversdale; Elim/Hesperus.

1. Who hath believed the tidings? Who?	John 16:9
Or felt the joys our words impart?	John 12:37–38
Gladly confessed our record true,	
And found the Saviour in his heart?	Rom 10:16–17
Planted in nature's barren ground,	
And cherished by Jehovah's care,	Ps 92:13
There shall the immortal Seed be found,	John 12:23–24
The Root Divine shall flourish there.	1 Pet 1:23–25
2. See the Desire of nations comes,	Hag 2:7
Nor outward pomp bespeaks Him near;	
A veil of flesh the God assumes,	Heb 10:20
A servant's form He stoops to wear:	Phil 2:7
He lays His every glory by;	
Ignobly low, obscurely mean,	Heb 5:8
Of beauty void, in reason's eye,	
The Source of loveliness is seen.	Song 5:16
3. Rejected and despised of men,	Luke 18:31–33
A man of griefs, inured to woe;	
His only intimate is pain,	Luke 24:26
And grief is all His life below.	
We saw, and from the irksome sight	
Disdainfully our faces turned;	John 19:5–6
Hell followed Him with fierce despite,	
And earth the humble Object scorned.	John 19:2–3
4. Surely for us He humbled was,	Phil 2:8
And grieved with sorrows not His own:	Matt 8:17; Heb 5:7
Of all His woes were we the cause,	
We filled His soul with pangs unknown.	Matt 26:38
Yet Him the Offender we esteemed,	

Part II: Psalms and Hymns arranged according to the Christian Year

Stricken by heaven's vindictive rod,	Gal 3:13
Afflicted for Himself we deemed,	
And punished by an angry God.	Ps 7:11; Rom 1:18

5. But O, with our transgressions stained,
For our offence He wounded was; — Rom 4:25
Ours were the sins that bruised and pained — 2 Cor 5:21
And scourged, and nailed Him to the cross. — John 19:1
The chastisement that bought our peace,
To sinners due, on Him was laid:
Conscience, be still! Thy terrors cease! — Heb 9:14
The debt's discharged; the ransom's paid. — Mark 10:45

6. What though we all as wandering sheep
Have left our God, and loved to stray, — Luke 15:4–7
Refused His mild commands to keep,
And madly urged the downward way?
Father, on Him Thy bolt did fall, — Rom 3:25
The mortal law Thy Son fulfilled, — Rom 8:3–4
Thou laid'st on Him the guilt of all,
And by His stripes we all are healed. — 1 Pet 2:24

7. Accused, His mouth He opened not; — Matt 26:62
He answered not, by wrongs oppressed.
Pure though He was from sinful spot, — Heb 7:26
Our guilt He silently confessed.
Meek as a lamb to slaughter led, — Acts 8:32–35
A sheep before His shearers dumb,
To suffer in the sinner's stead — 1 Pet 3:18
Behold the spotless Victim come! — 1 Pet 1:19

8. Who could His heavenly birth declare, — Mark 6:2–3
When bound by man He silent stood;
When worms arraigned Him at their bar, — Matt 26:59–60
And doomed to death the Eternal God? — Matt 26:63–65

Patient the sufferings to sustain,
The vengeance to transgressors due,   Isa 63:4
Guiltless He groaned and died for man:
Sinners, rejoice, He died for you.   Phil 4:4

9. For your imputed guilt He bled,   Rom 5:18
Made sin, a sinful world to save;   2 Cor 5:21
Meekly He sank among the dead:
The rich supplied an honoured grave!   Luke 23:50–53
For, O! devoid of sin, and free   Rev 1:5
From actual and entailed offence,
No sinner in Himself was He,   John 8:46
But pure and perfect innocence.

10. Yet Him the Almighty Father's will   Acts 2:23
With bruising chastisements pursued,
Doomed Him the weight of sin to feel,
And sternly just, required His blood.   Lev 17:11
But, lo! The mortal debt is paid,
The costly sacrifice is o'er;   Heb 10:10
His soul, for sin an offering made,
Revives, and He shall die no more.   Rom 6:9

11. His numerous seed He now shall see,   Heb 2:10
Scattered through all the earth abroad,   John 11:51–52
Blest with His immortality,
Begot by Him, and born of God.   John 1:13
Head to His Church o'er all below,
Long shall He here His sons sustain;   1 Pet 1:5
Their bounding hearts His power shall know,
And bless the loved Messiah's reign.   1 Cor 15:25–26

12. 'Twixt God and them He still shall stand,
The children whom His Sire hath given;   Heb 2:13; John 6:39

Part II: Psalms and Hymns arranged according to the Christian Year

Their cause shall prosper in His hand,	
While Righteousness looks down from Heaven:	Isa 54:17; Jer 23:6
While pleased He counts the ransomed race,	
And calls and draws them from above;	Rom 9:24
The travail of His soul surveys,	
And rests in His redeeming love.	John 10:16

13. 'Tis done! My justice asks no more,
The satisfaction's fully made: John 19:30
Their sins He in His body bore, Heb 9:28
Their Surety all the debt has paid.
My Righteous Servant and My Son Zech 3:8
Shall each believing sinner clear; Acts 13:38–39
And all who stoop to abjure their own,
Shall in His righteousness appear. Phil 3:9

14. Them shall He claim His just desert, Eph 1:10
Them His inheritance receive, Ps 2:8
And many a contrite humble heart Isa 57:15
Will I for His possession give.
Satan He thence shall chase away,
Assert His right, His foes o'ercome; Rev 19:20
Stronger than hell, retrieve the prey,
And bear the spoil triumphant home. John 6:39

15. For charged with all their guilt he stood,
Sinners from suffering to redeem;
For them he poured out all His blood, Matt 26:28
Their Substitute, He died for them. 1 Pet 3:18
He died, and rose His death to plead, 1 Cor 15:3–4
To testify their sins forgiven:
And still I hear Him intercede,
And still he makes their claim to heaven. Heb 7:25

H. Easter Sunday

This is the climax of the Christian Year, as it is the central article of faith of Christianity: that Christ Jesus, having been crucified and laid in a tomb, rose bodily from the dead on the third day after that doleful event, and left the tomb empty. "But now Christ has been raised from the dead, the firstfruits of those who are asleep." (1 Cor 15:20). Some of Wesley's best known and most triumphant hymns are those which proclaim this cardinal truth.

31. Psalm 16

This first appeared posthumously in *The Arminian Magazine*, 1799. Peter quotes this in his Pentecost sermon as referring to Christ's resurrection (Acts 2:25–28). Wesley sees in the psalm both Christ's resurrection and that of the saints at the Last Day. Meter: 8.8.6.D. Tunes: Traveller; Grosvenor; St. Justin.

1. O Lord, Thy faithful servant save,	
Faith in Thy name Thou knowest I have,	John 1:12
My soul hath called Thee mine:	Rom 10:13
My good cannot to Thee extend,	
My good did first from Thee descend,	1 John 4:10
And all I have is Thine.	1 Cor 4:7
2. I feel Thy yearning bowels move;	
Thy people for Thy sake I love,	Lam 2:11
In them alone delight;	
The saints who here Thine image bear,	2 Cor 3:18
Who here Thy spotless nature share,	Rom 8:29
And walk with Thee in white.	Rev 7:13
3. But those that serve the prince of hell,	John 14:30
His wretched slaves, I still repel,	
Nor in their offerings join;	Ps 106:28
My soul their fellowship disclaims,	
My lips shall never name their names,	Jas 4:4
Or call their pleasures mine.	Heb 11:25

Part II: Psalms and Hymns arranged according to the Christian Year

4. The Lord Himself my portion is;   Ps 119:57; Lam 3:24
Thou reachest out my cup of bliss,   Ps 116:13
And wilt no more remove;
My fair inheritance Thou art;   Col 1:12
The needful thing, the better part,   Luke 10:42
I find in perfect love.

5. The Lord I will forever bless;   Ps 34:1
The Counsellor and Prince of Peace,   Isa 9:6
He teaches me His will;
He doth with mighty pains chastise,   Heb 12:7, 11
And makes me to salvation wise   Ps 119:98–99
By every scourge I feel.

6. Him I have set before my face,   Dan 9:3
The pardoning God of boundless grace,   Dan 9:18
Of everlasting love;
By faith I always see Him stand;   Acts 7:55–56
And with Him placed on my right hand   Rev 1:17
I never shall remove.

7. Wherefore my heart doth now rejoice;   Ps 13:5
I wait to hear Thy quickening voice;   John 5:25
My flesh exults in hope;
Thou wilt not leave me in the grave;   John 5:28–29
Sure confidence in Thee I have
That Thou wilt raise me up.   John 6:40

8. As sure as God brought back our Head,
Our great Good Shepherd, from the dead,   Heb 13:20
I shall right early rise;   1 Thess 4:14
My soul shall no corruption see;
My soul, O Lord, shall rise with Thee,   2 Cor 5:1
And mount above the skies.   Heb 6:19–20

9. Thou wilt the path of life display,	Matt 7:14
And lead me in Thyself the Way,	John 14:6
Till all Thy grace is given:	
Fulness of joy with Thee there is;	Ps 21:6
Thy presence makes the perfect bliss,	Jude 24
And where Thou art is heaven.	

HYMNS ON OUR LORD'S RESURRECTION

32. "Christ the Lord is risen today"

This hymn first appeared in *Hymns and Sacred Poems*, 1739, within a year of his conversion. Originally the hymn did not have the "Hallelujah" at the end of each line, but with the publication of the *Foundery Collection of Tunes*, 1742, it was set to the now familiar tune "*Easter Hymn*" (called then "Salisbury"), with the now familiar *Hallelujahs*. This tune first appeared in a collection under the title *Lyra Davidica* in 1708, but it cannot be traced back any further. However, the tune's adaptation to this famous hymn on Christ's resurrection enhances the majestic and triumphant tone of Wesley's lines. Verses 6–9 have, sadly, long been omitted, but for Wesley Christ's resurrection had solid implications for Christian holiness in the present, as well as for the hope of resurrection at Christ's coming in the future. The final verse puts the capstone on Christ's triumphant return from death: He *is* the King of glory; this *is* everlasting life. Sadly, it has been omitted from many hymn-books. Meter: 7.7.7.7.

1. "Christ the Lord is risen today,"	Hallelujah	Luke 24:6
Sons of men and angels say!	"	Luke 24:34
Raise your joys and triumphs high;	"	
Sing ye heavens; and, earth, reply.	"	Isa 44:23
2. Love's redeeming work is done,	Hallelujah	Heb 10:12
Fought the fight, the battle won:	"	
Lo! Our Sun's eclipse is o'er;	"	Luke 23:44–45
Lo! He sets in blood no more.	"	

Part II: Psalms and Hymns arranged according to the Christian Year

3. Vain the stone, the watch, the seal;	Hallelujah	Matt 28:2–4
Christ has burst the gates of hell!	"	Rev 1:18
Death in vain forbids His rise:	"	Acts 2:24
Christ has opened Paradise.	"	
4. Lives again our glorious King:	Hallelujah	
Where, O death, is now thy sting?	"	1 Cor 15:55
Dying once, He all doth save:*	"	Rom 6:9
Where thy victory, O grave?	"	1 Cor 15:54
5. Soar we now where Christ has led?	Hallelujah	
Following our exalted Head,	"	Col 1:18
Made like Him, like Him we rise,	"	Phil 3:21
Ours the cross, the grave, the skies!	"	
#6. What though once we perished all,	Hallelujah	
Partners in our parents' fall?	"	Rom 5:12
Second life we all receive,	"	John 3:5–6
In our Heavenly Adam live.	"	1 Cor 15:45
#7. Risen with Him, we upward move;	Hallelujah	Col 3:1
Still we seek the things above;	"	
Still pursue, and kiss the Son	"	Ps 2:12
Seated on His Father's throne.	"	Heb 1:3
#8. Scarce on earth a thought bestow,	Hallelujah	
Dead to all we leave below;	"	1 Tim 6:7
Heaven our aim, and loved abode,	"	1 Tim 6:12
Hid our life with Christ in God!	"	Col 3:3
#9. Hid; till Christ, our Life, appear,	Hallelujah	Col 3:4
Glorious in His members here:	"	Eph 5:30
Joined to Him, we then shall shine	"	Eph 5:14
All immortal, all divine!	"	1 Cor 15:53

#10. Hail, the Lord of earth and heaven!	Hallelujah	Acts 17:24
Praise to Thee by both be given:	"	
Thee we greet triumphant now;	"	Matt 28:9
Hail, the Resurrection, Thou!	"	Rev 1:18
11. King of glory, soul of bliss,	Hallelujah	Ps 24:10
Everlasting life is this,	"	John 11:25–26
Thee to know, Thy power to prove,	"	Phil 3:10
Thus to sing, and thus to love!	"	

*1877 *Collection*, 1904, & 1933 *MHB* have here, "Once He died, our souls to save."

33. "O Jesus, our King"

From *Hymns for Our Lord's Resurrection*, 1746. Meter: 5.5.5.11. Tune: Ardwick, Derbe (repeat last line).

1. O Jesus, our King,	John 12:14–15
Thy glory we sing,	
Thy rising declare,	Acts 2:32
And join in the pomp, and the benefit share.	
2. Thy conquest we feel	Isa 25:7–8
O'er death and o'er hell,	
Redeemed from the grave,	Isa 26:19
We are bold to proclaim Thee almighty to save.	Isa 63:1; Zeph 3:17
3. We know that our Head	
Is risen indeed,	Luke 24:34
Thy record receive,	1 John 1:3
And raised by the power of Thy spirit we live.	Rom 8:11
4. Thy Spirit attests	
The truth in our breasts,	
Thy witness imparts	Rom 8:14–16

> *The first resurrection of faith to our hearts.**   Rev 20:5–6
>
> 5. *Thou hast conquered beneath*   Rev 1:18
> *The sharpness of death,*   Rom 1:4
> *Our souls to retrieve,*
> *And open the kingdom to all that believe.†*   Luke 23:42–43
>
> 6. *Believing on Thee*
> *We rise from the tree,*   John 3:36
> *And heavenward move,*
> *And fly to Thy throne on the wings of Thy love.*   Isa 40:31
>
> 7. *Thy love that o'ercame*
> *Our sorrow and shame,*
> *And ransomed our race,*   1 Tim 2:6
> *And sent Thee to God to prepare us a place.*   John 14:2–3
>
> 8. *Follow after, it cries,*   Luke 18:22
> *To your place in the skies*
> *By Immanuel led,*   Rev 7:17
> *Follow after, and suffer, and reign with your Head.*   2 Tim 2:9, 12

*Wesley here appears to adopt the a-millennial view of Revelation 20:5–6, whereby the "first resurrection" refers to the miracle of conversion when a dead sinner by God's action comes to life in Christ, cf. Ephesians 2:4–6.
†This verse has clear allusions to verse 17 of the *Te Deum*, "When Thou hadst overcome the sharpness of death, Thou didst open the Kingdom of Heaven to all believers."

34. "Break forth into praise"

This first also appears in the first edition of *Hymns for Our Lord's Resurrection* in 1746, and also in the second edition of 1748. Meter: 10.10.11.11. Tunes: Houghton; Hanover; St. Ignatius.

> 1. *Break forth into praise! Our Surety and Head,*   Col 1:18

His members to raise, Hath rose from the dead:	
The power of His Spirit Hath quickened our Lord,	Rom 8:11
That we by His merit May all be restored.	Rom 4:25
2. *Our Captain and King With shouts we proclaim,*	Heb 2:10
And joyfully sing The wonderful name;	
The name all-victorious We publish and feel,	Phil 2:10
Triumphantly glorious O'er sin, earth, and hell.	Rev 1:18
3. *The power of His rise We know and declare,*	Phil 3:10
And rapt to the skies, His happiness share;	
In heavenly places with Jesus we sit,	Eph 2:6
And Jesus's praises With angels repeat.	Rev 5:8–9
4. *We sing of His love While sojourning here,*	Heb 11:13, 16
Till Christ from above Our Saviour appear;	Titus 2:13
The heirs of salvation With triumph receive,	
In full consummation Of glory to live.	1 Pet 4:13

35. "I know that my Redeemer lives"

First appeared in *Hymns and Sacred Poems*, 1742. This lengthy hymn majors on two themes: Christian holiness, and the perseverance of the saints to final glory, both based on Christ's resurrection, as per 1 Pet 1:3–5. The best known and most appropriate tune setting, "Bradford" (see above), is adapted from the famous aria of the same title in *The Messiah* by Handel. Meter: C.M. Tune: Bradford.

1. *I know that my Redeemer lives,*	Job 19:25
And ever prays for me;	John 17:20
A token of His love He gives,	
A pledge of liberty.	2 Cor 3:17

Part II: Psalms and Hymns arranged according to the Christian Year

2. I find Him lifting up my head,	Ps 3:3
He brings salvation near,	Isa 46:13
His presence makes me free indeed,	John 8:36
And He will soon appear.	

(three verses omitted)

#6. With confidence I now look up,	Isa 45:22
His promised aid implore;	Rom 10:12–13
Sweetly revives my blasted hope,	
And I can doubt no more.	Ps 27:13–14

#7. He will perform the work begun;	Phil 1:6
Jesus, the sinner's Friend,	John 15:15
Jesus, the Lover of His own,	
Will love me to the end.	John 13:1

#8. No longer am I now afraid;	Ps 27:1
The promise must take place,	
Perfect His strength in weakness made,	2 Cor 12:9
Sufficient is His grace.	

#9. Unto salvation kept I am,	1 Pet 1:5
Through faith, by power Divine,	
Ready His nature, with His name,	2 Pet 1:4; Isa 44:5
To be revealed in mine.	

10. He wills that I should holy be;	1 Pet 1:15–16
Who can withstand His will?	
The counsel of His grace in me	1 Pet 5:10
He surely shall fulfil.	

#11. Confident now of faith's increase,	Luke 17:5
I all its fruits shall prove—	Gal 5:22–23
Substantial joy, and settled peace,	

And everlasting love.	Gal 5:6

#12. Yes, Lord, I put my trust in Thee,	
On Thee my soul and stay;	Ps 18:18
I know that Thou wilt come to me,	
And I shall see Thy day.	1 Cor 1:8

#13. With me, I know, Thy Spirit dwells,	John 14:17
Nor ever shall depart,	John 14:16
Till in me He Himself reveals	
And purifies my heart.	1 John 3:3

#14. He tells me He will quickly come	
And seal me His abode;	Eph 1:13
He now marks out His future home,	
The temple of my God.	1 Cor 6:19

15. Jesus, I hang upon Thy word;	Luke 19:48
I steadfastly believe	2 Cor 4:13
Thou wilt return and claim me, Lord,	
And to Thyself receive.	John 14:3

(One verse included of the remaining eight)

18. When God is mine, and I am His,	Song 2:16
Of paradise possessed,	Rev 2:7
I taste unutterable bliss	
And everlasting rest.	Heb 4:10

36. "I know that my Redeemer lives," Job 19:25–26

A short hymn, but full of assurance. From *Hymns and Sacred Poems*, Part II, 1742. Meter: L.M. Tune: Torquay (repeat last line); Pentecost.

1. *I know that my Redeemer lives;*

Part II: Psalms and Hymns arranged according to the Christian Year

He lives, and on the earth shall stand,	1 Thess 2:19
And though to worms my flesh He gives	
My dust lies numbered in His hand.	Eccl 12:7; Ps 102:14

2. *In this re-animated clay*
I surely shall behold Him near, — Ps 17:15
Shall see Him at the latter day — 1 Thess 4:16–17
In all His majesty appear. — 1 John 3:2

3. *I feel what then shall raise me up,* — Rom 6:5, 8:11
The Eternal Spirit lives in me;
This is my confidence of hope — Heb 6:18
That God I face to face shall see. — Rev 22:4

4. *Mine own and not another's eyes*
The King shall in His beauty view, — Isa 33:17
I shall from Him receive the prize, — Phil 3:14
And wear the crown to victors due. — 2 Tim 4:8; Rev 2:10

I. Ascensiontide

Ascension Thursday falls forty days after Easter Sunday, and the following Sunday is Ascension Sunday. Regrettably, it is all too often eclipsed in the modern church by "Mothers' Day," and thus this great event in our Lord's exaltation is obscured. However, when we look at the "Epistle" (really a sermon) to the Hebrews, its entire theological base is the Ascension, since it has brought to a triumphant conclusion Christ's atoning work. See in particular Hebrews 1:3, 6:20, 7:23–28, 9:24, 10:19–21.

We begin with Wesley's version of the final stanzas of Psalm 24, which has through the history of the Church been taken to refer prophetically to the Ascension.

37. Psalm 24:7–10

This first appeared in *Psalms and Hymns*, 1743. Meter: L.M. Tunes: Hermann (with *Hallelujah* to conclude each verse); Church Triumphant; Saul; Alstone.

1. *Our Lord is risen from the dead,*	Mark 16:6
Our Jesus is gone up on high;	Eph 4:8
The powers of hell are captive led,	Ps 68:18
Dragged to the portals of the sky.	
2. *There His triumphal chariot waits,*	2 Kgs 2:11; Ps 68:17
And angels chant the solemn lay:	Rev 5:11–12
"Lift up your heads, ye heavenly gates,	
Ye everlasting doors, give way!	
3. *"Loose all your bars of massy light,*	Rev 21:11–12
And wide unfold the ethereal scene;	
He claims these mansions as His right;	John 14:2
Receive the King of Glory in!"	Luke 24:51
4. *"Who is this King of Glory, who?"*	
"The Lord that all His foes o'ercame,	Col 2:15

Part II: Psalms and Hymns arranged according to the Christian Year

The world, sin, death, and hell o'erthrew:	Rev 1:18
And Jesus is the Conqueror's name."	Heb 12:2
5. *Lo! His triumphal chariot waits,*	See on v. 2
And angels chant the solemn lay—	
"Lift up your heads, ye heavenly gates;	
Ye everlasting doors, give way!"	
6. *"Who is this King of Glory, who?"*	
"The Lord of glorious power possessed,	Acts 10:38; Rom 1:4
The King of saints and angels too,	Rev 1:5, 8
God over all, forever blessed."	Rom 9:5

HYMNS FOR ASCENSIONTIDE

38. "Hail the day that sees Him rise"

This is the best known of Wesley's hymns on the Ascension, which first appeared in *Hymns and Sacred Poems*, 1739. Like Wesley's famous Easter hymn (above) it did not originally include the "Hallelujahs," but they were soon added, and the hymn was sung to "Salisbury" ("*Easter Hymn*"). In 1861, the church musician W. H. Monk matched it to the tune "*Ascension*" (the arrangement in both the 1904 *MHB* and the 1933 *MHB*). However, the tune "*Llanfair*," composed by Robert Williams (1781–1821) and published in 1817, was a comparative latecomer: it became attached to this hymn only in 1906, but several modern hymn-books now have it as their set tune.[5] Meter: 7.7.7.7.

1. *Hail the day that sees Him rise,*	Hallelujah	Acts 1:2
Ravished from our wistful eyes!	"	Acts 1:10
Christ, awhile to mortals given,	"	

---

5. The hymn has suffered a good deal from revisers of varying competence and insight over the decades, especially in the United States, with not altogether happy results. See John Hammond's discussion in "History of Hymns: 'Hail the day that sees Him rise,'" in:
http://www.gbod.org/resources/history-of-hymns-hail-the-day-that-sees-him-rise.

Psalms and Hymns with Introductory Notes

Re-ascends His native heaven!	"	John 6:62
2. *There the pompous triumph waits:*	Hallelujah	
"Lift your heads, eternal gates,	"	Ps 24:9
Wide unfold the radiant scene,	"	
Take the King of Glory in!"	"	John 17:5
#3. *Circled round with angel powers,*	Hallelujah	Rev 5:8–10
Their triumphant Lord, and ours,	"	
Conqueror over death and sin,	"	Rom 6:9–10
Take the King of Glory in!	"	
4. *Him though Highest heaven receives,*	Hallelujah	
Still He loves the earth He leaves;	"	John 17:26
Though returning to His throne,	"	
Still He calls mankind His own.	"	Heb 2:11–12
5. *See! He lifts His hands above!*	Hallelujah	
See! He shows the prints of love!	"	Luke 24:39f.
Hark! His gracious lips bestow	"	
Blessings on His Church below!	"	Luke 24:50f.
#6. *Still for us His death He pleads;*	Hallelujah	Heb 9:24
Prevalent, He intercedes;	"	
Near Himself prepares our place,	"	John 14:2
Harbinger of human race.	"	
#7. *Master, (will we ever say)*	Hallelujah	
Taken from our head today;	"	John 16:28
See Thy faithful servants, see!	"	
Ever gazing up to Thee.	"	Acts 1:11

Part II: Psalms and Hymns arranged according to the Christian Year

8. Grant, though parted from our sight,	Hallelujah	Acts 1:9
High above yon azure height,	"	
Grant our hearts may thither rise,	"	Heb 4:14
Following Thee beyond the skies.	"	
#9. Ever upward let us move,	Hallelujah	Col 3:2
Wafted on the wings of love;	"	
Looking when our Lord shall come,	"	1 Thess 1:10
Longing, gasping after home.	"	2 Pet 3:12
#10. There we shall with Thee remain,	Hallelujah	1 Thess 4:17
Partners of Thy endless reign;	"	John 12:26
There Thy face unclouded see,	"	1 Cor 13:12
Find our heaven of heavens in Thee!	"	

39. "Hail, Jesus, hail"

The following hymn, from *Hymns for Ascension Day*, 1746, is basically a paraphrase of Hebrews 9:11–28, albeit with intrusions of other Scriptures, notably from Isaiah 49:16 in verse 5. Meter: 8.8.8.8.8.8. Tunes: Stella; Colchester.

1. Hail, Jesus, hail, our great High Priest,	Heb 8:1
Entered into Thy glorious rest,	Luke 24:26
That holy happy place above!	
Thou hast the conquest more than gained,	Rom 8:37
The everlasting bliss obtained	
For all who trust Thy dying love.	Rom 8:31–32
2. The blood of goats and bullocks slain	
Could never purge our guilty stain,	Heb 10:4
Could never for our sins atone;	
But Thou Thine own most precious blood	Heb 9:12

Hast spilt to quench the wrath of God,	Rom 3:25
Hast saved us by Thy blood alone.	Rom 5:9

3. Shed on the altar of Thy cross,	
Thy blood to God presented was	Heb 10:12
Through the eternal Spirit's power:	Heb 9:14
Thou didst a spotless Victim bleed,	1 Pet 1:19
That we from sin and suffering freed,	Rev 1:5
Might live to God, and sin no more.	2 Cor 5:15

4. That we the promise might receive,	
Might soon with Thee in glory live,	Rom 5:2
Thou stand'st before Thy Father now!	Rev 5:6
For us Thou dost in heaven appear,	Heb 9:24
Our Surety, Head, and Harbinger,	
Our Saviour to the utmost Thou.	Heb 7:25

5. Not without blood—Thou prayest above:	Heb 9:22
The marks of Thy expiring love	
God on Thy hands engraven sees!	Isa 49:16
He hears Thy blood for mercy cry,	
And sends His Spirit from the sky,	John 15:26
And seals our everlasting peace.	Eph 4:30

6. Thankful we now the earnest take,	2 Cor 1:22
The pledge Thou wilt at last come back	Acts 1:11
And openly Thy servants own;	Matt 25:31, 34
To us, who long to see Thee here,	2 Pet 3:12
Thou shalt a second time appear,	Heb 9:28
And bear us to Thy glorious throne.	

40. "God is gone up on high"

Also from *Hymns for Ascension Day*, 1746. Meter: 6.6.6.6.8.8. Repeat the refrain after each verse. Tunes: Darwall; Gopsal.

Part II: Psalms and Hymns arranged according to the Christian Year

1. God is gone up on high,	Ps 68:18
With a triumphal noise!	
The clarions of the sky	
Proclaim the angelic joys!	Rev 5:11–12

Join all on earth, rejoice and sing;
Glory ascribe to glory's King. Ps 29:1–2

2. God in the flesh below,	1 Tim 3:16
For us He reigns above;	Rom 15:12
Let all the nations know	Ps 67:2
Our Jesu's conquering love!	

3. All power to our great Lord	Matt 28:18
Is by the Father given;	
By angel hosts adored,	
He reigns supreme in heaven.	Acts 2:34–36

4. High on His holy seat	
He bears the righteous sway;	Rev 11:16–17
His foes beneath His feet	Ps 110:1
Shall sink and die away.	Heb 10:12–13

5. His foes and ours are one:	1 Cor 15:25
Satan, the world, and sin;	
But He shall tread them down,	Isa 63:3
And bring His kingdom in.	

6. Till all the earth, renewed	Isa 65:17
In righteousness divine,	2 Pet 3:12
With all the hosts of God	Ps 103:21
In one great chorus sing:	

Join all on earth, rejoice and sing;

Glory ascribe to glory's King.　　　Ps 96:10

41. "Entered the holy place above"

This hymn on the Ascension and Priestly intercession of Christ first appeared in *Hymns and Sacred Poems*, 1740. Meter: 8.8.8.8.8.8. Tunes: Mount Sion; St. Petersburg.

1. *Entered the holy place above,*	Heb 9:12, 24
Covered with meritorious scars,	Luke 24:39–40
The tokens of His dying love	
Our great High-Priest in glory bears;	Heb 8:1
He pleads His passion on the tree,	Heb 7:25; Rom 8:34
He shows Himself to God for me.	
2. *Before the throne my Saviour stands,*	Rev 5:6
My Friend and Advocate appears;	1 John 2:1
My name is graven on His hands,	Isa 49:16
And Him the Father always hears;	John 11:42
While low at Jesu's cross I bow,	
He hears the blood of sprinkling now.	1 Pet 1:2
3. *This instant now I may receive*	
The answer of His powerful prayer;	Rom 8:35
This instant now by Him I live,	Rom 8:10
His prevalence* with God declare;	
And soon my spirit, in His hands,	
Shall stand where my Forerunner stands.	Heb 6:20

*This word has changed its meaning from that of the eighteenth century, when it meant, "prevailing," or, "having victorious effect."

Part II: Psalms and Hymns arranged according to the Christian Year

J. Whitsuntide (Pentecost)

Whitsuntide is a time for new converts to declare their faith in baptism. Traditionally, the candidates wore white; hence it became known as "White Sunday," shortened to "Whitsun." While all seasons are appropriate times for Gospel preaching, this is also a special time for such preaching, and for sinners to feel the force of Divine conviction, just as Peter's hearers were "cut to the heart" as a result of Peter's Pentecost sermon (Acts 2:37).

42. Psalm 130

Wesley's version of this psalm is therefore a timely song for the season. It first appeared in *Hymns and Sacred Poems*, 1740. Meter: C.M. Tunes: Belmont, Bishopthorpe.

1. *Out of the depths of self-despair*	Ps 42:5
To Thee, O Lord, I cry:	Isa 6:5
My misery mark, attend my prayer,	Rom 3:16
And bring salvation nigh.	Luke 18:13
2. *Death's sentence in myself I feel;*	Ps 32:3–4
Beneath Thy wrath I faint:	
O let Thine ear consider well	Dan 9:17, 19
The voice of my complaint.	
3. *If Thou art rigorously severe,*	Nah 1:3
Who may the test abide?	
Where shall the man of sin appear,	Job 4:17
Or how be justified?	Job 9:2
4. *But O! forgiveness is with Thee,*	Isa 55:7
That sinners may adore,	
With filial fear Thy goodness see,	2 Cor 7:1
And never grieve Thee more.	
5. *I look to see His lovely face,*	2 Cor 4:6

I wait to meet my Lord;	
My longing soul expects His grace,	Ps 84:2
And rests upon His word.	Ps 119:147

6. *My soul, while still to Him it flies,*	Ps 55:16–17
Prevents the morning ray:	
O that His mercy's beams would rise,	Luke 1:78
And bring the Gospel day!	

7. *Ye faithful souls, confide in God;*	Ps 27:14
Mercy with Him remains;	
Plenteous redemption in His blood,	Eph 1:7
To wash out all your stains.	Isa 1:18

8. *His Israel Himself shall clear,*	Luke 24:21
From all their sins redeem:	Luke 24:47
The LORD *Our Righteousness is near,*	Jer 23:6
And we are just in Him.	Isa 45:25

HYMNS FOR WHITSUNTIDE

43. "Granted is the Saviour's prayer"

This hymn first appeared in *Hymns and Sacred Poems*, 1739, as a hymn for Whitsunday. Meter: 7.7.7.7. Tunes: Savannah; Vienna.

1. *Granted is the Saviour's prayer,*	John 14:16
Sent the gracious Comforter;	
Promise of our parting Lord,	Luke 24:49
Jesus to His heaven restored.	

2. *Christ; who now gone up on high,*	Eph 4:10
Captive leads captivity;	Eph 4:8
While His foes from Him receive	Rom 5:10
Grace, that God with man may live.	

Part II: Psalms and Hymns arranged according to the Christian Year

3. *God, the everlasting God,*	Isa 40:28
Makes with mortals His abode;	
Whom the heavens cannot contain,	1 Kgs 8:27
He vouchsafes to dwell in man.	John 14:17

4. *Never will He thence depart,*	Isa 59:21
Inmate of an humble heart;	
Carrying on His work within,	1 Cor 3:16
Striving till He casts out sin.	Gal 5:5

5. *There He helps our feeble moans,*	Rom 8:26
Deepens our imperfect groans;	
Intercedes in silence there,	Rom 8:27
Sighs the unutterable prayer.	

6. *Come, Divine and peaceful Guest,*	1 John 4:13
Enter our devoted breast;	
Holy Ghost, our hearts inspire,	Gal 5:25
Kindle there the Gospel fire.	Matt 3:11

#7. *Crown and agonizing strife,*	
Principle, and Lord of life;	John 6:63; 2 Cor 3:6
Life Divine in us renew,	Titus 3:5
Thou the Gift and Giver too.	John 7:39

#8. *Now descend and shake the earth,*	Heb 12:26
Wake us into second birth;	John 3:8
Now Thy quickening influence give,	
Blow, and these dry bones shall live!	Ezek 37:3–10

#9. *Brood Thou o'er our nature's night,*	
Darkness kindles into light;	Acts 26:18
Spread Thy over-shadowing wings,	Gen 1:2

Psalms and Hymns with Introductory Notes

Order from confusion springs.

#10. *Pain, and sin, and sorrow cease;*	Isa 35:10
Thee we taste, and all is peace;	Ps 34:8
Joy Divine in thee we prove,	1 Pet 1:8
Light of truth, and fire of love.	John 16:13; Rom 5:5

The following two hymns first appeared in a collection entitled *Hymns of Petition and Thanksgiving for the Promise of the Father*, 1746, and subtitled *Hymns for Whitsunday*.

44. "Away with our fears, our troubles and tears"

Meter: 5.5.5.11. Tune: Ardwick.

1. *Away with our fears,*	Ps 34:4
Our troubles and tears:	
The Spirit is come,	Acts 2:4
The witness of Jesus returned to His home.	Acts 2:36
2. *The pledge of our Lord*	John 16:7
To His heaven restored	
Is sent from the sky,	Acts 1:5, 11:16–17
And tells us our Head is exalted on high.	Acts 5:31–32
3. *Our Advocate there*	1 John 2:1
By His blood and His prayer	
The gift hath obtained,	
For us He hath prayed, and the Comforter gained.	John 17:20
4. *Our glorified Head*	
His Spirit hath shed,	Acts 2:33
With His people to stay,	
And never again will He take Him away.	John 14:16

Part II: Psalms and Hymns arranged according to the Christian Year

5. *Our heavenly Guide*	John 16:13
With us shall abide,	
His comfort impart,	Phil 4:7
And set up His kingdom of love in the heart.	Col 1:13

6. *The heart that believes*	
His kingdom receives,	Matt 18:3
His power and His peace,	John 14:27
His life, and His joy's everlasting increase.	Rom 14:17

7. *Then let us rejoice*	Phil 4:4
In heart and in voice,	
Our Leader pursue,	Ps 23:2–3
And shout as we travel the wilderness through:	Isa 35:6–9

8. *With the Spirit remove*	Gal 5:5
To Zion above,	Heb 12:22
Triumphant arise,	Jer 31:12
And walk with our God, till we fly to the skies.	Gen 5:22

45. "Father of everlasting grace"

Meter 8.8.8.8.8.8. Tune: Stamford.

1. *Father of everlasting grace,*	Isa 54:8
Thy goodness and Thy truth we praise,	
Thy goodness and Thy truth we prove;	Jer 31:14
That hast, in honour of Thy Son,	John 14:26
The gift unspeakable sent down,	
The Spirit of life, and power, and love.	Zech 4:6

#2. *Thou hast the prophecy fulfilled,*	Joel 2:28–29
The grand original compact sealed,	
For which Thy word and oath were joined:	Heb 6:17
The promise to our fallen head,	Gen 3:15; Rom 5:17

Psalms and Hymns with Introductory Notes

To every child of Adam made,
Is now poured out on all mankind.   Acts 2:39

#3. The purchased Comforter is given,
For Jesus is returned to heaven,   John 16:7
To claim, and then the grace impart:
Our day of Pentecost is come,   Acts 2:1
And God vouchsafes to fix His home   John 14:23
In every poor expecting heart.   2 Cor 1:22

#4. Father, on Thee whoever call,   Rom 10:13
Confess Thy promise is for all,
While every one that asks receives,   Matt 7:8
Receives the gift, and Giver too,   Luke 11:13
And witnesses that Thou art true,
And in Thy Spirit walks, and lives.   Gal 5:25

#5. Not to a single age confined,   Matt 28:20
For every soul of man designed,
O God, we now Thy Spirit claim:
To us the Holy Ghost impart,   Luke 11:13
Breathe Him into our panting heart,   John 20:23
Thou hear'st us ask in Jesus's name.   John 14:13–14

6. Send us the Spirit of Thy Son,
To make the depths of Godhead known,   1 Cor 2:10
To make us share the life divine;
Send Him the sprinkled blood to apply,   1 Pet 1:2
Send Him our souls to sanctify,
And show and seal us ever Thine.   Eph 4:30

7. So shall we pray and never cease,   Eph 6:18
So shall we thankfully confess
Thy wisdom, truth, and power, and love;   Isa 11:2
With joy unspeakable adore,   1 Pet 1:8

Part II: Psalms and Hymns arranged according to the Christian Year

    And bless and praise Thee evermore,
    And serve Thee as Thy hosts above.   Ps 103:21; 1 Thess 1:9

    8. Till, added to that heavenly choir,
    We raise our songs of triumph higher,   Ps 107:1–3
    And praise Thee in a bolder strain,
    Out-soar the first-born seraph's flight,
    And sing, with all our friends in light,   Col 1:12
    Thy everlasting love to man.   John 3:16

46. "Filled with the Spirit of holiness"

Wesley's meditation on *Acts 2:4, 6* reveals his view of the role of tongues, i.e., as reversing the confusion of languages recorded in Genesis 11:1–9. This appears in *Scripture Hymns*, 1762, *Acts*. Meter: C.M.D. Tunes: Forest Green; Kingsfold; Old 44th.

    1. Filled with the Spirit of holiness,   Rom 1:4
    One family is joined
    With all the tongues of earth to praise   Rev 4:9
    The Saviour of mankind;
    Earnest of the whole world employed   Eph 1:14
    In their own tongues to sing,   Phil 2:11
    In season due, the Incarnate God,
    The saints' eternal King.*   Isa 33:22

    2. Tongues at first were multiplied,
    Proud, aspiring worms to abase,
    Rebels to confound, divide,
    Wide disperse the audacious race;   Gen 11:9
    God by different languages   Gen 11:7
    Baffled their gigantic power,
    Bade their impious project cease,
    Stopped the heaven-invading tower.   Gen 11:8

3. *Tongues are multiplied again*	
(While our God in love comes down)	
To collect the sons of men	1 Cor 14:22
Reconcile the world in one,	Zeph 3:9
Make us each with each agree,	1 Cor 1:10
Pride, the cause of strife remove,	
Teach our hearts humility,	Zeph 3:12–13
Join us all in faith and love.	1 Thess 5:8

*The reference is to Revelation 15:3, last line, where the KJV reads "King of the saints," but this is supported by only one late Greek miniscule, while most other Greek manuscripts and early versions read "King of the nations."

47. "Where shall my wondering soul begin?"

This is reputed to be the hymn Charles Wesley wrote on the occasion of his evangelical conversion in the home of John Bray of Little Britain, near Aldersgate Street, London, at Whitsuntide, May 21, 1738. He wrote in his journal, "Least of all would he [the enemy] have us tell what things God has done for our souls . . . In His name, therefore, and through His strength, I will perform my vows unto the Lord . . ." (Vol. 1, 94). It appears in the first volume of *Hymns and Sacred Poems*, 1739.

Three days later, his brother John came to a similar experience at an evening meeting of the Moravian Brethren, at the "Bible and Sun" meetinghouse in Aldersgate Street. Hence, Whitsuntide held a very special place in the Wesley brothers' memory and personal pilgrimage. The final two verses, referring to the "bleeding heart," "open side," and the "wounded side" of Christ reflects the strong emphasis of the Moravians on the "blood and wounds" of Christ. However, the message in the final verse, "only believe and all is yours," enshrines the central message of the Evangelical Revival.

This hymn first appeared in print in *Hymns and Sacred Poems*, 1739, entitled "Christ, the Friend of Sinners." Meter: 8.8.8.8.8.8. Tunes: Crucifixion; Old 23rd; St. Catherine; St. Petersburg.

1. *Where shall my wondering soul begin?*
How shall I all to heaven aspire?

Part II: Psalms and Hymns arranged according to the Christian Year

A slave redeemed from death and sin,	Ps 49:15; Hos 13:14
A brand plucked from the burning fire,	Amos 4:11; Zech 3:2
How shall I equal triumphs raise,	Ps 47:1
And sing my great Deliverer's praise?	Gal 1:4

2. *O, how shall I the goodness tell,*	
Father, which Thou to me hast showed?	
That I, a child of wrath and hell,	Eph 2:3
I should be called a child of God,	1 John 3:1
Should know, should feel my sins forgiven,	John 5:24
Blest with this antepast of heaven!	1 Pet 1:4

3. *And shall I slight my Father's love?*	Heb 10:29
Or basely fear His gifts to own?	
Unmindful of His favours prove?	Deut 32:18
Shall I, the hallowed cross to shun,	
Refuse His righteousness to impart,	Rom 1:16–17
By hiding it within my heart?	John 19:38

#4. *No—though the ancient dragon rage,*	Rev 12:3
And call forth all his hosts to war;	
Though earth's self-righteous sons engage;	Matt 23:34–35
Them, and their god, alike I dare:	2 Cor 4:4; Phil 3:19
Jesus, the sinner's Friend, proclaim;	Matt 11:19
Jesus to sinners still the same.	Heb 13:8

5. *Outcasts of men, to you I call,*	Isa 11:12
Harlots, and publicans, and thieves!	Mark 2:15
He spreads His arms to embrace you all;	
Sinners alone His grace receives:	Mark 2:17
No need of Him the righteous have;	Luke 5:32
He came the lost to seek and save.	Luke 19:10

(one verse omitted)
7. *Come, O my guilty brethren, come,*

Psalms and Hymns with Introductory Notes

Groaning beneath your load of sin!   Matt 11:28–30
His bleeding heart shall make you room,
His open side shall take you in;   John 20:27
He calls you now, invites you home: John 6:37
Come, O my guilty brethren, come!   Ezek 33:11

#8. For you the purple current flowed   1 John 1:7
In pardon from His wounded side: John 19:30, 34
Languished for you th' eternal God,
For you the Prince of Glory died.   1 Cor 2:8
Believe, and all your guilt's forgiven;   John 3:18
Only believe—and yours is heaven.   John 20:31

K. Trinity Sunday

This Sunday in the Christian Year climaxes the revelation of the Son in His Person and work (Christmas, Epiphany, Easter, Ascension), and the sending of the Spirit (Whitsun), and now the Persons of the Godhead are brought together. Hence subsequent Sundays are designated as "the nth Sunday after Trinity" until the close of the year.

Paraphrases of Scripture relating to the Trinity

The Trinity is a revelation of the New Testament, specifically by the Incarnation of the Son in the womb of the Virgin Mary, and the outpouring of the Holy Spirit at Pentecost. However, there are what are called "adumbrations" or hints of the Trinity in the Old Testament, where the plurality in the Godhead is revealed. Genesis 1:26 is one such text, which Wesley paraphrases as follows.

48. "Hail Father, Son, and Spirit, great"

This short hymn, based on the "us" and "our" in Genesis 1:26, first appeared in *Hymns on the Trinity*, 1767. Meter: C.M.D. Tunes: Noel; Petersham.

1. Hail Father, Son, and Spirit, great	
Before the birth of time,	Gen 1:1; John 1:1
Enthroned in everlasting state	Ps 90:2
Jehovah Elohim!	Gen 2:4
A mystical plurality	Gen 1:26
We in the Godhead own	
Adoring One in Persons Three	Isa 48:16
And Three in nature One.	Matt 28:19
2. From Thee our being we receive	Acts 17:28
The creatures of Thy grace,	
And raised out of the earth we live	Gen 2:7
To sing our Maker's praise:	Ps 8:1
Thy powerful, wise, and loving mind	
Did our creation plan,	Prov 3:19

And all the glorious Persons joined
To form Thy favourite, man.   Gen 1:26

49. "Jehovah, God the Father, bless"

The second such paraphrase, again from *Hymns on the Trinity*, 1767, is based on the Aaronic blessing, Numbers 6:24–26. Meter: C.M.D. Tunes: as above, or Varina.

1. *Jehovah, God the Father, bless,*	Ps 34:1
And Thy own work defend!	
With mercy's outstretched arms embrace,	Luke 15:20
And keep us to the end:	Jude 24
Preserve the creatures of Thy love	Ps 121:7
By providential care,	
Conducted to the realms above	2 Tim 4:18
To sing Thy goodness there.	
2. *Jehovah, God the Son, reveal*	Heb 1:3
The brightness of Thy face!	
And all Thy pardoned people fill	
With plenitude of grace:	John 1:16
Shine forth with all the Deity	John 1:4–5
Which dwells in Thee alone;	
And lift us up Thy face to see	Ps 17:15
On Thy eternal throne!	Acts 7:55f.
3. *Jehovah, God the Spirit, shine,*	2 Cor 3:17–18
Father and Son to show;	John 16:14
With bliss ineffable, Divine,	
Our ravished hearts o'erflow;	
Sure earnest of that happiness,	2 Cor 5:5
Which human thought transcends,	John 14:17
Be Thou our everlasting peace,	Phil 4:7
When grace in† *glory ends.*	Ps 84:11

Part II: Psalms and Hymns arranged according to the Christian Year

4. Thy blessing, grace, and peace we claim,	Rev 1:4–5
Great God in Persons Three,	
The incommunicable name	Exod 3:15
Ascribing now to Thee:	Isa 42:8
We soon shall join that harping host,	Rev 5:8
And sing, Thy saints among,	
To Father, Son, and Holy Ghost,	
The new, eternal song.	Rev 14:2–3

†Wesley has "and" here, but it is more correct to affirm that present grace will end in future glory.

HYMNS ON THE TRINITY

50. "Worship and praise belong"

We turn now to hymns on the Trinity based on New Testament texts. The first selection has strong overtones of Revelation 5:9-13. From *Hymns on the Trinity: Hymns and Prayers to the Trinity*, 1767, no. VIII. Meter: 6.6.6.6.8.8. Tunes: Adoration (St. John's); Wesley.

1. Worship and praise belong	Ps 33:1
To God the Lord most high:	
Who taught us the new song	Ps 40:3; Isa 42:10
His name we magnify,	Luke 1:46
The Trinity in One we bless,	2 Cor 13:14
The Unity in Three confess.	
2. Not from our creeds alone	
The doctrine we receive:	2 Thess 2:15
Jehovah three in one,	
He gives us to believe,	1 Pet 1:21
The God of truth Himself imparts,	1 Cor 2:12, 16
And writes His name upon our hearts.	Isa 44:5, 49:16

3. *His Son on us bestowed*	1 John 3:1
The Father hath revealed:	Matt 16:16–17
The Son His Father showed	
From mortal eye concealed;	1 Cor 2:14
The indwelling Comforter attests	John 15:26, 16:14
That One in Three, in faithful breasts.	
4. *Thrice holy God, in whom*	Isa 6:3
We live, and move, and are,	Job 12:10
To do Thy will we come,	Ps 40:8
Thy glory to declare,	
By all our converse here to show	2 Cor 5:16, 20
That God is manifest below.	
5. *Baptized into Thy name,*	Matt 28:19
Mysterious One in Three,	
Our souls and bodies claim	
A sacrifice to Thee:	Rom 12:1
We only live our faith to prove	Gal 2:20
The faith which works by humble love.	Gal 5:6
6. *O that our light may shine,*	Matt 5:16
And all our lives express	
The character Divine,	2 Pet 1:4–8
The real holiness!	
Then, then receive us up to adore	John 14:3
The Triune God forevermore.	Rev 7:15

51. "God of unexhausted grace"

This Hymn to the Trinity first appears in *Hymns and Sacred Poems*, 1742. In standard Reformed style he speaks of the Father's plan of salvation, the Son's atoning work, and the Spirit's application and seal. It concludes with an ascription of praise to the Three Persons in glorious unity. Meter: 7.6.7.6.D. Trochaic-iambic. Tune: Pelham.

Part II: Psalms and Hymns arranged according to the Christian Year

1. *God of unexhausted grace,*
Of everlasting love, — Jer 31:3
Overpowered before Thy face
I fall, and dare not move. — Job 42:5–6
What hast Thou for sinners done,
For so poor a worm as me? — Isa 41:14
Thou hast given Thine only Son, — 1 John 4:10
To bring us back to Thee. — 1 Pet 3:18

2. *Suffering, sin-atoning God,*
Thy hallowed name I bless; — Phil 2:9–10
Jesus, lavish of Thy blood — Eph 1:6, 8
To buy the sinner's peace, — Eph 2:14
Gushing from Thy sacred veins
Let it now my soul o'erflow, — Zech 13:1
Purge out all my sinful stains,
And wash me white as snow. — Isa 1:18

3. *Holy Ghost, set to Thy seal,* — Eph 1:13
The life of Jesus breathe; — 2 Cor 4:10
The deep things of God reveal, — 1 Cor 2:10
Apply my Saviour's death:
With the Father and the Son
Soon as one in Thee I am, — John 17:21
All my nature shall make known
The glories of the Lamb. — 1 Pet 2:9

4. *Father, Son, and Holy Ghost,*
Thy Godhead we adore, — 1 Tim 6:15–16
Join with the triumphant host
Who praise Thee evermore; — Rev 15:4
Live, by heaven and earth adored,
Three in One, and One in Three, — Isa 48:16
Holy, holy, holy Lord, — Isa 6:3

All glory be to Thee.	Rom 11:36; Heb 13:21

THE PERSONS OF THE GODHEAD ONE BY ONE

THE FATHER

52. Psalm 93

First published in 1854, by Rev. H. Fish, from a manuscript in his own possession. Meter: 6.6.7.7.7.7. Tunes: Fulneck; Devotion

1. *Jehovah reigns on high*	Ps 113:5
In peerless majesty;	
Boundless power His royal robe,	Isa 6:1
Purest light His garment is;	1 John 1:5
Rules His word the spacious globe,	Dan 4:17
'Stablished it in floating seas.	Ps 24:2
2. *Ancient of days! Thy name*	Dan 7:13
And essence is I Am;	Exod 3:14
Thou, O Lord, and Thou alone,	Deut 4:39; Isa 37:16
Gavest whate'er is to be;	
Stood Thine everlasting throne,	Ps 45:6
Stands to all eternity.	Ps 90:2
3. *The floods, with angry noise,*	Ps 46:6
Have lifted up their voice—	
Lifted up their voice on high;	
Fiends and men exclaim aloud;	Ps 2:1–3
Rage the waves, and dash the sky,	Luke 21:25
Hell assails the throne of God.	Rev 12:7–8, 13
4. *Their fury cannot move*	
The Lord who reigns above;	Ps 76:10

Part II: Psalms and Hymns arranged according to the Christian Year

Him the mighty waves obey,	Ps 65:7
Sinking at His awful will;	Ps 107:29
Ocean owns His sovereign sway,	
Hell at His command is still.	Rev 20:14

5. Thy statutes, Lord, are sure,	Ps 119:89
And as Thyself endure;	Ps 119:160
Thine eternal house above	John 14:2
Holy souls alone can see,	
Fitted here by perfect love,	
There to reign enthroned with Thee.	Matt 19:28

HYMNS TO THE FATHER

53. "Thee, O my God and King"

It will readily be seen that his hymn is based on the Parable of the Prodigal Son, in Luke 15:11–32. Wesley sees in the parable his own experience of return, forgiveness, and the Father's acceptance. This first appears in *Hymns and Sacred Poems*, 1739, under the heading "Hymn of Thanksgiving to the Father," Meter: 6.6.7.7.7.7. Tunes: Shaftesbury; Eccles.

1. Thee, O my God and King,	Ps 145:1
My Father, Thee I sing!	
Hear, well-pleased, the joyous sound,	Ps 89:15–16
Praise from earth and heaven receive;	Ps 103:21–22
Lost, I now in Christ am found,	Luke 15:6
Dead, by faith in Christ I live.	Rom 8:10

2. Father, behold Thy Son,	Matt 3:17
In Christ I am Thy own;	1 Cor 6:19
Stranger long to Thee and rest,	
See, the prodigal is come:	
Open wide Thine arms and breast,	Mark 10:16
Take the weary wanderer home!	Ps 107:4–6

3. Thine eye observed from far,	Jer 30:10
Thy pity looked me near:	
Me Thy bowels yearned to see,	
Me Thy mercy ran to find,	Eph 2:4
Empty, poor, and void of Thee,	Eph 2:12
Hungry, sick, and faint, and blind.	Isa 42:7
4. Thou on my neck didst fall,	
Thy kiss forgave me all:	
Still the gracious words I hear,	Luke 7:50
Words that made the Saviour mine,	John 20:28
"Haste! For him the robe prepare,	Isa 61:10
His be the righteousness divine!"	Phil 3:9

54. "O heavenly King, look down from above"

This first appears in *Hymns and Sacred Poems*, 1742. Meter: 10.10.11.11. Tunes: Houghton; Laudate Dominum.

1. O heavenly King, look down from above;	Ps 33:13–14
Assist us to sing Thy mercy and love:	Ps 136:1–26
So sweetly o'erflowing, so plenteous the store,	Isa 55:7
Thou still art bestowing and giving us more.	
2. O God of our life, we hallow Thy name;	Matt 6:9
Our business and strife is Thee to proclaim.	Acts 13:47
Accept our thanksgiving for creating grace;	
The living, the living shall show forth Thy praise.	Isa 38:19
3. Our Father and Lord, almighty art Thou;	Rev 11:17
Preserved by Thy word, we worship Thee now;	Prov 2:7–8
The bountiful Donor of all we enjoy,	
Our tongues to Thine honour, and lives we employ.	Ps 35:28

Part II: Psalms and Hymns arranged according to the Christian Year

4. But O above all Thy kindness we praise,
From sin and from thrall which saves the lost race;   Luke 19:10
Thy Son Thou hast given the world to redeem,   1 John 2:2
And bring us to heaven whose trust is in Him.   1 Pet 1:5

5. Wherefore of Thy love we sing and rejoice,   Eph 2:4
With angels above we lift up our voice: Ps 148:2, 12–13
Thy love each believer shall gladly adore,
For ever and ever, when time is no more.   Rev 22:6–7

THE SON

55. Psalm 125

From *Psalms and Hymns*, 1743. Meter: S.M.D. Tunes: Ishmael; Leominster.

1. Who in the Lord confide,   Ps 56:4
And feel His sprinkled blood,   1 Pet 1:2
In storms and hurricanes abide   Acts 27:20, 23–25
Firm as the mount of God: Isa 2:2–3
Steadfast, and fixed, and sure,
His Sion cannot move;   Isa 28:16; Rom 9:33
His faithful people stand secure
In Jesu's guardian love.   Rom 8:35, 38–39

2. As round Jerusalem
The hilly bulwarks rise,   Isa 26:1
So God protects and covers them
From all their enemies: Isa 26:2–4
On every side He stands,   Ps 91:1–2
And for His Israel cares;   Ps 121:7–8
And safe in His almighty hands
Their souls forever bears.   Deut 31:6; Heb 13:5

#3. For lo! The reign of hell

And hellish men is o'er;	Ps 56:11; Heb 13:6
They can persuade, they can compel,	1 Cor 11:19
The just to sin no more:	Eph 6:16
To devils, men, or sin,	
They need no more give place,	Jas 4:7
Nor ever touch the thing unclean	2 Cor 6:17
When cleansed by pardoning grace.	1 Tim 4:4

4. But let them still abide
In Thee, all gracious Lord,	John 15:4
Till every soul is sanctified	John 17:17
And perfectly restored.	
The men of heart sincere	Heb 10:22
Continue to defend,	
And do them good, and save them here,	Ps 7:10
And love them to the end.	John 13:1

#5. Who to their sins draw back,	Heb 10:26
And love again to stray,	
The narrow path of life forsake.	Matt 7:14
And throng the spacious way,	Matt 7:13
Back to their vomit turn,	2 Pet 2:22
And fall from pard'ning grace;	
The Lord to punish them hath sworn,	Heb 10:27
And drive them from His face.	Matt 7:23

#6. But peace, and power, and love	Ps 119:165
Shall Israel's portion be;	Gal 6:16
They all His promises shall prove,	2 Pet 1:4
And all His goodness see;	Ps 27:13
Holy and pure in heart	Matt 5:8
Obtain the perfect power:	
They can no more from God depart	Isa 54:10
When they can sin no more.	

Part II: Psalms and Hymns arranged according to the Christian Year

HYMNS TO THE SON

56. "O filial Deity"

The following hymn first appeared in *Hymns and Sacred Poems*, 1739, as "Hymn to the Son." The titles and roles of Christ, especially His threefold office of Prophet, Priest, and King, form the framework of the various verses. In this important respect this composition parallels the similar hymn of Isaac Watts, "Join all the glorious names." However, somewhat in contrast to Watts, there is here much more of the first person pronoun, and personal experience—the "felt Christ." Meter: 6.6.7.7.7.7. Tune: Eccles (repeat last line).

1. O **filial Deity**	Rom 8:15–16
Accept my new-born cry!	John 3:3, 5
See the travail of Thy soul,	
Saviour, and be satisfied;	Isa 53:11
Take me now, possess me whole,	Eph 1:14
Who for me, for me, hast died!	Gal 2:20
#2. **Of life** Thou art the **Tree**,	Rev 2:7, 22:2
My immortality!	1 Cor 15:53
Feed this tender branch of Thine,	
Ceaseless influence derive,	
Thou the true, the heavenly Vine,	John 15:4–5
Grafted into Thee I live.	Rom 11:17
3. *Of life the* **Fountain** *Thou,*	Jer 2:13; Zech 13:1
I know—I feel it now!	
Faint and dead no more I droop:	Isa 40:29
Thou art in me; Thy supplies,	
Every moment springing up,	John 4:14
Into life eternal rise.	John 7:38
4. *Thou the* **Good Shepherd** *art,*	John 10:10
From Thee I ne'er shall part;	Rom 8:38–39
Thou my Keeper and my Guide,	Ps 121:5

Psalms and Hymns with Introductory Notes

Make me still Thy tender care;	
Gently lead me by Thy side,	John 10:4
Sweetly in Thy bosom bear.	Isa 40:11

5. Thou art my **Daily Bread**;	John 6:35
O Christ, Thou art my Head;	Eph 1:22; Col 1:18
Motion, virtue, strength to me,	Phil 4:8
Me, Thy living member, flow;	1 Cor 12:27
Nourished I, and fed by Thee,	1 Pet 2:2
Up to Thee in all things grow.	Eph 4:15–16

6. **Prophet**, to me reveal	Isa 11:1–2
Thy Father's perfect will;	John 12:49
Never mortal spake like Thee,	John 7:46
Human prophet like Divine;	Acts 3:22–26
Loud and strong their voices be,	
Small, and still, and inward Thine.	1 Kgs 19:12

7. On Thee, my **Priest**, I call,	Isa 52:15; Zech 6:13
Thy blood atoned for all;	2 Cor 5:14
Still the Lamb as slain appears,	Rev 5:6
Still Thou stand'st before the throne,	
Ever offering up my* prayers,	Heb 7:25
These presenting with Thine own.	John 17:24; Rom 8:26–27

8. Jesu! Thou art my **King**;	Isa 9:7; Jer 23:5–6
From thee my strength I bring;	
Shadowed by Thy mighty hand,	Isa 51:16
Saviour, who shall pluck me thence?	John 10:28
Faith supports; by faith I stand,	1 John 5:4
Strong in Thy omnipotence.	2 Cor 12:9

Part II: Psalms and Hymns arranged according to the Christian Year

> 9. **O filial Deity** See v. 1
> *Accept my new-born cry!*
> *See the travail of Thy soul,*
> *Saviour, and be satisfied;*
> *Take me now, possess me whole,*
> *Who for me, for me, hast died!*

*Wesley originally had "thy" here, but in his final revision of 1782 he substituted "my," thus making his meaning clear, and bringing it into line with Romans 8:26–27 and Hebrews 7:25, where the Spirit's intercession for and with the believer is closely identified with the Son's before Father.[6]

57. "Jesus, the Name high over all"

Inscribed on the Wesley statue in Bristol are his oft-repeated words, "O let me commend my Savior to you." This hymn epitomizes that same message which Wesley delighted to preach to sinners across the country, and remains one of his best-loved compositions. It first appears in *Hymns and Sacred Poems*, 1749. Meter: C.M. Tune: Lydia.

> 1. *Jesus, the name high over all,*   Phil 2:9–10
> *In hell, or earth, or sky;*
> *Angels and men before it fall,*   Heb 1:6; Matt 28:9
> *And devils fear and fly.*   Col 2:15
>
> 2. *Jesus! The name to sinners dear,*   Col 1:13
> *The name to sinners given;*   1 John 5:12–13
> *It scatters all their guilty fear,*   Heb 9:14
> *It turns their hell to heaven.*
>
> 3. *Jesus! The prisoner's fetters breaks,*   Luke 4:18, 21
> *And bruises Satan's head;*   Gen 3:15; Rom 16:20
> *Power into strengthless souls it speaks,*
> *And life into the dead.*   Eph 2:5

---

6. Osborn, vol. 1, 99.

4. O that the world might taste and see	Col 1:27
The riches of His grace!	Eph 2:7
The arms of love that compass me	
Would all mankind embrace.	Col 1:23, 26
#5. O that my Jesu's heavenly charms	Ps 45:13
Might every bosom move!	
Fly, sinners, fly into those arms	Heb 6:18
Of everlasting love.	Deut 33:27
6. His only righteousness I show,	Rom 1:17
His saving grace proclaim;	Titus 2:11–12
'Tis all my business here below	
To cry: "Behold the Lamb!"	John 1:29
7. Happy, if with my latest breath,	2 Tim 4:1–2
I might but gasp His name;	
Preach Him to all, and cry in death,	Rev 12:11
"Behold, behold the Lamb!"	John 1:36

58. "O, for a thousand tongues to sing"

This famous hymn first appeared in *Hymns and Sacred Poems*, 1740, under the heading, "For the Anniversary Day of One's Conversion," for Wesley the most significant date in his own Christian pilgrimage. In the 1780 *Collection* it appears as Number 1 in the opening section entitled "Exhorting, and beseeching sinners to return to God." Since then it has occupied the first position in every Methodist hymnal.

The opening line as it stands recalls the comment of Peter Böhler to Charles Wesley, "Had I a thousand tongues, I would praise Him with them all," but the line probably goes back ultimately to Johann Mentzer (1658–1734), "O dass ich tausend Zungen hätte," and later translated by Catherine Winkworth in 1861.[7] However, in the original 1740 version the

---

7. H&B, 79–80 n. 1. The opening verse—of the total of fifteen from Mentzer—runs as follows, with Miss Winkworth's rendering on the right:

Part II: Psalms and Hymns arranged according to the Christian Year

opening verse was the doxology below, while the familiar opening line did not appear until verse 7. The original verses 2–6 are now reproduced below. Meter: C.M. Tunes: Richmond; Lyngham; Lydia.

1. *O for a thousand tongues to sing*
My dear Redeemer's praise! — Isa 44:22–23
The glories of my God and King, — Ps 145:1
The triumphs of His grace! — Zech 4:6, 12:10

2. *My gracious Master, and my God,* — 1 Pet 2:3
Assist me to proclaim,
To spread through all the earth abroad — 1 Thess 1:8
The honours of Thy name. — Rev 5:12

3. *Jesus, the name that charms our fears,* — Rev 1:17
That bids our sorrows cease; — John 16:20; 1 Thess 4:13
'Tis music in the sinner's ears,
'Tis life, and health, and peace! — Ps 67:2; John 14:27

4. *He breaks the power of cancelled sin,* — Rom 8:1–2
He sets the prisoner free, — John 8:36
His blood can make the foulest clean— — 1 Pet 1:18–19
His blood availed for me.

5. *He speaks; and listening to His voice,* — John 5:25
New life the dead receive, — Eph 2:5
The mournful, broken hearts rejoice, — Isa 61:3

O! daß ich tausend zungen hätte   Oh would I had a thousand tongues,
Und einen tausend sachen mund   To sound Thy praise o'er land and sea!
So stimmt' ich damit um die wette   Oh! rich and sweet should be my songs,
Vom allertiefsten herzensgrund   Of all my God has done for me!
Ein loblied nach dem andern an   With thankfulness my heart must often swell,
Von dem was Gott an mir gethan.   But mortal lips Thy praises faintly tell.

(From: http://www.hymnary.org/text/o_that_i_had_a_thousand_voices_to_sound/)

Psalms and Hymns with Introductory Notes

The humble poor believe.	Matt 5:3, 11:5

#6. Hear Him, ye deaf; His praise, ye dumb,	Isa 35:5–6, 42:18
Your loosened tongues employ;	
Ye blind, behold your Saviour come,	Luke 4:18, 21
And leap, ye lame, for joy!	Acts 3:8, 16

#7. Look unto Him, ye nations, own	Isa 11:10; Rom 15:12
Your God, ye fallen race!	Isa 45:22
Look, and be saved through faith alone,	Rom 3:22
Be justified by grace!	Rom 3:24

8. See all your sins on Jesus laid:	Isa 53:6
The Lamb of God was slain,	Rev 5:6
His soul was once an offering made	Isa 53:10
For every soul of man.	
(four verses omitted)	

In the Draft Collection of 1778, verse 1, line 2 read, "My great Redeemer's praise," and from 1798 the line also read this way. Likewise, in Wesley's 1753 *Collection*, verse 2, line 1 read "My glorious Master."

Some modern hymn-books conclude with Wesley's doxology (originally placed at the beginning):

Glory to God, and praise, and love	1 Chr 29:11
Be ever, ever given,	Ps 30:12
By saints below, and saints above,	Ps 96:7–9
The Church in earth and heaven.	Rev 5:9–10

After this doxology come verses 2–6, commemorating his conversion (omitted from 1933 *MHB*). Verses 5 and 6 in particular give expression to the dictum of Martin Luther: "The heart of religion lies in its personal pronouns."

On this glad day the glorious Sun	
Of Righteousness arose;	Mal 4:2

Part II: Psalms and Hymns arranged according to the Christian Year

On my benighted soul He shone,	Gal 1:15–16
And filled it with repose.	Jer 6:16; Matt 11:28

Sudden expired the legal strife;	Rom 3:28; Titus 3:5
'Twas then I ceased to grieve;	
My second, real, and living life	1 Pet 1:23
I then began to live.	Rom 6:4

Thee with my heart I first believed,	Rom 10:10
Believed with faith Divine;	1 Pet 1:21
Power with the Holy Ghost received	1 Thess 1:5
To call the Saviour mine.	

I felt my Lord's atoning blood	Heb 10:22
Close to my soul applied;	
Me, me He loved—the Son of God	Gal 2:20
For me, for me He died!	Rom 14:8–9

I found, and owned the promise true	2 Cor 1:20
Ascertained of my part;	
My pardon passed in heaven I know,	Isa 55:7
When written on my heart.	2 Cor 3:3

THE HOLY SPIRIT

59. Psalm 143:8–12

This first appeared in *The Arminian Magazine* in 1798. The excerpt here picks up from verse 8 in the Biblical text. Meter: 8.8.6.D. Tunes; Pembroke; Purleigh.

7. O God, in whom I trust, appear!	Ps 56:4
Give me Thy pardoning voice to hear,	John 8:11
Thy saving health to see;	Jer 8:22
The glorious Gospel light display,	2 Cor 4:3–4

And lead into the perfect way	Ps 139:24
A soul that looks to Thee.	
8. *For refuge, Lord, to Thee I fly!*	Isa 4:6; Heb 6:18
On Thee alone for help rely,	
For pardon, peace, and power.	Eph 1:19, 2:14
From all my foes and sins release,	
And teach me thus my Lord to please,	2 Cor 5:9
And bid me sin no more.	Col 1:22
9. *O reach me out Thy Spirit's hand!*	Gal 5:16
Into that good and pleasant land	Jer 3:19
Of holy quiet lead;	
Quicken me, for Thy mercy's sake:	Ps 119:40
From sin and Satan's dungeon take,	
And make me free indeed.	John 8:36
10. *In mercy take these sins away,*	Hos 14:2
And all my foes forever slay,	Ps 27:2
That now my soul oppress!	
Receive me, Saviour, for Thine own,	Ps 49:15
And let me serve the Lord alone,	Matt 4:10
The Lord my Righteousness.	Jer 23:6

HYMNS TO THE HOLY SPIRIT

60. "Hear, Holy Spirit, hear"

This first appeared in *Hymns and Sacred Poems*, 1739, but it is reproduced here in the later, slightly altered form from *Hymns for those to Whom Christ is All in All*, 1761 (published anonymously). This latter work is important for Charles's view of the Perfection controversy around 1760–61, and is discussed in Part III.A.3 on Perfectionism. Meter: 6.6.7.7.7.7. Tunes: Fulneck; Devotion, Eccles.

Part II: Psalms and Hymns arranged according to the Christian Year

1. *Hear, Holy Spirit, hear,*
My inward Comforter! — 2 Tim 1:14
Loosed by Thee, my stammering tongue — Mark 7:35
First assays to praise Thee now;
This the new, the joyful song: — Isa 42:10
Hear it in Thy temple, Thou! — Ps 18:6

2. *Long o'er the formless soul*
The dreary waves did roll; — Ps 42:7
Void I lay, and sunk in night:
Thou, the overshadowing Dove, — Gen 1:2
Called the chaos into light, — 2 Cor 4:6
Bad'st me be, and live, and love. — John 9:25, 38

(two verses omitted)

5. *Fruit of the Saviour's prayer,* — John 14:16
My promised Comforter!
Thee the world cannot receive, — John 14:17
Thee they neither know nor see, — 1 Cor 2:14
Dead is all the life they live,
Dark their light, while void of Thee. — Mic 3:6

6. *Yet I partake Thy grace*
Through Christ my righteousness; — 1 Cor 1:30
Mine the gifts Thou dost impart,
Mine the unction from above, — 1 John 2:20
Pardon written on my heart,
Light, and life, and joy and love. — John 1:4–5; 1 John 4:7

7. *Thy gifts, blest Paraclete,* — Rom 12:6–8
I glory to repeat:
Sweetly sure of grace I am, — 1 John 5:10
Pardon to my soul applied,
Interest in the spotless Lamb; — 1 Pet 1:19

Dead for all, for me He died.	2 Cor 5:14
8. *Thou art Thyself the seal;*	Eph 1:13–14
I more than pardon feel,	
Peace, unutterable peace,	Isa 26:3
Joy that ages ne'er can move,	John 16:33
Faith's assurance, hope's increase,	Heb 10:22
All the confidence of love!	
9. *Pledge of Thy promise given,*	2 Cor 1:22
My antepast of heaven;	
Earnest Thou of joys Divine,	
Joys Divine on me bestowed,	Rom 15:13
Heaven, and Christ, and all is mine,	1 Cor 3:22–23
All the plenitude of God.	Eph 3:19
10. *Thou art my inward Guide,*	1 Cor 3:16
I ask no help beside:	
Arm of God, to Thee I call,	Isa 51:9
Weak as helpless infancy!	
Weak I am—yet cannot fall,	2 Cor 12:9
Stayed by faith, and led by Thee!	Rom 8:14

61. "Rejoice, rejoice, ye fallen race"

This first appeared in *Hymns and Sacred Poems*, 1742 as "A Hymn for the Day of Pentecost." As several verses in this hymn make clear, both Wesley and the early Methodists believed that the coming of the Spirit was not a "once-for-all" event restricted to the original Pentecost, but a phenomenon which could happen many times in God-given "seasons of refreshing" (Acts 3:19), as indeed they have happened many times in the history of the Church, in the form of revivals. Moreover, they believed firmly in the immediate sovereignty of the Spirit's activity as per John 3:8. However, despite what might appear from verses 5 and 7, there is not here the notion of

Part II: Psalms and Hymns arranged according to the Christian Year

"tarrying meetings," a practice begun by Hugh Bourne and William Clowes, founders of the "Primitive Methodists" in the early nineteenth century.

Selected verses, altered and somewhat rearranged, appear in 1933 *MHB*, no. 274, with verse 5 below as its first verse. Meter: L.M. Tunes: Winchester New; Newhaven.

1. *Rejoice, rejoice, ye fallen race,*	Rom 15:10
The Day of Pentecost is come;	
Expect the sure descending grace,	
Open your hearts to make Him room.	Rev 3:20
2. *Our Jesus is gone up on high,*	Eph 4:8
For us the blessing to receive:	Eph 4:11–13
It now comes streaming from the sky;	
The Spirit comes, and sinners live.	Ezek 36:26–28
3. *To every one whom God shall call*	
The promise is securely made;	Acts 2:39
To you far off, He calls you all;	Eph 2:17–18
Believe the word which Christ has said.	Acts 16:31
4. *"The Holy Ghost, if I depart,*	
The Comforter shall surely come,	John 16:7
Shall make the contrite sinner's heart	John 16:8–11
His loved, his everlasting home."	John 14:23
5. *Lord, we believe to us and ours*	
The apostolic promise given;	Acts 3:19–20
We wait to taste the heavenly powers,*	Isa 64:1–2
The Holy Ghost sent down from heaven.	1 Pet 1:12
6. *Ah! Leave us not to mourn below,*	John 16:20
Or long for Thy return to pine;	
Now Lord, the Comforter bestow,	John 20:22
And fix in us the Guest Divine.	Luke 19:7; 1 Cor 3:16

Psalms and Hymns with Introductory Notes

7. *Assembled here with one accord,*   Acts 2:1
Calmly we wait the promised grace,
The purchase of our dying Lord: Acts 20:28
Come Holy Ghost, and fill the place.   Acts 4:31

8. *If every one that asks may find,*   Luke 11:13
If still Thou art to sinners given,†
Come as a mighty rushing wind;   Acts 2:2
To shake our earth come down from heaven.   Acts 4:31

9. *Behold, to Thee our souls aspire,*   Isa 26:9
And languish Thy descent to meet:
Kindle in each the living fire,   Lev 6:12–13; Matt 3:11
And fix in every heart Thy seat.

10. *Wisdom and strength to Thee belongs—*   Isa 11:2
Sweetly within our bosoms move,
Now let us speak with other tongues,
The new, strange language of Thy love.   Zeph 3:9; 1 Cor 13:1

11. *Spirit of faith, within us live,*   1 Cor 12:3; 2 Cor 4:13
And strike the crowd with fixed amaze;
Open our mouths, and utterance give,   Acts 2:4
To publish our Redeemer's praise.   Acts 9:17, 20

12. *To testify the grace of God,*   Acts 20:24
Today as yesterday the same,   Heb 13:8
And spread through all the earth abroad,
The wonders wrought by Jesu's name.   Heb 2:3–4

*In 1933 *MHB*: "We wait the Pentecostal powers"
†In 1933 *MHB* the second and last lines read: "If still Thou dost on sinners fall"; and: "Great grace be now upon us all."

Part II: Psalms and Hymns arranged according to the Christian Year

62. "Come, Holy Ghost, our hearts inspire"

This first appeared in *Hymns and Sacred Poems*, 1740, in a section entitled "Before reading the Scriptures." Meter: C.M. Tunes: Richmond; St. Columba.

1. Come, Holy Ghost, our hearts inspire,	1 John 2:27
Let us Thine influence prove,	
Source of the old prophetic fire,	Jer 5:14
Fountain of life and love.	Jer 2:13
2. Come, Holy Ghost (for moved by Thee	
The prophets wrote and spoke);	2 Pet 1:21
Unlock the truth, Thyself the key,	1 Cor 2:13–14
Unseal the sacred book.	2 Pet 1:20
3. Expand Thy wings, celestial Dove,	Matt 3:16
Brood o'er our nature's night;	
On our disordered spirits move,	
And let there now be light.	John 12:46
4. God through Himself we then shall know,	1 Cor 2:10–11
If Thou within us shine;	
And sound, with all Thy saints below,	Eph 3:18
The depths of love Divine.	Eph 3:19

63. "Come, Holy Ghost, all-quickening fire!"

This first appeared in *Hymns and Sacred Poems*, 1739, entitled "Hymn to the Holy Ghost." Meter: 8.8.8.8.8.8. Tunes: Tarsus; Arne's.

1. Come, Holy Ghost, all-quickening fire,	Isa 4:5
Come, and my hallowed heart inspire,	
Sprinkled with the atoning blood;	1 Pet 1:2
Now to my soul Thyself reveal,	
Thy mighty working let me feel,	Eph 1:19

Psalms and Hymns with Introductory Notes

And know that I am born of God.	1 John 5:1

#2. Thy witness with my spirit bear	Rom 8:16
That God, my God, inhabits there,	
Thou with the Father and the Son	
Eternal light's coeval beam;	1 Tim 6:16
Be Christ in me, and I in Him,	John 17:21
Till perfect we are made in one.	Eph 4:13, 16

#3. When wilt Thou my whole heart subdue?	Mic 3:19; Rom 8:13
Come, Lord, and form my soul anew,	Ezek 36:26–27
Emptied of pride, and wrath, and hell:	1 John 2:16
Less than the least of all Thy store	
Of mercies, I myself abhor;	
All, all my vileness may I feel.	Rom 7:24

4. Humble, and teachable, and mild,	
O may I, as a little child,	Matt 18:3–4
My lowly Master's steps pursue!	
Be anger to my soul unknown;	Jas 1:20
Hate, envy, jealousy, be gone!	Prov 6:16–19
In love create Thou all things new.	2 Cor 5:17

5. Let earth no more my heart divide;	
With Christ may I be crucified,	Rom 6:6
To Thee with my whole soul aspire;	Matt 22:37–38
Dead to the world and all its toys,	Gal 6:14
Its idle pomp and fading joys,	1 John 2:17
Be Thou alone my one desire.	Ps 27:4

#6. Be Thou my joy, be Thou my dread;	Isa 8:13
In battle cover Thou my head,	Ps 91:4, 7
Nor earth nor hell I then shall fear;	Ps 27:1
I then shall turn my steady face;	
Want, pain defy, enjoy disgrace,	

Part II: Psalms and Hymns arranged according to the Christian Year

Glory in dissolution near.   2 Cor 5:1

7. My will be swallowed up in Thee;   Luke 22:42
Light in Thy light still may I see,   Ps 36:9
Beholding Thee with open face: 2 Cor 3:18
Called the full power of faith to prove,   Rom 12:2
Let all my hallowed heart be love,
And all my spotless life be praise.   Heb 13:15

#8. Come, Holy Ghost, all-quickening fire,   See v. 1
My consecrated heart inspire,
Sprinkled with the atoning blood;
Still to my soul Thyself reveal,
Thy mighty working may I feel,
And know that I am one with God!

PSALMS AND HYMNS WITH INTRODUCTORY NOTES

L. From Trinity to Advent

This section includes psalms and hymns on the theme of the expansion of Christ's Kingdom, the Communion of saints, Christian service, and Christian pilgrimage.

PSALM SELECTIONS

64. "My heart is full of Christ, and longs"

The latter part of this version of Psalm 45 (verses 1–7, from *Psalms and Hymns*, 1743) occurs above in the section under Christmas, but this opening part is also suitable for that occasion. The first line says it all for Wesley's life and Christian experience, just as verse 4 does for the progress of the great Evangelical Revival. Meter: 8.8.8.8.8.8. Tune: Worsley.

1. My heart is full of Christ, and longs	Phil 1:21
Its glorious matter to declare!	
Of Him I'll make my loftier songs,	Eph 5:19
I cannot from His praise forbear;	
My ready tongue makes haste to sing	1 Cor 14:15
The glories of my heavenly King.	Rev 1:12–17
2. Fairer than all the earth-born race	
Perfect in comeliness Thou art;	
Replenished are Thy lips with grace,	Luke 4:22
And full of love Thy tender heart:	Luke 7:13
God ever blest! We bow the knee,	Heb 1:8; Rev 1:17
And own all fullness dwells in thee.	Col 2:9
3. Gird on thy thigh the Spirit's sword,	Isa 49:2; Rev 2:12
And take to Thee Thy power divine;	
Stir up Thy strength, almighty Lord,	Ps 80:2–3
All power and majesty are Thine:	Matt 28:18
Assert Thy worship and renown;	
O all-redeeming God, come down.	Isa 44:3, 5, 64:1

153

Part II: Psalms and Hymns arranged according to the Christian Year

4. Come and maintain Thy righteous cause,
And let Thy glorious toil succeed;   Rev 12:10–11
Dispread the victory of Thy cross,   John 12:31–32
Ride on, and prosper in thy deed;
Through earth triumphantly ride on   Rev 19:11
And reign in every heart alone.   Rom 5:21

65. Psalm 2

Also from *Psalms and Hymns*, 1743. Meter: L.M. Tunes: Duke Street; Holly; Maryton.

1. Why do the Jews and Gentiles join   Rev 16:14, 16
To execute a vain design,   Acts 4:25–28
Idly their utmost powers engage,
And storm with unavailing rage?

2. Earth's haughty kings their Lord oppose;   2 Kgs 19:22
The rulers list themselves His foes,
To fight against their God agree,   Ps 83:4–5
And slay the Incarnate Deity: Matt 2:16

3. As sworn their Maker to dethrone,   Isa 45:9
And Jesus, His anointed Son,
To rise from all subjection freed,   Luke 19:14
And reign almighty in His stead.

4. The Lord that calmly sits above,   Ps 99:1
Enthroned in everlasting love,
Shall all their feeble threats deride, Ps 59:8
And laugh to scorn their hateful pride.

5. Then shall He in His wrath address
And vex His baffled enemies;

Psalms and Hymns with Introductory Notes

"Yet I have glorified My Son,   Acts 13:33
And placed Him on His Father's throne.   Rev 3:21

6. "Conqueror of sin, and death, and hell,   Rev 1:18
He reigns a Prince invincible:
All power is now to Jesus given,   Matt 28:18
Triumphant on the hill of heaven."

7. "I publish the Divine decree,
That all shall live who trust in Me: John 6:47
Look unto Me, ye ransomed race,   Isa 45:22
Believe, and ye are saved by grace.   Rom 10:9

8. "I heard My gracious Father say,
'Thou art My Son; on this glad day
Thou art declared My Son with power,   Rom 1:4
Raised from the dead, to die no more.   Rom 6:9

9. "'Ask, and the Gentile world receive;
All, all I to Thy prayer will give;
So dearly bought with blood Divine,   Acts 20:28
Lo! every soul of man is Thine.   1 Tim 2:6

10. "'Whoe'er withstand a pardoning God   Mic 7:18
Shall groan beneath Thine iron rod: Rev 19:15
Whoe'er their Advocate repel,   2 Thess 1:8–9
The anger of their Judge shall feel.'"   Matt 25:41

11. Wherefore to Him, ye kings, submit;   Isa 52:15
Be wise to fall and kiss His feet;   Luke 7:38
With awful joy revere His sway,
Ye rulers of the earth, obey.   Phil 2:10–11

12. Worship the co-eternal Son,   Heb 1:6
Lest you in anger He disown,   Matt 7:23

Part II: Psalms and Hymns arranged according to the Christian Year

His light withhold, His grace deny,	
And leave you in your sins to die.	John 8:24

13. *Thrice happy all who trust in Him,*	Ps 40:4
All good, almighty to redeem!	
They only shall His mercy prove,	Isa 26:5, 7
Loved with an everlasting love.	Jer 31:3

HYMN SELECTIONS FOR THE PERIOD AFTER TRINITY

66. "Earth, rejoice! Our Lord is King"

The following hymn first appeared in *Hymns and Sacred Poems*, 1740, with the title, "To be sung in a tumult." The later tumults in Cornwall and at Devizes come to mind here. Meter: 7.7.7.7. Tunes: Ephraim; University College; Monkland.

1. *Earth, rejoice, our Lord is King!*	Ps 98:4–6
Sons of men, His praises sing;	
Sing ye in triumphant strains,	
Jesus the Messiah reigns!	1 Cor 15:25

2. *Power is all to Jesus given,*	Matt 28:18
Lord of hell, and earth, and heaven,	
Every knee to Him shall bow;	Isa 45:23; Phil 2:10
Satan, hear, and tremble now!	

#3. *All Thy hosts to battle bring:*	Rev 19:14
Shouts in us a stronger King,	
Lifts our hearts and voices high—	Isa 40:9
Hark, the morning stars reply!	Job 38:7

4. *Angels and archangels join,*	
All triumphantly combine,	Rev 5:12–13
All in Jesu's praise agree,	Eph 1:6
Carrying on His victory.	

5. Though the sons of night blaspheme,   1 Thess 5:5; Isa 52:5
More there are with us than them;   2 Kgs 6:16
God with us, we cannot fear –   Isa 8:10
Fear, ye fiends, for Christ is here!

6. Lo! To faith's enlightened sight,
All the mountain flames with light;   2 Kgs 6:17
Hell is nigh, but God is nigher,
Circling us with hosts of fire.   Ps 34:7

7. Christ the Saviour* is come down,
Points us to the victor's crown,   2 Tim 4:7–8
Bids us take our seats above,   Eph 2:6
More than conquerors in His love.   Rom 8:37

#8. Yes, the future work is done,
Christ the Saviour reigns alone,   Acts 7:55–56
Forces Satan to submit,
Bruises him beneath our feet.   Rom 16:20

*Charles Wesley has here in the original version "Our Messias," but his brother John altered this to "Christ the Saviour" for later collections, albeit this hymn was omitted from the 1780 *Collection*. In all, six verses have been omitted above from Wesley's original composition, and here the numbering adjusted accordingly.

67. "Ye servants of God"

This familiar hymn on Christian service, urges humble obedience to our heavenly Master for work in His "glorious" kingdom in publication of the Gospel of Christ and His salvation, in singing His praise, and honoring Him in all that we do—even in the face of persecution. The final verse reminds us that such service is His right, since He has "all glory and power, all honor and blessing" (note the verses from Revelation). This first appeared in *Hymns for Times of Trouble and Persecution*, 1744, in a sub-section of

Part II: Psalms and Hymns arranged according to the Christian Year

four hymns under the title, "Hymns to be Sung in a Tumult," one of which is a twenty-verse meditation on Hosea 14. The year 1744 was among the worst for mob violence against the Wesleys' preaching, as reflected in verses 2 and 3. Meter: 5.5.5.5.6.5.6.5. Tune: Hanover; Laudate Dominum.

1. *Ye servants of God,*	Ps 134:1
Your Master proclaim,	Acts 13:38–39
And publish abroad	
His wonderful name;	Luke 24:47
The name all-victorious	Phil 2:9–10
Of Jesus extol;	
His kingdom is glorious,	Dan 7:14
And rules over all.	Ps 22:28
#2. *The waves of the sea*	
Have lift up their voice,	Ps 93:3–4
Sore troubled that we	
In Jesus rejoice:	1 Pet 4:12–14
The floods they are roaring;	Ps 69:1–2
But Jesus is here:	Acts 18:10
While we are adoring	
He always is near.	Ps 145:18
#3. *Men, devils engage;*	Rev 12:12
The billows arise,	
And horribly rage,	Ps 46:6
And threaten the skies:	
Their fury shall never	Isa 7:4
Our steadfastness shock,	Col 2:5
The weakest believer	
Is built on a Rock.	Matt 7:24–25
4. *God ruleth on high,*	Ps 103:19
Almighty to save,	Isa 63:1
And still He is nigh;	Ps 34:18
His presence we have.	

The great congregation	Ps 22:25
His triumph shall sing,	Ps 111:1
Ascribing salvation	2 Tim 1:10
To Jesus our king.	Rev 19:16
5. Salvation to God,	Rev 7:10
Who sits on the throne,	Rev 4:2–3
Let all cry aloud,	
And honour the Son!	John 5:23
The praises of Jesus*	
The angels proclaim,	Rev 4:11–12
Fall down on their faces,	Rev 7:11
And worship the Lamb.	Rev 4:8
6. Then let us adore,	2 Thess 1:10
And give Him His right,	Rev 5:5
All glory and power,	
All wisdom and might;	
All honour and blessing,	Rev 5:12
With angels above,	
And thanks never ceasing,	Rev 7:12; 1 Cor 15:57
And infinite love.	Eph 6:24

*Wesley's original line here was *Our Jesu's praises*, but the altered line above has now become standard.

The last two verses of the associated Hosea 14 meditation are worth including here, since they reflect Wesley's confidence in the Lord for preserving the converts who came from and endured the violent mobs. Meter: L.M.

19. Beneath my love's almighty shade,	Isa 4:6
O Israel, sit, and rest secure,	Deut 33:12, 28
On me thy quiet soul be stayed,	
'Till pure as I thy God am pure.	1 John 3:3
20. Surely I will my people save;	Deut 33:29
Who on my faithful word depend;	Ps 130:5

Part II: Psalms and Hymns arranged according to the Christian Year

Their fruit to holiness shall have,	John 15:5
And glorious-all to heaven ascend.	

68. "Behold the servant of the Lord"

Here Wesley is the deeply humble servant of Christ, ready to do the Master's will, and equipped by Divine grace. The following first appeared in 1745, at the conclusion of "A Farther Appeal to Men of Reason and Religion" by John Wesley, and later included in *Hymns and Sacred Poems*, vol. 2, 1749. Meter: 8.8.8.8.8.8. Tune: Mozart.

1. *Behold the servant of the Lord!*	Luke 1:38
I wait thy guiding eye to feel,	
To hear and keep Thy every word,	Ps 119:57; Jas 1:22
To prove and do Thy perfect will;	Rom 12:1–2
Joyful from my own works to cease,	Heb 9:14
Glad to fulfil all righteousness.	Matt 3:15
2. *Me, if Thy grace vouchsafe to use,*	Rom 12:3
Meanest of all Thy creatures, me;	Prov 3:34
The deed, the time, the manner choose,	
Let all my fruit be found of Thee;	Eph 5:8–10
Let all my works in Thee be wrought,	1 Cor 3:14
By Thee to full perfection brought.	
3. *My every weak, though good design,*	Phil 2:2
O'errule, or change, as seems Thee meet;	Ps 90:17
Jesus, let all my work be Thine!	Rom 8:3–4
Thy work, O Lord, is all complete,	
And pleasing in thy Father's sight;	John 8:29
Thou only hast done all things right.	
4. *Here then to Thee my own I leave;*	
Mould as Thou wilt Thy passive clay;	Isa 64:8
But let me all Thy stamp receive,	1 Cor 6:18–19

But let me all Thy words obey;	Rom 6:17
Serve with a single heart and eye,	Col 3:23–24
And to Thy glory live and die.	Rom 14:8

69. "Except the Lord conduct the plan"

Yet another hymn on Christian service, based on Psalm 127. This first appeared in *Hymns for the Use of Families*, 1767, and entitled "For a Family of Believers." Meter: 8.8.6.D. Tunes: Purleigh; St. Justin.

1. *Except the Lord conduct the plan,*	Ps 127:1
The best concerted schemes are vain,	Isa 8:10, 19:11–12
And never can succeed;	Gen 11:8
We spend our wretched strength for nought:	Ps 127:2
But if our works in Thee be wrought,	John 3:21
They shall be blessed indeed.	Rev 14:13
2. *Lord, if Thou didst Thyself inspire*	Col 3:15
Our souls with this intense desire	
Thy goodness to proclaim,	Isa 52:7
Thy glory if we now intend,	Ps 86:12
O let our deed begin and end	
Complete in Jesu's name!	Col 1:28, 2:10
3. *In Jesu's name behold we meet,*	Matt 18:20
Far from an evil world retreat,	Luke 5:16, 6:12
And all its frantic ways;	
One only thing resolved to know,	Ps 27:4; Luke 10:42
And square our useful lives below	
By reason and by grace.	Eccl 12:13; 1 Cor 15:58
4. *Not in the tombs we pine to dwell,*	Mark 5:5
Not in the dark monastic cell,	John 17:15
By vows and grates confined;	

Part II: Psalms and Hymns arranged according to the Christian Year

Freely to all ourselves we give,	2 Cor 4:2
Constrained by Jesu's love to live,	2 Cor 5:14
The servants of mankind.	2 Cor 4:5

5. Now Jesus, now Thy love impart,	Rom 5:5
To govern each devoted heart,	
And fit us for Thy will:	2 Tim 3:17
Deep founded in the truth of grace,	
Build up Thy rising church, and place	Matt 16:18
The city on the hill.	Matt 5:14

6. O let our faith and love abound!	1 Thess 5:8
O let our lives to all around	
With purest lustre shine!	Phil 2:15
That all around our works may see,	Matt 5:16
And give the glory, Lord, to Thee,	
The heavenly light Divine.	John 8:12

70. "All praise to our Redeeming Lord"

This hymn first appeared in a collection entitled *Hymns for Those that Seek and Those that Have Redemption in the Blood of Jesus Christ*, 1747, titled in particular, "At the Meeting of Friends." The hymn displays the true nature of Christian fellowship, as opposed to mere socializing. Meter: C.M. Tunes: Lucius; Edgeware.

1. All praise to our redeeming Lord	Rom 3:24
Who joins us by His grace,	Eph 4:16
And bids us, each to each restored,	
Together seek His face.	Col 2:2

2. He bids us build each other up;	Eph 4:12
And, gathered into one,	Eph 4:4
To our high calling's glorious hope	Phil 3:14
We hand in hand go on.	

3. The gift which He on one bestows,	Eph 4:7
We all delight to prove;	
The grace through every vessel flows,	1 Pet 4:10
In purest streams of love.	1 Pet 1:22
4. Even now we think and speak the same,	Rom 12:16
And cordially agree;	Rom 15:5
Concentred all, through Jesu's name	
In perfect harmony.	Phil 2:2
5. We all partake the joy of one,	
The common peace we feel,	Eph 4:3
A peace to sensual minds unknown,	John 14:27
A joy unspeakable.	1 Pet 1:8
6. And if our fellowship below	1 John 1:3, 7
In Jesus be so sweet,	2 Cor 2:14
What heights of rapture shall we know	
When round His throne we meet.	Rev 7:14–15

71. "Captain of Israel's host, and Guide"

The pilgrim Church was a vital concept in Wesley's thought. He saw the Christian pilgrimage both collectively, as the Church, and personally for each Christian, as in Bunyan's famous allegory, *The Pilgrim's Progress*. We see also in these selections how Charles differed from his brother John in affirming the Perseverance of the saints, that every true Christian would reach the "home above" after traveling through "this weary world," led by God's "unerring Holy Spirit."

This appeared in *Scripture Hymns*, 1762, based on the appearance of the Captain of the Lord's Host in Josh 5:14. However, it has strong overtones of Matthew Henry's comment *in loc.* on Exodus 13:17–22, where he writes: "They needed not to fear missing their way who were thus led, or being lost who were thus directed . . . They who make the glory of God their end, and

Part II: Psalms and Hymns arranged according to the Christian Year

the Word of God their rule, the Spirit of God the guide of their affairs, may be confident that 'the Lord goes before them.'"[8] Meter: 8.8.8.8.8.8. Tune: Marienlyst; Jena.

1. Captain of Israel's host, and Guide	Josh 5:14
Of all who seek the land above,	
Beneath Thy shadow we abide,	Isa 4:6, 32:2
The cloud of Thy protecting love;	Isa 4:5
Our strength, Thy grace; our rule, Thy word;	Mic 5:4; 2 Tim 3:16
Our end, the glory of the Lord.	John 17:24
2. By Thine unerring Spirit led,	Rom 8:14
We shall not in the desert stray;	Isa 35:8
We shall not full direction need*,	Ps 23:2–3; Isa 26:7
Nor miss our providential way;	
As far from danger as from fear,	Rom 8:35, 38–39
While love, almighty love, is near.	John 17:11, 26

*The word "need" here is in the archaic sense of "lack," not the modern sense of "require."

72. "Leader of faithful souls, and Guide"

Similar lines in the same vein occur in the following hymn, described as the marching song of the pilgrim church, where its members press on through the "vale of woe" to the new Jerusalem, that "city out of sight," having "no abiding city here." Cf. the hymn "Come on, my partners in distress" (below), where Wesley describes the beatific vision which beckons the Christian onwards. This first appears in *Hymns for those that seek, and those that have Redemption*, 1747. Meter: 8.8.8.8.8.8. Tune: Mount Beacon; Marienlyst.

1. Leader of faithful souls, and Guide	Heb 12:2
Of all that travel to the sky	
Come, and with us, even us, abide,	

---

8. H&B, 472 n. 5–12. Harman makes the same observation on this hymn, and on others which owe their inspiration to Matthew Henry. See Harman, "Impact of Matthew Henry," 8.

Psalms and Hymns with Introductory Notes

Who would on Thee alone rely:	Isa 26:13, 28:16
On Thee alone our spirits stay,	Isa 37:16
While held in life's uneven way.	Ps 42:4–5

2. Strangers and pilgrims here below,	Heb 11:13
This earth, we know, is not our place;	Heb 13:14
But hasten through the vale of woe,	Ps 84:6
And, restless to behold Thy face,	Ps 17:15
Swift to our heavenly country move,	Heb 11:16
Our everlasting home above.	

3. We have no abiding city here,	Heb 13:14
But seek a city out of sight;	Heb 11:10
Thither our steady course we steer,	
Aspiring to the plains of light,	Isa 60:19–20
Jerusalem, the saints' abode,	Rev 21:2–3
Whose founder is the living God.	Zech 2:5

4. Patient the appointed race to run,	Heb 12:1
This weary world we cast behind;	Phil 3:13
From strength to strength we travel on	Ps 84:7
The new Jerusalem to find*;	Gal 4:26
Our labour this, our only aim,	
To find the New Jerusalem.	Rev 3:12

#5. Thither in all our thoughts we tend,	Matt 7:13–14; 1 Tim 4:10
And still with longing eyes look up,	Luke 21:28
Our hearts and prayers before us send,	
Our ready scouts of faith and hope,	1 Pet 1:3, 21
Who bring us news of Sion near,	
We soon shall see the towers appear.	Ps 48:12–14

6. Through Thee, who all our sins hast borne,	1 Pet 2:24
Freely and graciously forgiven,	Eph 1:7

Part II: Psalms and Hymns arranged according to the Christian Year

With songs to Zion we return,   Isa 35:10
Contending for our native heaven;
That palace of our glorious King,   Ps 45:15
We find it nearer while we sing.   Rom 13:11

(one verse omitted)
8. Raised by the breath of love Divine,   Ezek 37:5
We urge our way with strength renewed;
The Church of the first-born to join,   Heb 12:23
We travel to the mount of God,   Isa 2:3
With joy upon our heads arise,   Isa 51:11
And meet our Captain in the skies.   Heb 2:10

*In the sense of "attain to," "obtain."

M. The Lord's Supper

The early Methodists revived the love-feast, or *agape*-feast, from early Christian times, but apart from this they placed great importance on the Lord's Supper. In these hymns we see the mystical dimension of the Supper as taught by the English Reformers, whereby Christ's "Real Presence" is not in the elements in any physical or quasi-physical sense, but yet He is present to faith in the believing recipient. This view goes back at least to a treatise by Bertram (Latinized to Ratramnus) in the ninth century, and reflects the dimension of Pauline teaching in 1 Corinthians 10:16, where both the bread and the wine are a "communion" (κοινωνια) in the body and blood of Christ.

The hymns below are selections from *Hymns on the Lord's Supper*, published 1745, containing 166 hymns in all. The arrangement, however, is most interesting. It follows the introductory treatise *The Christian Sacrament and Sacrifice* by a Dr. Daniel Brevint (d. 1695), born on the island of Jersey, and educated at Oxford, but who emigrated to France to become pastor of a French Protestant congregation in Normandy, and afterwards chaplain to Marshal Turenne in the court of Louis XIV. At the request of many, including the Princess of Turenne, he wrote a treatise on the Lord's Supper, in which he on one hand explained and refuted the Roman Catholic Mass, but on the other hand in a positive vein expounded the Scriptural doctrine of the Supper, with its mystical dimension, intended as a preparation for partaking at the Lord's table. Theologically, Dr. Brevint absorbed the theology of the University of Saumur, a mediating position between strict Calvinistic Puritanism, and the Arminianism now becoming fashionable in the seventeenth century, albeit it was more of a modified Calvinism than the rationalism inherent the Arminian outlook à la William Laud.

Whatever, the doctrine of the Supper in this treatise stands clearly in the Reformed stream, and at the outset Brevint expounds it in the following way, which in turn provides his outline (emphases his):

> "The Lord's Supper was chiefly ordained as a *Sacrament*. (1) To represent the sufferings of Christ which are past, whereof it is a *memorial*. (2) To convey the first-fruits of those sufferings, in present graces, whereof it is a *means*. And (3) To assure us of glory to come, whereof it is an infallible *pledge*."[9]

These three aspects occupy Sections II to V. However, there is more:

---

9. As in Osborn, 186.

Part II: Psalms and Hymns arranged according to the Christian Year

Section VI: Concerning the Sacrament as it is a sacrifice; first, of the Commemorative Sacrifice;

Section VII: Concerning the Sacrifice of Ourselves;

Section VIII: Concerning the Sacrifice of our Goods.

Wesley follows this outline, with hymns arranged accordingly:

1. (The Lord's Supper) as it is a Memorial of the Sufferings of and Death of Christ (27 hymns)
2. (The Lord's Supper) as it is a sign and a Means of Grace (65 hymns)
3. (The Lord's Supper) a Pledge of Heaven (23 hymns)
4. The Holy Eucharist as it implies a Sacrifice (12 hymns)
5. Concerning the Sacrifice of our Persons (30 hymns)
6. After the Sacrament (9 hymns)

The Editor (Dr. G. Osborn) comments:

> "The genius of the Wesleys has given wings to the thought and feeling of Dr. Brevint; the handful of corn shakes like Lebanon. And while "the Great Monarch" (i.e., Louis XIV) and the splendours of his court are forgotten ... the Protestant worshippers will minister, by the agency of the Wesleys, to the devotion of multitudes ..."[10]

73. "Come, all who truly bear"

This hymn appears in Section I, no. XIII. When Wesley speaks of the "sacramental seal" in this and subsequent hymns below, the reference is to Romans 4:11 in regard to Old Testament circumcision, and thereby to the Gospel sacraments in general, but beyond that it is not to any specific text, but to theology. Meter: S.M.D. Tunes: Leominster; Fairfield.

1. *Come, all who truly bear,*	
The name of Christ your Lord,	1 Cor 1:2
His last mysterious supper share,	Matt 26:26

---

10. Ibid., 184.

Psalms and Hymns with Introductory Notes

And keep His kindest word:	Matt 26:28
Hereby your faith approve	Heb 11:39
In Jesus crucified,	
In memory of my dying love	
Do this, He said, and died.	1 Cor 11:25

2. The badge and token this,
The sure confirming seal — Rom 4:11
That He is ours, and we are His, — Song 2:16
The servants of His will,
His dear peculiar ones, — 1 Pet 2:9
The purchase of His blood; — Mark 10:45
His blood which once for all atones, — Heb 9:28
And brings us now to God. — Heb 2:10

3. Then let us still profess
Our Master's honoured name, — Rom 10:9–10
Stand forth His faithful witnesses, — Rev 12:11
True followers of the Lamb: — Rev 14:4
In proof that such we are — 1 John 3:1
His saying we receive,
And thus to all mankind declare — 1 Thess 1:8
We do in Christ believe. — 1 Thess 1:3

4. Part of His church below, — 1 Cor 12:27
We thus our right maintain,
Our living membership we show, — 1 Pet 2:5
And in the fold remain; — John 10:16
The sheep of Israel's fold — Mic 5:4
In England's* pastures fed,
And fellowship with all we hold — 1 John 1:3
Who hold it with our Head. — Eph 4:15

---

*One may substitute "worldwide" here, to avoid the parochialism of Wesley's line.

Part II: Psalms and Hymns arranged according to the Christian Year

74. "Jesu, at whose supreme command"

This hymn appears in section II (the longest single section), no. XXX. Meter: C.M. Tunes: Arnold's; Hampstead.

1. *Jesu, at whose supreme command*	1 Cor 11:24, 25
We thus approach to God,	
Before us in Thy vesture stand,	Rev 5:8
Thy vesture dipped in blood.	Isa 63:2
2. *Obedient to Thy gracious word,*	
We break the hallowed bread,	Acts 20:7
Commemorate Thee, our dying Lord,	Luke 22:19
And trust on Thee to feed.	John 6:35, 54
3. *Now Saviour, now Thyself reveal,*	
And make Thy nature known;	John 16:14
Affix the sacramental seal,	
And stamp us for Thine own.	2 Cor 1:22
4. *The tokens of Thy dying love*	Luke 22:19–20
O let us all receive,	
And feel Thy quickening Spirit move,	Col 2:13
And sensibly believe.	
5. *The cup of blessing, blest by Thee,*	1 Cor 10:16
Let us Thy blood impart;	
The bread Thy mystic body be,	Matt 26:26
And cheer each languid heart.	
6. *The grace which sure salvation brings*	Titus 3:5
Let us herewith receive;	
Satiate the hungry with good things,	Luke 1:53
The hidden manna give.	Rev 2:17
7. *The living Bread sent down from heaven*	John 6:50

Psalms and Hymns with Introductory Notes

In us vouchsafe to be;
Thy flesh for all the world is given,   John 6:51
And all may live by Thee.

8. Now, Lord, on us Thy flesh bestow,   John 6:51
And let us drink Thy blood,   John 6:54
Till all our souls are filled below   Eph 3:19
With all the life of God.   2 Cor 4:10

75. "Author of Life Divine"

This hymn appears in Section II, no. XL. Its opening verse recalls the words of dispensation in the Prayer Book formulary, "The body of our Lord Jesus Christ, which was given for thee, preserve thy body and soul unto everlasting life: take and eat this, in remembrance that Christ died for thee, and feed on Him in thy heart by faith with thanksgiving." Meter: 6.6.6.6.8.8., Tunes: Wesley; St. Godric.

1. Author of life Divine,   Acts 3:15
Who hast a table spread,   1 Cor 10:21
Furnishèd with mystic wine,   John 6:63
And everlasting bread,
Preserve the life Thyself hast given,   2 Tim 4:18
And feed and train us up for heaven.   John 6:27

2. Our needy souls sustain   Ps 23:3
With fresh supplies of love,
Till all Thy life we gain,   Phil 3:8
And all Thy fullness prove,   Eph 3:19
And, strengthened by Thy perfect grace   Eph 3:16
Behold without a veil Thy face.   2 Cor 3:18

Part II: Psalms and Hymns arranged according to the Christian Year

76. "Jesus, we thus obey"

This hymn appears also in Section II, no. LXXXI. The wording of this hymn has been altered considerably in the 1933 *MHB*, albeit without altering the general sense. Meter: S.M.D. Tunes: S.M. St. Augustine; S.M.D. Llanllyfni.

1. Jesus, we thus obey	
Thy last and kindest word;	1 Cor 11:24–25
Here in Thine own appointed way,	Luke 22:19
We come to meet our Lord:	1 Cor 10:16
The way thou hast enjoined	
Thou wilt therein appear;	Matt 18:20; John 6:48
We come with confidence to find	
Thy special presence here.	John 6:58
2. Our hearts we open wide,	
To make the Saviour room;	2 Pet 3:18
And lo! The Lamb, the Crucified,	Rev 13:8
The sinner's Friend, is come.	Matt 11:19
His presence makes the feast;	Matt 28:20
And now our bosoms feel	
The glory not to be expressed,	
The joy unspeakable.	1 Pet 1:8
3. With pure celestial bliss	
He doth our spirits cheer;	John 16:33
Thy house of banqueting is this,	
And He hath brought us here:	Song 2:4
He doth His servants feed	John 6:55
With manna from above,	John 6:49–50
His banner over us is spread	
His everlasting love.	2 Tim 1:9
#4. He bids us drink and eat	Matt 26:26–27
Imperishable food,	
He gives His flesh to be our meat,	John 6:51

And bids us drink His blood:	John 6:53
Whate'er the Almighty can	
To pardoned sinners give,	
The fullness of our God made man	John 1:1, 14
We here with Christ receive.	John 1:16

77. "In Jesus we live"

This hymn appears in Section III, no. XCV. Meter: 10.10.11.11. Tunes: Lyons; Montgomery.

1. In Jesus we live, In Jesus we rest,	Matt 11:29
And thankful receive His dying bequest;	Heb 9:15
The cup of salvation His mercy bestows,	Psalm 116:13
And all from His passion our happiness flows.	

2. With mystical wine He comforts us here,	
And gladly we join, Till Jesus appear,	1 Cor 11:26
With hearty thanksgiving His death to record;	
The living, the living, should sing of their Lord.	Isa 38:19

3. He hallowed the cup which now we receive,	Mark 14:23
The pledge of our hope with Jesus to live,	Matt 26:28–29
(Where sorrow and sadness shall never be found,)	Rev 21:4
With glory and gladness eternally crowned.	

4. The fruit of the vine (the joy it implies)	
Again we shall join to drink in the skies,	Mark 14:25
Exult in His favour, our triumph renew;	Rom 5:2, 11
And I, saith the Saviour, will drink it with you.	Matt 26:29

Part II: Psalms and Hymns arranged according to the Christian Year

78. "Victim Divine"

This hymn appears in Section IV, no. CXVI. Meter: 8.8.8.8.8.8. Tunes: Euphony; St. Chrysostom: Pater Omnium.

1. Victim Divine, Thy grace we claim,	Gal 1:4
While thus Thy precious death we show:	1 Cor 11:26
Once offered up, a spotless Lamb;	Isa 53:7
In Thy great temple here below,	
Thou didst for all mankind atone,	1 Tim 2:6
And standest now before the throne.	Heb 7:25; Rev 5:6
2. Thou standest in the holy place,	Heb 9:24
As now for guilty sinners slain:	1 Tim 1:15
The blood of sprinkling speaks, and prays,	Heb 12:24
All prevalent for helpless man;	
Thy blood is still our ransom found,	Ps 49:7; Matt 20:28
And speaks salvation all around.	Titus 2:11
#3. The smoke of Thy atonement here	Eph 5:2
Darkened the sun, and rent the veil,	Luke 23:45
Made the new way to heaven appear,	Heb 10:20
And showed the great Invisible;	1 Tim 1:17
Well pleased in Thee, our God looked down,	
And calls His rebels to a crown.	1 Cor 1:27–28
#4. He still respects Thy sacrifice,	Rom 4:25
Its savour sweet doth always please;	Eph 5:2
The offering smokes through earth and skies,	
Diffusing life, and joy, and peace;	2 Cor 2:14
To these Thy lower courts it comes,	
And fills them with divine perfumes.	Ps 45:8; 2 Cor 2:15
5. We need not now go up to heaven,	
To bring the long-sought Saviour down;	Rom 10:6–7
Thou art to all already given,	Rom 10:12

Thou dost even now Thy banquet crown: 1 Cor 5:7
To every faithful soul appear,
And show us Thy real presence here.   1 Cor 10:16

79. "Let Him to whom we now belong"

This hymn appears in Section V, no. CLVII, *Concerning the Sacrifice of Ourselves*, but could equally belong in the final section, *After the Sacrament*. Oddly, the hymn appears in the 1780 *Collection* in the section entitled "For Believers Saved," and in the 1933 *MHB*, no. 382, as a hymn of Dedication, in each case isolated from its original Eucharistic context. Meter: C.M. Tunes: Jackson; Byzantium; Tiverton.

1. *Let Him to whom we now belong*	1 Cor 3:23; Gal 5:24
His sovereign right assert,	Rom 12:1–2
And take up every thankful song,	Eph 5:19–20
And every loving heart.	
2. *He justly claims us for His own*	1 Cor 6:19
Who bought us with a price:	1 Cor 6:20
The Christian lives to Christ alone,	Rom 14:8
To Christ alone He dies.	
3. *Jesu, Thine own at last receive;*	Ps 73:24
Fulfil our heart's desire,	Ps 37:4
And let us to Thy glory live,	Eph 1:12, 14
And in Thy cause expire.	2 Cor 5:8–9
4. *Our souls and bodies we resign,*	1 Thess 5:23
With joy we render Thee	
Our all, no longer ours, but Thine	John 17:9–10
Through all eternity.	Rev 22:5

Part II: Psalms and Hymns arranged according to the Christian Year

N. Advent

As the Christian Year closes and turns again to Advent and the lead-up to the celebration of Christ's first coming, attention at this time (late November and into early December) also turns to eschatology: the Second Coming, the Last Judgment, the World to Come, etc. Many of Wesley's hymns affirm and reflect the hope of Christ's glorious return, which he describes with joyous anticipation. However, one will find no hint of a pre-tribulation "secret," or sudden and unobtrusive rapture—the doctrine commonly known as "Darbyism"—anywhere in these verses (or any others on the Second coming), since that notion did not arise until the 1830s, long after Wesley's death.

80. Psalm 98

This is an appropriate psalm with which to begin the selections, since its closing verses speak of the coming of the Lord for judgment. This version first appeared in *The Arminian Magazine*, 1798. Meter: 7.6.7.6.7.7.7.6. Tunes: Hatfield; Josiah.

1. Sing we to our conquering Lord	
A new triumphant song;	2 Cor 2:14
Joyfully His deeds record,	Ps 66:1, 5
And with a thankful tongue:	
Wonders His right hand hath wrought;	Rom 15:19
Still His outstretched arm we see;	Jer 27:5
He alone the fight hath fought,	
And got the victory.	Rev 1:18, 2:9
2. God, the Almighty God, hath made	
His great salvation known;	Eph 3:5–6
Openly to all displayed	
His glory in His Son:	Eph 3:11–12
Christ hath brought the life to light,	2 Tim 1:10
Bade the glorious Gospel shine,	
Showed in all the heathen's sight	Rom 3:29–30
His righteousness Divine.	Rom 3:22

3. *He to Israel's chosen race*	Acts 3:26, 13:33
His promise hath fulfilled:	Gal 3:29
Mindful of His word of grace,	Eph 1:13
His saving health revealed:	Ps 67:2
He to all the sons of men	Rom 1:14–15
Hath His truth and mercy showed;	Ps 25:10
Earth's remotest bounds have seen	Luke 2:30–31
The pardoning love of God.	
4. *Make a loud and cheerful noise*	Ps 100:1
To Him that reigns above;	1 Pet 3:22
Earth, with all Thy sons, rejoice	
In the Redeemer's love:	Rom 15:10–11
Raise your songs of triumph high,	
Bring Him every tuneful strain,	Eph 5:19
Praise the Lord who stooped to die,	John 10:18
To ransom wretched man.	Matt 20:28
5. *Him with lute and harp record,*	Ps 33:2–3
With shawms and trumpets praise;*	Isa 51:3
Sing, rejoice, before the Lord,	
And glory in His grace:	Rev 5:8–9
Hymn His grace, and truth, and power;	1 Tim 3:16
Give Him thanks, rejoice, and sing;	Heb 13:15
Praise Him, praise Him evermore,	
And triumph with your King.	1 Cor 15:57
6. *Ocean roar, with all thy waves*	Ps 96:11
In honour of His name;	
He who all creation saves	Ps 36:6
Doth all their homage claim:	
Clap your hands, ye floods! Ye hills,	Isa 55:12
Joyful all His praise rehearse;	
Praise Him till His glory fills	Isa 6:3

Part II: Psalms and Hymns arranged according to the Christian Year

The vocal universe.	Ps 72:19

7. *Lo! He comes with clouds, He comes*	Rev 1:7
In dreadful pomp arrayed!	Matt 24:31
All His glorious power assumes,	
To judge the world He made:	Matt 25:31ff.
Righteous shall His sentence be:	Matt 16:27
Think of that tremendous bar!	Acts 17:30–31
Every eye the Judge shall see!	
And thou shalt meet Him there!	Rom 2:16

*"Shawm": a mediaeval wind instrument

HYMNS ON THE SECOND COMING, ETC.

81. "We believe that Christ our Head"

This hymn, composed for a funeral, first appeared in *Hymns and Sacred Poems*, 1742, the first line being, "Let the world lament their dead," and is essentially a paraphrase of 1 Thessalonians 4:13–18. We pick it up at the second verse. Meter: 7.6.7.6.7.7.7.6. Tunes: Leamington; Russell Place; St. Hilary.

2. *We believe that Christ our Head*	Eph 4:15
For us resigned His breath,	Luke 23:46
He was numbered with the dead,	Isa 53:12; Luke 22:37
And dying, conquered death;	
Burst the barriers of the tomb;	Matt 28:2
Death could Him no longer keep:	Acts 2:24
He is the first-fruits become	1 Cor 15:23
Of those in Him that sleep.	Rev 14:13
3. *God, who Him to life restored,*	Acts 3:15
Shall all His members raise,	Phil 3:21
Bring them quickened with their Lord,	
The children of His grace.	Rom 8:11
We who then on earth remain	1 Cor 15:51

Shall not sooner be brought home;	
All the dead shall rise again	John 5:28–29
To meet the general doom.	Rev 20:12, 15
4. Jesus, faithful to His word,	Mark 13:23; Gal 1:12
Shall with a shout descend;	Acts 1:11
All heaven's host their glorious Lord	
Shall pompously attend.	Mark 8:38
Christ shall come with dreadful noise,	2 Pet 3:10
Lightnings swift, and thunders loud,	Isa 24:19–21
With the great archangel's voice,	Matt 24:31
And with the trump of God.	1 Cor 15:52
5. First the dead in Christ shall rise;	Isa 26:19
Then we that yet remain	
Shall be caught up to the skies,	
And see our Lord again.	Job 19:26; 1 John 3:2
We shall meet Him in the air,	2 Thess 2:1
All rapt up to heaven shall be,	John 14:3
Find, and love, and praise Him there,	Rev 7:15–17
To all eternity.	Rev 11:15
6. Who can tell the happiness	
This glorious hope affords?	1 John 3:3
Joy unuttered we possess	John 15:11
In these reviving words.	Rom 15:13
Happy, while on earth we breathe,	Ps 65:4
Mightier bliss ordained to know,	1 Thess 5:9–10
Trampling down sin, hell, and death,	
To the third heaven we go!	2 Cor 12:2

82. "The great archangel's trump shall sound"

This first appeared in *Hymns and Sacred Poems*, 1749. The occasion is interesting: Charles was preaching on March 14, 1744, in an upper room in

Part II: Psalms and Hymns arranged according to the Christian Year

Leeds, when the floor suddenly collapsed. CW relates the incident in his Journal, "I met the brethren at Leeds, and many others in an old upper-room. After singing, I shifted my place, to draw them to the upper end. One desired me to come nearer the door, that they might hear without. I removed again, and drew the weight of the people after me. In that instant the floor sank. I lost my senses, but recovered them in a moment, and was filled with power from above. I lifted up my head first, and saw the people under me heaps upon heaps. I cried out, 'Fear not: the Lord is with us; our lives are all safe!' and then, 'Praise God, from whom all blessings flow.'" Wesley records further that while there were injuries, no one was killed.[11] Meter: L.M. Tunes: Truro; Church Triumphant; Rimington.

1. *The great archangel's trump shall sound* 1 Thess 4:16
   (While twice ten thousand thunders roar), 2 Pet 3:10
   Tear up the graves, and cleave the ground, Dan 12:2; John 5:28–29
   And make the greedy sea restore.

2. *The greedy sea shall yield her dead,* Rev 20:13
   The earth no more her slain conceal,
   Sinners shall lift their guilty head, 2 Thess 1:9
   And shrink to see a yawning hell. Matt 25:41, 46

3. *But we who now our Lord confess,* Rom 10:9
   And faithful to the end endure, Matt 24:13
   Shall stand in Jesu's righteousness, Phil 3:9
   Stand as the Rock of Ages sure. Isa 32:2

4. *We, while the stars from heaven shall fall,* Mark 13:25
   And mountains are on mountains hurled, Rev 6:14
   Shall stand unmoved amidst them all, 2 Thess 1:7
   And smile to see a burning world.

5. *See the celestial bodies roll* Matt 24:29
   In spires of smoke beneath our feet!
   They shrivel as a parchment scroll! Rev 6:14

11. CWJ, entry for March 14, 1744.

The elements melt with fervent heat.	2 Pet 3:12

6. *The earth, and all the works therein,*	2 Pet 3:7
Dissolve, by raging flames destroyed,	2 Pet 3:10
While we survey the awful scene,	Rev 19:20
And mount above the fiery void.	2 Pet 3:13

7. *By faith we now transcend the skies,*	2 Cor 5:7
And on that ruined world look down;	
By love above all height we rise,	Eph 2:6
And share the everlasting throne.	2 Tim 2:12

83. "Lo! He comes with clouds descending"

This hymn is of multiple authorship: the original version comes from the young John Cennick (see Appendix A), who, allied with George Whitefield, contributed to the Methodist work in Bristol in its early days. Charles Wesley modified Cennick's hymn in *Hymns of Intercession for All Mankind*, 1758, while Martin Madan made some further alterations in 1760. Comparison with Cennick's original version reveals only a broad correspondence: it is fair to say that Wesley has certainly received inspiration from Cennick's original, but apart from verses 3 and 4 the hymn is essentially Wesley's own composition. Meter: 8.7.8.7.4.4.7. Tunes: Helmsley; Regent Square; Neander.

1. *Lo! He comes with clouds descending,*	1 Thess 4:16
Once for favored sinners slain;	John 10:11
Thousand thousand saints attending,	Deut 33:2
Swell the triumph of His train:	Matt 25:31
Hallelujah! Hallelujah!	
God appears on earth to reign.	1 John 2:28

2. *Every eye shall now behold Him*	Rev 1:7
Robed in dreadful majesty;	
Those who set at naught and sold Him,	Luke 23:18

Part II: Psalms and Hymns arranged according to the Christian Year

Pierced and nailed Him to the tree,	Luke 23:33; John 19:37
Deeply wailing, deeply wailing,	Zech 12:10ff.
Shall the true Messiah see.	Matt 26:64

#3. Every island, sea, and mountain,	Rev 16:20
Heav'n and earth, shall flee away;	Rev 20:11
All who hate Him must, confounded,	2 Thess 1:8
Hear the trump proclaim the day:	1 Cor 15:52
Come to judgment! Come to judgment!	Acts 17:31
Come to judgment! Come away!	

#4. Now redemption, long expected,	Heb 9:28
See in solemn pomp appear;	Rev 19:14
All His saints, by man rejected,	John 15:19
Now shall meet Him in the air:	1 Thess 4:17
Hallelujah! Hallelujah!	
See the day of God appear!	1 Thess 5:2

#5. Answer Thine own bride and Spirit,	Rev 22:17
Hasten, Lord, the general doom!	
The new Heaven and earth to inherit,	Isa 65:17; 2 Pet 3:13
Take Thy pining exiles home:	Heb 11:16
All creation, all creation,	Rom 8:22
Travails, groans, and bids Thee come!	Rom 8:21

6. The dear tokens of His passion	Luke 24:39-40
Still His dazzling body bears;	Luke 9:2-3; 2 Pet 1:16
Cause of endless exultation	
To His ransomed worshippers;	1 Pet 4:13
With what rapture, with what rapture	
Gaze we on those glorious scars!	2 Thess 1:10

7. Yea, Amen! let all adore Thee,	2 Pet 3:18
High on Thine eternal throne;	Heb 12:2
Savior, take the power and glory,	Rev 19:1, 16

Claim the kingdom for Thine own;	Rev 11:15
O come quickly! O come quickly!	Rev 22:20
Everlasting God, come down!	

84. "I would not, Lord, Thy Spirit bind"

This hymn first appeared in *Scripture Hymns*, 1762. As is well known, our Lord Himself refused to give a date for His coming in glory (Matt 24:36; Mark 13:32), but that has not deterred would-be date predictors through the centuries, to our own time. Wesley is adamant against any such endeavor in these lines based on Acts 1:7. Meter: 8.8.8.8.8.8. Tunes: Mozart; Giessen.

1. *I would not, Lord, Thy Spirit bind,*	
Or rashly bold prescribe to Thee,	Isa 40:13; 1 Cor 2:16
But wait submissive and resigned	Jas 5:7
Thy kingdom, when Thou wilt, to see;	1 Thess 5:1–2
The seasons of Thy grace are known,	2 Cor 6:2
The times of love to Thee alone.	

2. *Thy promised grace I dare not say*	
Thou wilt—Thou must—this instant give,	Rom 9:33–36
But humbly for Thy coming stay,	1 Thess 1:10
My misery with Thy mercy leave,	
Thy wisdom trust, and truth, and power,	Prov 3:5
Which sets the day, and sees the hour.	Zech 14:7

3. *No more presumptuous to foretell*	John 21:23
Or fix the appearing of my Lord;	
Till Thou these heavy clouds dispel,	Dan 7:13
Darkly I hang upon Thy word;	1 Cor 13:12
Each moment for Thy presence sigh	Phil 3:20
Whose glory fills both earth and sky.	Isa 6:3; John 12:41

4. *Surely if Thou direct my heart*	1 Sam 7:3; 2 Thess 3:5

Part II: Psalms and Hymns arranged according to the Christian Year

Into the expectation true,	Luke 12:40
Thou wilt to me Thy grace impart,	Eph 3:16
Thy Spirit's power in season due	1 Thess 1:5
The forfeited dominion give,	
And King in all Thy servants live.	Eph 3:17

85. "Thou Judge of quick and dead"

Now, on a more somber but necessary note, the Last Judgment, as indicated in Jude 6. This first appeared in *Hymns and Sacred Poems*, 1749, in a section entitled "Hymns for the Watchnight." Meter: S.M.D. Tunes: Leominster; Ich halte treulich still.

1. *Thou Judge of quick and dead,*	2 Tim 4:1
Before whose bar severe,	
With holy joy, or guilty dread,	Isa 8:13
We all shall soon appear;	2 Cor 5:10
Our cautioned souls prepare	
For that tremendous day,	Jude 6
And fill us now with watchful care,	Matt 24:42; Mark 13:35
And stir us up to pray.	Mark 14:38
2. *To pray, and wait the hour,*	1 Thess 1:10
That awful hour unknown,	Zech 14:6–7
When robed in majesty and power	
Thou shalt from heaven come down,	1 Thess 4:16
The immortal Son of Man,	Dan 7:13; Matt 26:64
To judge the human race,	Matt 25:32
With all Thy Father's dazzling train,	Matt 16:27
With all Thy glorious grace.	
#3. *To damp our earthly joys,*	2 Pet 3:11
To increase our gracious fears,	Luke 21:34
Forever let the archangel's voice	
Be sounding in our ears!	Joel 2:11; 1 Thess 4:16

The solemn midnight cry,	Matt 25:6
"Ye dead, the Judge is come;	
Arise, and meet Him in the sky,	1 Thess 4:17
And meet your instant doom!"	Matt 7:23

4. O may we thus be found	
Obedient to His word,	Matt 24:45–47
Attentive to the trumpet's sound,	1 Thess 4:16
And looking for our Lord!	2 Pet 3:12
O may we thus ensure	
A lot among the blest,	2 Pet 1:10–11
And watch a moment, to secure	Luke 21:36
An everlasting rest!	Heb 4:11

86. "Ye virgin souls arise"

Finally, the need to be watchful for His Coming, based on the Parable of the Ten Virgins in Matthew 25:1–13. This hymn first appeared in *Hymns and Sacred Poems*, 1749, in the section entitled "Hymns for the Watchnight." Meter: 6.6.6.6.8.8. Tunes: Christchurch; Crofts 136th; Trumpet.

1. Ye virgin souls arise,	
With all the dead awake,	Dan 12:2
Unto salvation wise,	Heb 9:28
Oil in your vessels take:	
Upstarting at the midnight cry,	1 Thess 5:6
Behold the heavenly Bridegroom nigh.	Isa 62:5

2. He comes, He comes to call	
The nations to His bar,	Ps 96:13; Matt 25:32
And raise to glory all	1 Cor 15:43
Who fit for glory are;	Rom 9:23
Made ready for the full reward,	2 John 8
Go forth with joy to meet your Lord.	

Part II: Psalms and Hymns arranged according to the Christian Year

3. Go meet Him in the sky,	1 Thess 4:17
Your everlasting Friend;	John 15:15
Your Head to glorify,	
With all His saints ascend:	
Ye pure in heart, obtain the grace	Matt 5:8
To see without a veil His face.	2 Cor 3:18

4. Ye that have here received	
The unction from above,	1 John 2:27
And in his spirit lived	Rom 8:11
Obedient to His love,	
Jesus shall claim you for His bride;	Eph 5:26–27
Rejoice with all the sanctified!	Heb 10:14

5. The everlasting doors	Ps 24:7, 9
Shall soon the saints receive,	Jas 5:8; Rev 1:3
Above yon angel powers	
In glorious joy to live;	
Far from a world of grief and sin,	Rev 21:27
With God eternally shut in.	Rev 21:3

6. Then let us wait to hear	1 Thess 1:10
The trumpet's welcome sound,	1 Thess 4:16
To see our Lord appear,	1 Pet 5:4
Watching let us be found;	
When Jesus doth the heavens bow,	Matt 24:30
Be found—as, Lord Thou find'st us now!	1 John 2:28

PSALMS AND HYMNS WITH INTRODUCTORY NOTES

O. New Year

From the outset of the Evangelical Revival, converts from both Whitefield's and Wesley's preaching would gather on December 31st for earnest prayer and seeking God's favor for the New Year. Thus New Year's Eve, 1738, saw a great outburst of Divine blessing at the love-feast of the Fetter Lane Society, at which the Wesleys and Whitefield were present, such that "the power of God came mightily upon us, inasmuch as many cried out for exceeding joy and many fell to the ground."[12] The Watch-night became an institution in Methodism from that time on.

87. Psalm 71:14-24

First published 1854, from a manuscript in the possession of Rev. H. Fish. A Psalm wherein the psalmist looks back to his younger years, with thankfulness to God, and hence is suitable for New Year. Part II, vv. 8–14. Meter: 8.8.8.8.8.8. Tunes: Solid Rock; Monmouth; Stella.

8. *I wait to prove Thine utmost grace,*	
To love and praise Thee evermore;	Ps 52:9
My mouth shall show Thy righteousness,	Ps 35:28
The riches of Thy saving power:	Rom 5:9
But who Thy saving power can tell?	
Its riches are unsearchable.	Eph 3:8
9. *Yet will I in Thy strength go forth,*	Isa 40:31
And spread Thy Righteousness Divine;	
Trample on all the creatures' worth;	
Merit and good are only Thine:	1 John 1:5
Impute it, and Thy sin's forgiven;	Rom 4:6–8
Implant, and man is meet for heaven.	2 Cor 7:1; Heb 12:14
10. *Me from my youth Thou, Lord, hast taught,*	2 Tim 3:15
And still I have Thy wonders shown;	Ps 77:14
Feeble and old, forsake me not	Ps 92:14

---

12. JWJ, entry for Jan 1, 1739, vol. 1, 161, where Wesley appears to be recounting the events of the previous night. Also cited in Heitzenrater, *Wesley and the People*, 90.

Part II: Psalms and Hymns arranged according to the Christian Year

Till I Thy saving power make known,
To this, and distant times record   Ps 22:31
My glorious, all-redeeming Lord.   Isa 4:2

11. *Thy righteousness is far above*   Ps 36:6
The human or angelic ken: 1 Pet 1:12
Who can express Thy mighty love,
Thy wonders towards the sons of men?   Ps 107:8, 15, 21, 31
What earthly power, or heavenly, dare   Isa 40:22–23
With Thee, the God of gods, compare?   Isa 40:18, 25

12. *Thee, Saviour of mankind, I bless,*
And thank thee for my troubles past;   2 Tim 3:11
Out of the depth of sore distress   Ps 130:1
Thy love shall bring me up at last;   2 Tim 4:18
Quicken, increase my faith, and guide,   Luke 17:5–6
And comfort me on every side.   Isa 12:1, 52:9

13. *Wherefore I will Thy goodness sing,*   Isa 12:5
Thy faithfulness with joy record;
My harp, and every tuneful string,   Ps 33:2
Shall sound the mercies of my Lord,   Ps 89:1
The Holy One of Israel praise,   Isa 12:6
The pardoning God of truth and grace.   Mic 7:18

14. *My lips shall glory in the song,*   Ps 63:3, 119:171
My soul in Thy redeeming love;
Thy righteousness shall all day long   Phil 3:9
The matter of my triumph prove;   Rom 1:16–17
For all the tempter's rage is o'er,   Rev 12:10–11
And sin and sorrow are no more.   Rev 21:4

HYMNS FOR NEW YEAR

88. "Come let us anew, our journey pursue"

This hymn was written originally for New Year's Day, 1750, a last-minute inclusion in *Hymns for New Year's Day*, 1749 (publ. early in 1750). Although intended for New Year, it looks back on the whole of life's journey in the light of eternity and Christ's coming in glory. It bids us take note of "the fugitive moment," and exhorts us to "improve our talents" ("improve" in the old sense of "build on" or "develop"), in what remains of our life. Meter: 5.5.5.11. Tunes: Ardwick; Derbe (repeat last line).

1. *Come, let us anew*	
Our journey pursue,	Ps 84:5; Heb 12:1
Roll round with the year,	Jas 4:13–15
And never stand still till the Master appear.	1 John 3:2–3
2. *His adorable will*	Rom 12:2
Let us gladly fulfil,	Col 1:9–10
And our talents improve,	
By the patience of hope, and the labour of love.	1 Thess 1:3
3. *Our life is a dream*	Job 20:8
Our time as a stream	
Glides swiftly away,	Ps 90:10
And the fugitive moment refuses to stay.	Ps 73:19
4. *The arrow is flown,*	
The moment is gone;	2 Cor 4:17
The millennial year*	
Rushes on to our view, and eternity's here.	Jude 20, 21
5. *O that each in the day*	
Of His coming may say:	Phil 2:16
I have fought my way through,	2 Tim 4:7
I have finished the work Thou didst give me to do!	John 17:4

Part II: Psalms and Hymns arranged according to the Christian Year

6. *O that each from his Lord*	
May receive the glad word:	2 Tim 4:8
Well and faithfully done;	Matt 25:21
Enter into my joy, and sit down on my throne!	Luke 22:29–30

*Whether this line indicates Premillennial belief on Wesley's part remains an open question. Probably not, however, since very next line would seem to indicate that the Second Coming ushers in eternity, rather than the halfway house of a millennium.

89. "Come let us arise, and press to the skies"

While this appears in *Hymns and Sacred Poems*, 1749, Charles originally wrote this specifically for his bride, Sally Gwynne, whom he married that year. Far from being just another romantic sonnet, Wesley here commits his life and that of his bride to his heavenly Master to guide and keep them through all the years of marriage ahead, a prayer that was abundantly fulfilled in their nearly thirty-nine years of wedlock. Moreover, Wesley shows in verses 5 and 6 a proper understanding of Matthew 25:31–46 as showing kindness to and service for Christian saints ("Christ's brethren," cf. Gal 6:10), rather than as mandating the modern "social gospel." In the 1780 *Collection* it appears as four eight-line verses. Meter: 5.5.5.11. Tune: Ardwick, Derbe.

1. *Come, let us arise,*	Eph 5:14
And press to the skies;	Phil 3:14
The summons obey,	
My friends, my beloved, and hasten away.	3 John 1:15
2. *The Master of all*	
For our service doth call,	Matt 24:45–46
And deigns to approve,	2 Tim 2:15
With smiles of acceptance our labour of love.	1 Cor 13:13; 1 Thess 1:3
3. *His burden we bear,*	Gal 6:17
Who alone can declare	
How easy His yoke,	Matt 11:30

While to love and good works we each other provoke.	Heb 10:24

4. *By word and by deed,*	Isa 50:4; Jas 2:17
The bodies in need,	Luke 10:33–34
The souls to relieve,	
And freely as Jesus hath given to give.	Acts 20:35; Matt 10:8

5. *Then let us attend*	Prov 19:17; Heb 6:10
Our heavenly Friend,	John 15:15
In His members distressed,	Matt 25:40
By want, or affliction, or sickness oppressed.	

6. *The prisoner relieve,*	
The stranger receive,	
Supply all their wants,	Matt 25:35–36
And spend and be spent in assisting His saints.	2 Cor 9:12

7. *Thus while we bestow,*	
Our moments below,	
Ourselves we forsake,	Luke 9:23
And refuge in Jesus's righteousness take.	Phil 3:9

8. *His passion alone,*	
The foundation we own;	Gal 6:14
And pardon we claim,	Rom 8:1
And eternal redemption, in Jesus's name.	Heb 9:15

90. "Sing to the great Jehovah's praise"

Hymn VII in a short collection of *Hymns for New Year's Day*, 1750. Originally three eight-line verses. Meter: C.M. Northrop (repeat last line); Richmond.

1. *Sing to the great Jehovah's praise;*	Ps 148:1
All praise to Him belongs;	

Part II: Psalms and Hymns arranged according to the Christian Year

Who kindly lengthens out our days,	Isa 46:4
Demands our choicest songs.	Isa 38:20; Eph 5:19

2. His providence hath brought us through	Jude 1:24
Another various year;	
We all with vows and anthems new	Ps 116:14
Before our God appear.	

3. Father, Thy mercies past we own;	Lam 3:22
Thy still continued care;	Phil 4:19
To Thee presenting, through Thy Son,	2 Cor 4:14
Whate'er we have or are.	

4. Our lips and lives shall gladly show	Heb 13:15–16
The wonders of Thy love,	
While on in Jesu's steps we go	1 Pet 2:21
To see Thy face above.	Rev 22:4

5. Our residue of days or hours	
Thine, wholly Thine, shall be;	1 Chr 29:11, 14
And all our consecrated powers	
A sacrifice to Thee.	Rom 12:1

#6. Till Jesus in the clouds appear	Rev 1:7
To saints on earth forgiven,	Heb 9:28
And bring the grand sabbatic year,	Heb 4:9
The jubilee of heaven.	Lev 25:8, 11

Psalms and Hymns with Introductory Notes

P. General Devotional Psalms and Hymns

Despite Charles Wesley's commitment to his brother John's perfectionist views—from which he distanced himself in later life (on this see Part III.A.3 below), his myriad array of hymns for worship, holy living, Christian service, union with Christ, pilgrimage and perseverance rank among the greatest ever written. In this section is reproduced a selection of two psalm versions and nine of his hymns to illustrate the depth and breadth, and the mystical dimension, of his Christian devotion.

91. Psalm 23

This first appeared in *The Arminian Magazine*, 1800, and was included in the 1933 *MHB* (no. 621), with verses 4 and 5 omitted. Meter: 7.7.7.7.7.7. Tunes: Redhead; Wells; Ratisbon.

1. Jesus the Good Shepherd is;	John 10:11
Jesus died the sheep to save;	John 10:15
He is mine, and I am His;	Song 2:16
All I want in Him I have—	
Life, and health, and rest, and food,	
All the plenitude of God.	Eph 1:23
2. *Jesus loves and guards His own;*	John 6:39
Me in verdant pastures feeds;	Ezek 34:14
Makes me quietly lie down,	Ps 3:5
By the streams of comfort leads:	Isa 12:2; 2 Cor 1:5
Following Him where'er He goes,	John 10:4
Silent joy my heart o'erflows.	
3. *He in sickness makes me whole,*	Luke 7:48
Guides into the paths of peace;	Luke 1:79
He revives my fainting soul,	Ps 119:25
'Stablishes in righteousness;	Isa 54:14
Who for me vouchsafed to die,	Isa 53:7; John 10:15
Loves me still—I know not why!	

Part II: Psalms and Hymns arranged according to the Christian Year

#4. Unappalled by guilty fear,
Through the mortal vale I go;   Job 10:21–22
My eternal Life is near;   Job 23:10–11; Luke 1:79
Thee my Life in death I know;   John 5:24
Bless my chastening, cheering rod,   Heb 12:10
Die into the arms of God!   Deut 33:27

#5. Till that welcome hour I see,   Rev 19:9
Thou before my foes dost feed;
Bid'st me sit and feast with Thee,   Rev 3:20
Pourest my oil upon my head;   Ps 92:10
Givest me all I ask, and more,   Eph 3:20
Makest my cup of joy run o'er.   Ps 16:5

6. Love Divine shall still embrace,   2 Thess 3:5
Love shall keep me to the end;   Phil 1:6
Surely all my happy days
I shall in Thy temple spend,   Ps 27:4
Till I to thy house remove,   2 Cor 5:1
Thy eternal house above.   2 Cor 5:8

NINE DEVOTIONAL HYMNS

(N.B. three of the following appear elsewhere in this book.)

92. "Thou hidden source of calm repose"

Herein is the full range of Christian experience—in this life. Hence when Wesley talks of weakness, toil, grief, war, loss, want, and so on, he is of course speaking of this present world. His happy soul is kept above (v. 2), while in all the miseries which belong to this world, and from which the Christian cannot escape, he looks to Christ as his sustaining comfort. Originally, the last line of verse 4 read, "my heaven in hell," by which he meant both the "heaven-on-earth" and the "hell-on-earth" experiences, which are the are but the tastes of each in this present world and life experience, just as Bunyan describes in his famous allegory *Pilgrim's Progress*. This first appears in *Hymns and Sacred Poems*, 1749. Meter: 8.8.8.8.8.8. Tunes: Pater Omnium; St. Chrysostom; Stella.

1. Thou hidden source of calm repose,	Matt 11:29
Thou all-sufficient love Divine,	2 Cor 12:9
My help and refuge from my foes,	Isa 25:4; Ps 46:1
Secure I am, if Thou art mine;	John 17:9, 11
And lo! From sin, and grief, and shame	
I hide me, Jesus, in Thy Name.	Ps 17:8
2. Thy mighty name salvation is,	Matt 1:21
And keeps my happy soul above;	Col 3:1, 3
Comfort it brings, and power, and peace,	2 Cor 1:3, 5
And joy, and everlasting love;	Isa 35:10
To me, with Thy dear name, are given	Isa 56:5
Pardon, and holiness, and heaven.	1 Cor 1:30
3. Jesu, my all in all Thou art;	1 Cor 3:22–23
My rest in toil, my ease in pain,	
The medicine of my broken heart,	Prov 17:22
In war my peace, in loss my gain,	
My smile beneath the tyrant's frown,	Acts 5:41
In shame my glory and my crown.	Gal 6:14
4. In want my plentiful supply,	Phil 4:12
In weakness my almighty power,	2 Cor 12:9
In bonds my perfect liberty,	Phil 1:13, 19
My light in Satan's darkest hour,	
In grief my joy unspeakable,	1 Pet 1:8
My life in death, my heaven, my all.*	Phil 1:21

*This line is a recent alteration from what Wesley originally wrote (see above).

Part II: Psalms and Hymns arranged according to the Christian Year

93. "Jesu, lover of my soul"

This hymn first appeared in *Hymns and Sacred Poems*, 1741, Part I, and while John Wesley included it in an early collection, *Hymns and Spiritual Songs*, published 1753, he did not include it in his *Collection* of 1780, because he considered it "too sentimental." However, due to its popularity, it reappeared in the revised *Collection* of 1797 (after John Wesley's death), and then in the *Collection with Supplement* in 1831. Since then it has appeared in all Methodist hymnals, and also in those of many denominations.

For all John's disapproval this has become one of Charles Wesley's best known and most loved hymns, as it speaks to Christian experience as few others do. We see here the love of Christ to the soul acutely conscious of sin, and our security of Christ as we face the "storms of life." Many are the wonderful stories of the blessing wrought by this hymn. One relates how in the American Civil War a Union sentry was on duty at night, and across the river a Confederate marksman took aim at him to shoot him dead, but then he heard the sentry singing this hymn. On hearing those strains the Confederate lowered his musket and refused to fire. Many years later the latter met that same sentry, told him his story, and the two former enemies were reconciled in love.[13]

Some have found difficulty with line 3 in verse 1, viz. "the nearer waters." Julian writes, "In life, as in nature, storms are local. One ship may be dashed hither and thither by the fury of 'the nearer waters,' whilst another is sleeping in the far distance on a throbless sea. Men cry for help, not against dangers which are both distant and undefined; but out of the depths of their immediate troubles."[14] Verse 3, usually omitted, is herein included. Meter: 7.7.7.7.D. Tunes: Hollingside; Aberystwyth; Everlasting Love (repeat the last two lines).

1. *Jesu, Lover of my soul,*	John 13:1
Let me to Thy bosom fly,	John 13:23
While the nearer waters roll,	
While the tempest still is high:	Mark 4:37

---

13. See Grace Church, *Life and Hymns*, at the 48:30 mark. The story about the origin and occasion of this hymn, whereby a bird flew in through a window from a storm and into Wesley's bosom (given in the lecture prior to this story), Julian discounts: see Julian, vol. 1, 591.

14. Julian, vol. 1, 591.

Psalms and Hymns with Introductory Notes

Hide me, O my Saviour, hide,	Ps 27:5
Till the storms of life be past;	
Safe into the haven guide,	Heb 6:19–20
O receive my soul at last.	Ps 73:24
2. Other refuge have I none,	Ps 46:1; Heb 6:18
Hangs my helpless soul on Thee;	
Leave, ah! Leave me not alone,	John 14:18
Still support and comfort me:	2 Cor 1:4
All my trust on Thee is stayed,	Ps 71:5; 2 Cor 3:4
All my help from Thee I bring;	
Cover my defenceless head	
With the shadow of Thy wing.	Ps 91:4
#3. Wilt Thou not regard my call?	
Wilt Thou not accept my prayer?	Ps 55:1
Lo! I sink, I faint, I fall—	Matt 14:30; Heb 12:3
Lo! On Thee I cast my care:	1 Pet 5:7
Reach me out Thy gracious hand!	Matt 14:31
While I of Thy strength receive,	
Hoping against hope I stand,	Rom 4:18; 1 Thess 1:3
Dying, and behold, I live!	2 Cor 6:9
4. Thou, O Christ, art all I want,	Phil 3:8, 14
More than all in thee I find.	
Raise the fallen, cheer the faint,	
Heal the sick, and lead the blind:	Mark 1:34; Isa 42:7
Just and holy is Thy name,	Luke 1:49
I am all unrighteousness;	Rom 7:14
False and full of sin I am,	Rom 3:13
Thou art full of truth and grace.	John 1:14
5. Plenteous grace with Thee is found,	John 1:16
Grace to cover all my sin;	
Let the healing streams abound,	Jer 8:22; Mal 4:2

Part II: Psalms and Hymns arranged according to the Christian Year

Make and keep me pure within:	1 Tim 5:22
Thou of life the fountain art,	John 4:14
Freely let me take of Thee,	
Spring Thou up within my heart,	John 7:38
Rise to all eternity.	

94. "O love Divine, how sweet Thou art"

Here Wesley takes us into the arms of Christ's abiding love, using the examples of Mary (sister of Martha), Peter, and John. Wesley sought earnestly to comprehend the length and breadth and height and depth of the love of God, but never did, and never could, having to conclude in the words of this hymn, "God only knows the love of God."[15] The threefold "Thou knowest that Thee I love" in verse 5 reflects the words of Peter in John 21:15–17. This hymn first appeared in *Hymns and Sacred Poems*, 1749, in the section entitled "Desiring to love." Meter: 8.8.6.D. Tunes: Pembroke; Praise.

1. O Love divine, how sweet thou art!	Eph 3:19
When shall I find my willing heart	1 Chr 28:9
All taken up by thee?	Matt 26:41
I thirst, I faint, I die to prove	John 7:37
The greatness of redeeming love,	
The love of Christ to me.	Gal 2:20
2. Stronger His love than death or hell;	Rom 8:38–39
Its riches are unsearchable;	Eph 3:8
The first-born sons of light	John 12:36
Desire in vain its depths to see;	
They cannot reach the mystery—	Phil 4:7
The length, and breadth, and height.	Eph 3:18–19
3. God only knows the love of God;	1 Cor 2:11
O that it now were shed abroad	Rom 5:5

---

15. As J. R. Watson observes in the DVD by Mohan, *Heart Set Free: Life, Ministry*, at the 1:22:25 mark and following.

Psalms and Hymns with Introductory Notes

In this poor, stony heart!*	Ezek 36:26
For love I sigh, for love I pine,	
This only portion, Lord, be mine,	Isa 61:7
Be mine this better part.	

4. *O that I could forever sit*	
With Mary at the Master's feet;	Luke 10:39
Be this my happy choice;	Luke 10:42
My only care, delight, and bliss,	
My joy, my heaven on earth, be this	Rom 14:17
To hear the Bridegroom's voice.	John 3:29

#5. *O that with humbled Peter, I*	
Could weep, believe, and thrice reply	Luke 22:61–62
My faithfulness to prove,	1 Cor 4:2
Thou knowest (for all to Thee is known),	Ps 139:1–5
Thou knowest, O Lord, and Thou alone,	
Thou knowest that Thee I love.	John 21:15–17

#6. *O That I could with favoured John*	
Recline my weary head upon	
The great Redeemer's breast!	John 21:20
From care, and sin, and sorrow free,	1 Pet 5:10
Give me, O Lord, to find in Thee	Matt 11:28
My everlasting rest.	Jer 6:16; Heb 4:1

#7. *Thy only love do I require,*	John 15:9
Nothing in earth beneath desire,	Luke 18:22; Phil 3:7
Nothing in heaven above;	Ps 73:25
Let earth, and heaven, and all things go,	
Give me Thy only love to know,	Phil 3:8, 10
Give me Thy only love.	

*Charles Wesley originally had here, ". . . cold, stony heart." John revised this to the reading above in the 1780 *Collection*.

Part II: Psalms and Hymns arranged according to the Christian Year

95. "Thou Shepherd of Israel and mine"

From *Scripture Hymns*, 1762, on Song of Songs 1:7. There is sound theology here, as well as intimate mysticism, and both blend beautifully (see below, Part III.B.2). Rattenbury remarks, "The hymn is beyond analysis, at least for me. To pull it to pieces would be sacrilege... it does show how the mystical and imaginative soul leaps over time... (and) realizes not only a Savior whom the mind of Charles Wesley taught him was in heaven at the right hand of God, but (also) an everyday companion..."[16] Meter: 8.8.8.8.D. Anapaestic. Tunes: Trewen; Llangristiolus.

1. Thou Shepherd of Israel and mine,   Ps 80:1
The joy and desire of my heart,   Phil 3:10
For closer communion I pine,
I long to reside where Thou art: Phil 1:23
The pasture I languish to find
Where all, who their Shepherd obey,   John 10:3–4
Are fed, on Thy bosom reclined,   John 13:23, 25
And screened from the heat of the day.   Isa 4:6, 32:2

2. Ah! Show me that happiest place,
The place of Thy people's abode,   Rev 21:3–4
Where saints in an ecstasy gaze,
And hang on a crucified God;   1 Cor 2:8
Thy love for a sinner declare,   Rom 5:8
Thy passion and death on the tree;   1 Pet 2:24
My spirit to Calvary bear,
To suffer and triumph with Thee.   1 Pet 4:13

3. 'Tis there, with the lambs of Thy flock, Isa 40:11
There only, I covet to rest,
To lie at the foot of the rock,   Isa 32:2
Or rise to be hid in Thy breast;
'Tis there I would always abide,   John 15:4
And never a moment depart,

---

16. Rattenbury, *Evangelical Doctrines*, 184.

Concealed in the cleft of Thy side,   John 19:34; 20:27
Eternally held in Thy heart.   John 17:24

96. "O Thou who camest from above"

This hymn, discussed above in Part I (p. 39), expresses Wesley's overwhelming desire for the Divine fire to energize him for the Lord's work. From *Scripture Hymns*, 1762, based on Leviticus 6:12–13. Meter: L.M. Tunes: Wilton; Hereford.

> 1. *O Thou who camest from above*
> *The pure, celestial fire to impart,*
> *Kindle a flame of sacred love*
> *On the mean altar of my heart.*
>
> 2. *There let it for Thy glory burn*
> *With inextinguishable blaze;*
> *And trembling to its source return,*
> *In humble prayer and fervent praise.*
>
> 3. *Jesus, confirm my heart's desire*
> *To work, and speak, and think for thee;*
> *Still let me guard the holy fire,*
> *And still stir up Thy gift in me.*
>
> 4. *Ready for all Thy perfect will,*
> *My acts of faith and love repeat,*
> *Till death Thy endless mercies seal,*
> *And make the sacrifice complete.*

97. "Happy the man that finds the grace"

This hymn, also discussed above (p. 40), is a paraphrase of Proverbs 3:13–18, but with Christian themes woven through it. From *Hymns for those that Seek, and those that Have Redemption in the Blood of Jesus*, 1747. Meter: L.M. Tune: Blockley.

> 1. *Happy the man that finds the grace,*
> *The blessing of God's chosen race,*
> *The wisdom coming from above,*
> *The faith that sweetly works by love.*

2. Happy beyond description he,
Who knows, the Saviour died for me,
The gift unspeakable obtains,
And heavenly understanding gains.

3. Wisdom divine! Who tells the price
Of wisdom's costly merchandise?
Wisdom to silver we prefer,
And gold is dross compared to her.

4. Her hands are filled with length of days,
True riches, and immortal praise:
Riches of Christ on all bestowed,
And honour, that descends from God.

5. To purest joys she all invites,
Chaste, holy, spiritual delights;
Her ways are ways of pleasantness,
And all her flowery paths are peace.

6. Happy the man who wisdom gains;
Thrice happy who his guest retains;
He owns, and shall forever own,
Wisdom, and Christ, and heaven are one.

98. "Love Divine, all loves excelling"

This hymn saw a checkered and controversial path even in Wesley's own lifetime. It first appeared in *Hymns for those that Seek and those that Have Redemption in the Blood of Christ*, 1747, but John Wesley omitted verse 2 from the 1780 *Collection* because to him it appeared to contradict what he taught in his *A Plain Account of Christian Perfection (1725–1777)*. This issue is discussed further in Part III.A.3. For all the controversy, however, this hymn ranks among Wesley's most loved, and is widely sung even today, notably at the wedding of Prince William and Kate Middleton (April 29, 2011). Meter: 8.7.8.7.D. Tunes: Love Divine; Blaenwern.

1. *Love Divine, all loves excelling,*	Hos 11:9; John 3:16
Joy of heaven, to earth come down;	Phil 2:6–7
Fix in us Thy humble dwelling,	John 14:23
All Thy faithful mercies crown!	
Jesu, Thou art all compassion,	Luke 7:13

Pure, unbounded love Thou art;
Visit us with Thy salvation!   Isa 62:11; Luke 1:68
Enter every trembling heart.

#2. *Breathe, O breathe Thy loving Spirit   John 20:22
Into every troubled breast,
Let us all in Thee inherit,   Heb 6:12; Rev 21:7
Let us find that second rest;
Take away our power of sinning,
Alpha and Omega be,   Rev 1:8, 22:13
End of faith, as its beginning,   1 Pet 1:9; Heb 3:14
Set our hearts at liberty.

3. Come, almighty to deliver,   Matt 6:13; Rom 7:24
Let us all Thy grace receive;   John 1:16
Suddenly return, and never,
Never more Thy temples leave.   1 Cor 3:16
Thee we would be always blessing,   Ps 16:7–8
Serve Thee as Thy hosts above,
Pray, and praise Thee, without ceasing,   1 Thess 5:17–18
Glory in Thy perfect love.

4. Finish then Thy new creation,   2 Cor 5:17
Pure and spotless let us be;
Let us see Thy great salvation   Heb 2:3
Perfectly restored in Thee;
Changed from glory into glory,   2 Cor 3:18
Till in heaven we take our place,
Till we cast our crowns before Thee,   Rev 4:10
Lost in wonder, love, and praise.   Rev 7:11–12

*Some modern hymn-books incorporate an altered version of verse 2, as follows:

     2. Breathe, O breathe Thy loving Spirit

Part II: Psalms and Hymns arranged according to the Christian Year

Into every troubled breast;
Let us all in Thee inherit;
Let us find the promised rest.   Heb 4:10–11
Take away the love of sinning;
Alpha and Omega be;
End of faith, as its beginning,
Set our hearts at liberty.

99. "Christ, my hidden life, appear"

From *Hymns and Sacred Poems*, 1742 (six verses in all). Also discussed below in Part III.B.1, under the theme of "The Hidden Life." Meter: 7.6.7.6.7.7.7.6. Tunes: Leamington; Hatfield.

#1. Christ, my hidden life, appear,	Col 3:3–4
Soul of my inmost soul;	
Light of life, the mourner cheer,	John 1:4
And make the sinner whole.	John 5:14
Now in me Thyself display,	1 Tim 1:16
Surely Thou in all things art;	
I from all things turn away,	
To seek Thee in my heart.	Jer 29:13
2. Open, Lord, my inward ear,	Ps 40:6
And bid my heart rejoice,	
Bid my quiet spirit hear	
Thy comfortable voice,	Isa 30:21
Never in the whirlwind found,	
Or where earthquakes rock the place;	1 Kgs 19:11–12
Still and silent is the sound,	1 Kgs 19:12
The whisper of Thy grace.	Isa 30:15
3. From the world of sin, and noise,	
And hurry, I withdraw;	Matt 6:6

Psalms and Hymns with Introductory Notes

For the small and inward voice	
I wait with humble awe:	
Silent am I now, and still,	1 Kgs 19:13
Dare not in Thy presence move;	Ps 41:12
To my waiting soul reveal	
The secret of Thy love.	Ps 25:14

4. Thou hast undertook for me,	
For me to death wast sold:	Rom 8:32
Wisdom in a mystery	1 Cor 2:7
Of bleeding love unfold;	
Teach the lesson of Thy cross,	Heb 12:2
Let me die with Thee to reign,	2 Tim 2:12; Rev 3:21
All things let me count but loss	Phil 3:8
So I may Thee regain.	

5. Show me, as my soul can bear,	
The depth of inbred sin;	Ps 139:23–24
All the unbelief declare,	
The pride that lurks within;	Mark 7:22
Take me, whom Thyself hast bought;	1 Pet 1:18–19
Bring into captivity	
Every high aspiring thought	
That would not stoop to Thee.	2 Cor 10:5

6. Lord, my time is in Thy hand,	Ps 31:15
My soul to Thee convert;	
Thou canst make me understand	Luke 24:45
Though I am slow of heart.	Luke 24:25–27
Thine, in whom I live and move,	Acts 17:28
Thine the work, the praise is Thine;	Eph 2:10
Thou art wisdom, power, and love,	
And all Thou art is mine.	1 Cor 4:21–23

Part II: Psalms and Hymns arranged according to the Christian Year

100. "Come on, my partners in distress"

This first appeared in *Hymns and Sacred Poems*, 1749. In the 1780 *Collection* it appears under the heading, "For Believers Suffering," and is intended to comfort those Christians facing hard times in life in general, and in their Christian life in particular. Yet when in verse 7 he bids us "conspire our rapture to complete," he desires us to transcend our lowly status and condition to the glories which await us. So then, shining through here are the themes of Christian pilgrimage, and at its end the beatific vision—something philosophers and mystics have long sought, but which Wesley has found—and can only be found—in Christ, which for now he anticipates in its fullness for the future. These words truly lift us to the heights! Meter: 8.8.6.D. Tune: Praise* (repeat the last line, then the last three lines); Habakkuk.

Psalms and Hymns with Introductory Notes

1. Come on, my partners in distress,   Ps 18:6; Isa 25:4
My comrades through this wilderness,   Isa 43:19
Who still your bodies feel;
A while forget your griefs and fears,   Ps 31:9
And look beyond this vale of tears   Ps 84:6
To that celestial hill.   Mic 4:1

2. Beyond the bounds of time and space,   2 Cor 4:18
Look forward to that happy place,   Rev 21:4
The saints' secure abode;
On faith's strong eagle pinions rise,   Isa 40:31
And force your passage to the skies,
And scale the mount of God.   Rev 3:12

#3. See, where the Lamb in glory stands,   Rev 14:1
Encircled with His radiant bands,
And join the angelic powers,   Ps 148:1–2, 12–13
For all that height of glorious bliss
Our everlasting portion is,   Isa 45:17; Lam 3:24
And all that heaven is ours.   1 Pet 1:4; Rev 21:7

4. Who suffer for their Master here,   Phil 1:29; 1 Pet 4:12
We shall before His face appear,   Rev 22:4
And by His side sit down:
To patient faith the prize is sure,   Phil 3:14
And all that to the end endure   Matt 16:24, 24:13
The cross, shall wear the crown.   2 Tim 4:8

5. Thrice-blessed, bliss-inspiring hope!   1 Pet 1:3–4
It lifts the fainting spirit up,   Rom 5:5
It gives life to the dead: John 5:21
Our conflicts here shall soon be past,   Rom 8:18
And you and I ascend at last
Triumphant with our Head.   Eph 1:22; Rev 19:14

Part II: Psalms and Hymns arranged according to the Christian Year

6. That great mysterious Deity	Ps 139:6, 147:4–5
We soon with open face shall see:	
The beatific sight	Rev 21:22–23
Shall fill the heavenly courts with praise,	Rev 11:15–17
And wide diffuse the golden blaze	
Of everlasting light.	Isa 60:19
7. The Father shining on His throne,	Rev 4:2–3
The glorious co-eternal Son,	Matt 17:1–2
The Spirit One and Seven,	John 14:26; Rev 1:4
Conspire our rapture to complete;	
And lo! We fall before His feet,	Rev 5:8
And silence heightens heaven.	Rev 8:1–2
8. In hope of that ecstatic pause,	Titus 2:13
Jesus, we now sustain Thy cross,	Matt 16:24
And at Thy footstool fall,	
Till Thou our hidden life reveal,	Col 3:3–4
Till Thou our ravished spirits fill,	Eph 3:19
And God is all in all.	1 Cor 15:28

*Music is included here for the benefit of American readers who may not be familiar with this stirring tune.

101. "Praise the Lord, who reigns above"

Finally, to round off the entire selection, we conclude with Wesley's version of *Psalm 150*, from *Psalms and Hymns*, 1743 (1933 *MHB*, no. 14). Meter: 7.6.7.6.7.7.7.6. Tunes: Russell Place; Amsterdam.

1. Praise the Lord, who reigns above,	Ps 97:1
And keeps His court below;	Ps 65:4
Praise the holy God of love;	Ps 138:2
And all His greatness show!	
Praise Him for His noble deeds,	Judg 5:11; Ps 145:4
Praise Him for His matchless power;	

Psalms and Hymns with Introductory Notes

Him, from whom all good proceeds,	Isa 63:7
Let earth and heaven adore.	Ps 103:21–22

#2. Publish, spread to all around	Rom 15:9–12
The great Jehovah's name;	Ps 148:13
Let the trumpet's martial sound	Matt 24:31
The Lord of Hosts proclaim!	2 Chr 15:12, 14
Praise Him in the sacred dance,	
Harmony's full concert raise;	
Let the virgin choir advance,	Ps 45:14–15
And move but to His praise.	

3. Celebrate the eternal God	Isa 57:15
With harp and psaltery;	
Timbrels soft, and timbrels loud,	Ps 149:3–4
In His high praise agree;	
Praise Him every tuneful string,	Hab 3:19
All the reach of heavenly art;	
All the power of music bring,	Ezra 3:10–11
The music of the heart.	Eph 5:19

4. Him in whom they move and live,	Acts 17:28
Let every creature sing;	
Glory to their Maker give,	Ps 149:2
And homage to their King!	Ps 95:6
Hallowed be His name beneath,	
As in heaven on earth adored;	Matt 6:9–10
Praise the Lord in every breath;	
Let all things praise the Lord!	Eph 1:10

PART III

Theological Issues and Themes in Christian Experience

A. Theological Issues

1. Wesley and Incarnational Theology

The Incarnational hymn, "Let earth and heaven combine" (no. 19 above) includes the following verse:

> *He deigns in flesh to appear,*
> *Widest extremes to join;*
> *To bring our vileness near,*
> *And make us all divine.*
> *And we the life of God shall know,*
> *For God is manifest below.*

I commented above that this has definite overtones of the Incarnational theology of the Eastern Orthodox churches. It will be appropriate here to explain what this theology is, and to what extent Wesley came under its influence.

The Eastern view of the Incarnation and salvation traces back to the divinization ($\theta\varepsilon\omega\sigma\iota\varsigma$)[17] concept of Gregory of Nazianzus and Gregory of Nyssa in the later fourth century, and then passed on through the Greek fathers, notably John of Damascus, and down to the present day.[18] By this view, the very Incarnation of the Word (John 1:14) makes possible man's union with the Divine, no less than his deification. The Incarnation of the Word is the fulfillment of the entire redemptive process. Philip Kariatlis of St. Andrew's Theological College (Greek Orthodox Archdiocese of Australia) states the doctrine as follows:

> The *hypostatic union* of divine and human accomplished in Christ, was the very *foundation* of the *deification of humanity.* Since Christ took on human nature and bestowed upon it the fullness of grace, He made humanity capable of ascending to God.[19]

The idea is held to begin with Athanasius (296–373 AD) in his affirmation, "For He was made man that we might be made God,"[20] but that famous

---

17. $\theta\varepsilon\omega\sigma\iota\varsigma$: *Deification, divinization*; see Lampe, 649. Cf. $\theta\varepsilon\iota\omega\varsigma$, 1. *Divinely*; ibid.

18. The basic idea also came into the West, albeit in a more heretical, pantheistic form, through John Scotus Erigena (c.810–c.877). See Schaff, *History of the Christian Church*, vol. 5, 486–87.

19. Kariatlis, "Credible Presentation of Redemption." Emphasis original.

20. Athanasius, "The Incarnation of the Word," § 54 in *NPNF*, 65.

opponent of Arianism is also very clear on Christ dying for our sins, in our place, as our Representative and Substitute, as Protestantism has always held.[21] Rather, it is with the "Cappadocian fathers" (Basil the Great, Gregory of Nazianzus, and Gregory of Nyssa) that the "divinization" concept proper begins, and in turn Gregory of Nyssa will be a useful starting point.

Although outstanding in expounding and defending orthodox Christianity against the Arians and various other heretics, for which he will be forever honored, Gregory's view of salvation sees the Incarnation itself as pivotal in this regard. For Gregory, man is fallen and his nature corrupt, but salvation is thought of in remedial terms: "healing," "medicine," "therapy," and the like, and consequently for the individual salvation is a process, not an event or a state. Here is where the Incarnation comes in: the Son of God became the Son of man so that men might become God, and ascend to God. By virtue of the Incarnation, man becomes a sharer in His Divinity, and that is a process of deification which begins here on earth but reaches its fullest expression and union with God in the world to come.[22]

While much of this theology is essentially speculative and rather thin on Scripture support, two key texts form the backbone of the Eastern view: John 17:23, "I in them, and Thou in Me, that they may be perfected into one"; and also 2 Peter 1:4, ". . . you may become partakers of the divine nature." However, in the latter Peter has in mind regeneration by the Holy Spirit, but he does not link this with the Incarnation as such. As to the John 17 text, it is true that Christ indwells believers through the advent of the Holy Spirit into their lives, as this text teaches, but this does not amount to "divinization," nor is there any link there with the Incarnation as the means to this end.

More could be said on this theme, but the question here is, how did this kind of theology come into England, and within the purview of the Wesleys? The answer lies in the viewpoints of the Non-juror party, whose mystical outlook attracted them *inter alia* to Eastern theology. The Non-jurors represented the quintessence of seventeenth century high-church Anglicanism: mystical, ascetic, moralistic, and sacramental, while politically they refused the Oath of Allegiance to William III, and later to George I. Among their number were several devout bishops, and also William Law,

---

21. See ibid., §§ 9–10, 20 (40–41, 47). Kariatlis, in line with the teaching of the Greek Orthodox Church, rejects this understanding of the Cross as penal substitution in his "Credible presentation." Athanasius, however, clearly teaches this but does not lay emphasis on it since it was not a major issue in the fourth century.

22. See Dunstone, *Atonement in Gregory of Nyssa*, 14–17.

A. Theological Issues

author of *A Serious Call to a Devout and Holy Life*. They were aware of and admired Eastern Orthodox theology, made contacts with their leaders, and even desired a union with their branch of Christendom.[23]

Susannah Wesley likewise had strong sympathies with the Non-jurors, and she transmitted their views to her own children. Hence, Law's *Serious Call* exercised a profound influence on John in the 1720s, while Charles also demonstrated the influence of Law's book, plus other literature beloved of the Non-jurors. These influences moved him to shake off the dissolute lifestyle of the university, and to establish the Holy Club. Hence, indirect contacts with Eastern theology would have been part of the "mix" of ideas in those early days, but the evangelical conversion of the Wesley brothers in 1738 changed their outlook profoundly. Justification by faith caused both to break with the false mysticism of their upbringing and early influences. However, it was not a complete break, and Charles felt able to combine some elements of the Eastern view with his evangelical experience, and his thorough understanding of Scripture, at least as far as they did not come into direct conflict.

Hence in the Incarnational hymn quoted above, Wesley might on one hand reflect the Eastern outlook up to a point, yet in the line which talks about "making us all divine" he only reflects here the teaching of 2 Peter 1:4. Furthermore, the Incarnation in the plan of redemption simply opens the gate to "the life of God" and being "made perfect first in love;" but it does not of itself effect this change. Put another way, his view has a "salvation history" orientation; that the Incarnation begins the outworking of God's plan of salvation, through the cross and resurrection, to ultimate glory. The Incarnation is the beginning of that grand sequence of events, in which every believer participates (Rom 6:4–5, 8), through "the cross, the grave," and reaching its climax in "the skies":

> *Soar we now where Christ has led,*
> *Following our exalted Head;*
> *Made like Him, like Him we rise,*
> *Ours the cross, the grave, the skies.*

Likewise with the process of sanctification, whereby "our vileness" is "brought near": the Incarnation is indeed the doorway to this in the Divine plan, but Wesley does not state that the Incarnation is "the fulfillment of the entire redemptive process"—not here, and certainly not elsewhere.

---

23. Toon, Peter. "Nonjurors," in *NIDCC*, 714.

Part III: Theological Issues and Themes in Christian Experience

The Cross for Wesley is central, as Manning put it so well, "He (Wesley) is always at Calvary; no other place in the universe matters..."[24]

Eastern "Incarnational theology" indeed has its useful insights, but suffers too much from philosophical and theological speculation, and from its appeal to tradition and the opinions of certain Church Fathers rather than Scripture.

---

24. Manning, 43.

2. Theopaschitism

Something of a long-standing problem in Wesley's hymns is the oft-occurring theme of God suffering on the cross, and even of God dying thereon. How are we to grapple with the jarring and seemingly aberrant theology in such lines as these:

> O Love divine, what hast Thou done?
> The immortal God hath died for me!
> The Father's co-eternal Son
> Bore all my sins upon the tree;
> The immortal God for me hath died!
> My Lord, my Love is crucified.

Or again, in the very familiar verse:

> Amazing love! How can it be,
> That Thou my God shouldst die for me?

An ancient heresy in the Church is called Patripassianism, usually associated with Praxeas in the late second century, whereby God the Father suffered on the cross, and it is into this error that Wesley is sometimes alleged to have fallen. However, to be more accurate, the error (if such it be) is that of Theopaschitism, a corollary of the later Monophysitism of the Alexandrian theologians, whereby Christ as the Divine Logos absorbed the human nature such that He was simply the one Divine Person, and could properly be called "God."[25] Hence it was God who suffered on the cross. The famous Council of Chalcedon, 451 AD, rejected this view and set forth its formula that Christ is one divine Person in two natures. Wesley, as a result of his theological training at Oxford, would have been well aware of these Christological issues, and subscribed to the 39 Articles, Article II of which enshrines the Chalcedonian Formula.[26]

Handley Moule remarks in this connection:

> "The Human Nature of the Son never, for a moment, stood or
> stands apart from His Divine nature and Person. God sent forth
> His Son, born of a woman (Gal 4:4). He did not send His Son to

---

25. See Robert Wilken, "Monophysitism," in *EEC*, 620–21.
26. "The Son, which is the Word of the Father . . . took Man's nature in the womb of the blessed Virgin, of her substance: so that two whole and perfect Natures, that is to say, the Godhead and the Manhood, were joined together in one Person, never to be divided, whereof is one Christ, very God, and very Man; who truly suffered, was crucified, dead, and buried, to reconcile His Father to us . . ." (Art. II)

> join a man born of a woman; which would have been an alliance of two persons, not a harmony of two natures in relation to one Person. The Manhood was, and is, never independently personal. It is better to say Christ is *man*, than Christ is *a man*."[27] (Emphasis his)

An esteemed minister once remarked about the above excerpt from *And can it be*: "These heresies you sing in your hymns! One may indeed say that 'God manifest in human flesh died for me,' but not that 'God died for me.'" However, this is too slick. Despite the venerable minister's citation of 1 Timothy 3:16 (KJV) in this connection, are we to say that Christ as the Son of God "morphed" Himself into a man, albeit a very special man, and that this resultant hybrid is the one who died on the cross? Or alternatively, is it that Christ was some sort of "split personality"—Divine and human, and that only the human side of Him was what suffered and died?

If labels be of any use, the former is the modern "Kenotic" heresy, whereby the Son laid aside His essential Deity in order to become man (according to a misinterpretation of εκενωσεν in Phil 2:7): in other words, Deity reduced! The second is the ancient Nestorian heresy, which saw Christ as essentially a man in whom the Divine Logos (of John 1:1) dwelt in a special way—where "special way" is undefined. In other words we would have a schizophrenic Christ, two persons in one body; or perhaps even a refined form of Adoptionism, the view that Christ was basically a man who "adopted" the Divine Spirit at some stage of his life (usually seen as at His baptism).

On the contrary, the classic doctrine of the incarnation and the two natures is of one, indivisible Person with two natures, Divine and human, who ceased not to be what He was, i.e., the eternal Son of God; but who became what He was not, i.e., the man, Jesus of Nazareth. Thus He cannot in principle be "carved up" in any simplistic manner. The Person of Christ is a mystery, beyond human understanding, and that mystery must be preserved at all costs, but not "solved." To attempt the latter is indeed to invite heresy.

Does Wesley then flirt with the Monophysite and the consequent Theopaschitic heresy? Having been thoroughly schooled in theology at Oxford, and in particular in regard to these ancient heresies, it is not only highly doubtful, but really a nonsense proposition to assert that he does. Therefore, let us consider another aspect of the issue of Christ's Divine-human

---

27. See Moule, *Outlines of Christian Doctrine*, 61–62.

A. Theological Issues

Person, often overlooked, i.e., what theologians call the "communication of the attributes" (Latin: *communicatio idiomatum*), whereby the attributes of Christ's humanity may be referred to Him in His Divine Person, and *vice versa*. Louis Berhkof explains it as follows:

> "*A communication of properties.* This means that the properties of both, the human and the divine natures, are now the properties of the one Person, and are therefore ascribed to the one Person. The Person can be said to be almighty, omniscient, omnipresent and so on, but can also be called a man of sorrows, of limited knowledge and power, and subject to human want and miseries."[28]

This is the standard Reformed position, but against this is the Lutheran view, which Berkhof explains as an actual transference of attributes, usually understood as the divine to the human.[29] One can see how this does indeed veer toward the Monophysite position (although Lutherans would deny this). This being the case, we must predicate all actions and sufferings of the one Person of Christ, the Divine Person in His impersonal human nature, and hence affirm, "God suffered"; "God died." A mystery indeed, as Wesley himself both confesses and adores:

> *'Tis mystery all: the Immortal dies!*
> *Who can explore His strange design?*
> *In vain the first-born seraph tries*
> *To sound the depths of love Divine.*
> *'Tis mercy all! Let earth adore!*
> *Let angel minds inquire no more!*

Not only angel minds, but human minds as well: let them "inquire no more," but adore the mystery!

Both Wesleys were well acquainted with the "communication-of-attributes" issue also, and we may remark that the Anglican position on the *communicatio* in general follows the Reformed line (as noted in the quotation from Moule) rather than the Lutheran. John Wesley shows his awareness of the issue as various passages in his sermons indicate, but a reference in his *Notes on the New Testament* (on John 3:13) likewise attests this awareness, as follows:

---

28. Berkhof, *Systematic Theology*, 324.
29. Ibid., 325.

> "Therefore He is omnipresent: else He could not be in heaven and on earth at once. This is a plain instance of what is usually termed the communication of properties between the divine and the human nature, whereby what is proper to the divine nature is spoken concerning the human; and what is proper to the human is, as here, spoken of the divine."[30]

In using the word "spoken" Wesley clearly sides with the Reformed position as opposed to the Lutheran view of an actual transference. After some discussion, Deschner concludes that while Wesley has points of affinity with both Lutheran and Reformed, in general he is on-side with the Reformed view.[31] Whatever the precise details here, it is in this aspect of the doctrine of Christ's Person that we must resolve the apparent difficulty posed by Wesley's hymns. We might note that even the New Testament in two places uses Wesley-type language in regard to Christ's death, viz. Acts 20:28, ". . . the church of God which He purchased with His own blood";[32] and again in 1 Corinthians 2:8, ". . . they crucified the Lord of glory."

Bernard Manning remarks on these attempts to impugn Wesley's orthodoxy:

> "Wesley's orthodoxy, it is true, some of your modern theologians have been rash enough to question. With puny daring, they suggest he denies the true humanity of the Son and flirts with patripassianism. This is a feeble and unconvincing display by men who wince before the strength of his doctrine. Let them master the doctrine of the communication of attributes, as Wesley mastered it, and fears for his orthodoxy will give place to fears for their own."[33]

Let us therefore identify with the robust doctrine of the Incarnation in Wesley's lines, and not be afraid to sing them with conviction.

---

30. Wesley, *Explanatory Notes NT*, comm. *in loc.* on John 3:13, 312.

31. Deschner, *Wesley's Christology*, 33–35.

32. The text is admittedly difficult here, as the manuscripts vary, some reading "church of God," others reading "church of the Lord." Also, the manuscript testimony divides between "His own blood" and "blood of His own." Bruce Metzger, *Textual Commentary on the Greek NT*, 480–82, after a lengthy discussion opts for the reading above.

33. Manning, 28.

A. Theological Issues

3. Perfectionism

Much has been written on the subject of John Wesley's doctrine of Christian perfection, which both he and Charles called "perfect love," and I do not here propose to add to that voluminous discussion in respect of its theology. My purpose here is simply a historical-biographical one, i.e., to explore to what extent his hymns express this view, and whether he moved away from it in later life.

When the controversy over predestination erupted in 1740, the fracas was not only over that issue, but also this teaching of "perfect love," the belief that God would, with those who diligently sought and strove, root out all sin in the believer this side of glory. "The gradual process is interrupted . . . by the direct intervention of God, which in a single instant raises man to a higher plane."[34] We see this in such verses as these:

Verse 5 of his paraphrase of Psalm 45 (published in *Psalms and Hymns*, 1743):

> *Still let the word of truth prevail,*
> *The Gospel of Thy general grace,*
> *Of mercy mild that ne'er shall fail,*
> *Of everlasting righteousness;*
> *Into the faithful soul brought in,*
> *To root out all the seeds of sin.*[35]

In a collection prior to this, Wesley sings of "the rest" which remains to all God's people (*Hymns and Sacred Poems*, 1740; 1780 *Collection*, no. 311; 1933 *MHB*, no. 563):

> *A rest, where all our soul's desire*
> *Is fixed on things above;*
> *Where fear, and sin, and grief expire,*
> *Cast out by perfect love.*

The same hope and belief appears in these verses from *Hymns and Sacred Poems*, 1742 (1780 *Collection*, no. 394; 1933 *MHB*, no. 557):

> *I wait, till He shall touch me clean,*
> *Shall life and power impart,*

---

34. Lindström, *Wesley and Sanctification*, 121; also quoted in Wood, *Burning Heart*, 267.

35. Osborn, vol. 8, 103.

Part III: Theological Issues and Themes in Christian Experience

> *Give me the faith that casts out sin*
> *And purifies the heart.*
> *This is the dear redeeming grace,*
> *For every sinner free;*
> *Surely it shall on me take place,*
> *The chief of sinners, me.*[36]

We could go on multiplying examples, but the picture should be clear: both Wesleys taught a "second blessing," which issued in Christian perfection, although Charles understood this somewhat differently from his brother. The original wording of verse 2 of the famous hymn "Love Divine, all loves excelling" gives expression to this view:

> *Breathe, O breathe Thy loving Spirit*
> *Into every troubled breast,*
> *Let us all in Thee inherit,*
> *Let us find that second rest;*[37]

However, it is significant that neither Charles nor John ever claimed this "perfect love" experience for themselves. In response to a challenge from the Bishop of London to produce examples of such people, John could only say that it was true of certain others, and believed that he could point them out, e.g., John Fletcher of Madeley, but he never claimed it for himself. In short, this factual side of his teaching always caused him much perplexity. Charles's hymns likewise may express the *desire* for perfect love, and even the belief that God *would* bestow it, but they never express any claim to be in possession of it.[38] Charles had from his pre-conversion days taught this doctrine, as in a sermon preached on board ship in October 1735, while en route to Georgia: "Christian perfection is the goal of our religious race . . . Hitherto must all our desires be bent; hitherto must all our endeavors tend."[39]

By such striving, yearning, and praying, Wesley was confident that a time would come when:

> *Selfish and vain desires in me*
> *Shall never more reside,*
> *When Thou, with all Thy purity*

---

36. Ibid., vol. 2, 304–5.
37. Ibid., vol. 4, 219.
38. As observed by Lloyd-Jones, "New Developments," 88.
39. Cited in Tyson, *Assist Me to Proclaim*, 232.

A. Theological Issues

Dost in my heart abide.
Thy uttermost salvation then
I in thy presence prove;
The crown of righteousness obtain,
The heights and depths of love.[40]

During the 1750s, however, Charles was growing apart from his brother in a number of respects: his meddling in John's marital affairs caused friction, while also his theological move in Whitefield's direction likewise caused tensions. Indeed, Whitefield as early as September 1747, writing from Philadelphia, remarks in a letter to John Wesley that both were (apparently) speaking "more moderately with respect to sinless perfection."[41] Then as the 1760s dawned, there was an outburst of apparent blessing in a number of John Wesley's congregations, first in Yorkshire and then in London, when several testified to receiving this gift of "perfect love."[42] Charles was suspicious of these claims from the outset, however, which he thought to be nothing more than vain boasting, and that the truly perfect would boast only that Christ was to them their "all in all."

Hence in the year 1761, Wesley published anonymously a collection of hymns commenting on the perfection doctrine, i.e., *Hymns for Those to Whom Christ is All in All*. Wesley states in his "Advertisement," that these hymns are peculiarly designed for those who . . . "love the Lord their God with all their heart, and their neighbor as themselves." They labor to "abstain from all appearance of evil," and are "zealous of good works." And they daily "grow in grace and in the knowledge of our Lord Jesus Christ."[43] Such sentiments every astute Christian would endorse. Moreover, these caveats urging "labor," "zeal," "growth in grace," etc., had been standard

---

40. Cited in ibid., 235, and is part of the hymn "Fain would I wash my soul from sin," based on Jer 4:14, in *Scripture Hymns*, 1762, Osborn, vol. 10, no. 1291, 11–12. However, in the catalogue of Wesley's *Scripture Hymns* in the Wesley Center Online it should come between 1179 and 1180, but is omitted. [Herein a correction to n. 17 in my article in *RTR* 74 (August 2015) 101, where I incorrectly stated that this hymn came from the early 1740s.]

41. Letter from Rev. George Whitefield, in Baker, *Wesley, Letters*, 261. He pleads therein for reconciliation with both the Wesley brothers.

42. Wesley recounts some of these experiences in his journal for late February and early March 1760, JWJ, vol. 2, 498–99. Noteworthy are the testimonies of an unnamed person, and also of a certain Elizabeth Longmore, ibid., 500–502. Tyson also summarizes this episode in *Assist Me to Proclaim*, 243–45.

43. C. Wesley, "Advertisement" to *Hymns for those to Whom Christ is All in All*, in Maddox, Wesley Centre Online.

fare for both Wesleys in their holiness teaching from the outset; they were no friends of any "let go, and let God" theology, a view more akin to the quietism of certain Moravians, which they both trenchantly criticized.

Important in this connection are the hymns composed at the same time, i.e., during his illness of 1760–61, where we gain an insight into his thoughts on the subject in more mature years. Charles in his preface to these *Hymns on Select Passages of the Holy Scriptures* (published 1762; cited here as *Scripture Hymns*) assures the readers, "Several of the hymns are intended to prove, and several to guard, the doctrine of Christian perfection."[44] However, in the light of the various verses cited below, it is to be questioned what precisely he was safeguarding: the conventional Reformed doctrine of sanctification, i.e., a process not completed in this life, but in which a maturity is certainly possible; or is it his brother's view of a second blessing of "perfect love" (however that is defined) coming this side of glory? We here examine some selected excerpts to ascertain his thinking at this stage.

In the verse cited above ("Selfish and vain desires in me . . ."), from the hymn based on the text, "Wash your heart that you may be saved" (Jer 4:14), Wesley further on expresses his deep longing:

> *Come then, O Lord, into my heart,*
> *That sin forever may depart,*
> *With every low desire;*
> *That on the wings of faith and love*
> *I may to those bless'd realms above*
> *In every thought aspire.*[45]

This may seem at first glance to be his perfection doctrine, but on reflection all he is affirming here is the truth that "without holiness no-one will see the Lord" (Heb 12:10). There is no claim either to present possession of this state, or that he may confidently expect it in this life. In fact, in the very next verse he yearns for the glory which awaits both him and all the saints, a glory which comes with perfect holiness:

> *O could I now in garments white*
> *Ascend, and greet the sons of light*
> *Who through Thy cross o'ercame,*
> *Thy dazzling face with transport see,*

---

44. *Scripture Hymns*, 1762, ibid., vol. 1, 2 (immediately after the Table of Contents).
45. Osborn, vol. 10, 13.

A. Theological Issues

> *And sing through all eternity*
> *Salvation to the Lamb!*[46]

Again, in the following meditations on Isaiah 30:18, from *Scripture Hymns*, 1762, he awaits this "second blessing," or so it might appear:

> *He waits, that we from sin may turn,*
> *May deeply for His comforts mourn;*
> *Ready His grace to give . . .*
> *Thou waitest still, when Thee I know,*
> *A larger blessing to bestow,*
> *A second gift impart,*
> *(The sinless mind, the farther rest) . . .*[47]

But crucially, when shall this "second gift" be bestowed? For the time being, Wesley is patient, content to leave it to God's sovereign will:

> *The time I to Thy wisdom leave;*
> *When, as, Thou wilt the blessing give,*
> *The full felicity!*

However, two verses further on, in meditating on Isaiah 30:19, the picture becomes clear:

> *Thrice happy all who wait for Thee!*
> *Thee, Lord, we in Thy church shall see,*
> *Thy spotless church below;*
> *We at **Jerusalem** shall dwell,**
> *Where Thou dost all Thy truths reveal,*
> *And all Thy glories show.*
>
> *Hasten, O God, the joyful day,*
> *Appear to wipe our tears away,*
> *The blessing we implore!*
> *The fullness of Thy graces give*
> *In perfect love, and bid us grieve,*
> *And bid us sin no more.*[48]

*Emphasis his—he refers here to the heavenly Jerusalem, Hebrews 12:22. Hence this "second gift" comes in glory, and in particular at the Second coming, "the joyful day," when all tears are wiped away, and perfect love is at last fully realized. We see the same theme of eradicating the "root" of

46. Ibid.
47. Ibid., vol. 9, 396.
48. Ibid., 397.

sin finding expression in a short hymn of a later date, again from *Scripture Hymns*, 1762, on Revelation 1:11:

> *Jesus the first and last,*
> *On Thee my soul is cast:*
> *Thou didst Thy work begin*
> *By blotting out my sin;*
> *Thou wilt the root remove,*
> *And perfect me in love.*[49]

This sounds like the "perfect love" doctrine of his early days, yet the second verse seems at first glance to contradict the first:

> *Yet when the work is done,*
> *The work is but begun:*
> *Partaker of Thy grace,*
> *I long to see Thy face:*
> *The first I prove below,*
> *The last I die to know.*

However, there is no real contradiction, as the verses teach two phases of the sinner's redemption: "the first," which is the "blotting out (of) my sin," i.e., by justifying faith. This takes place here in this life ("below"), where he "proves" it, i.e., verifies by personal experience and assurance through the inward witness of the Spirit (on which more below). Then there is "the last," which takes place at death, when he shall "fully know" (cf. 1 Cor 13:12), and shall have that "perfect love" which he so much craves. This is now clearly the orthodox Protestant position on sanctification. It is evident here that while John still clung to the doctrine as he claimed to have taught it from 1725, Charles had either given up on it, or at the very least he is uncertain, He seems now to affirm Christian maturity this side of glory, but perfection awaits the final Day.

Tyson puts it this way:

> "Where John had come to stress a qualified conception of perfection, that could and should be expected *now*, instantaneously, Charles preferred to emphasize an unqualified perfection . . . that was gradually received over the course of a Christian's life and most fully experienced when he or she laid the mortal body down in death."[50]

49. Ibid., vol. 13, 221.
50. Tyson, *Assist Me to Proclaim*, 251.

A. Theological Issues

In all these examples the dating is all-important: we can see his earlier hymns not only express a *longing* for holiness, but assert a confidence that God *will* remove the root of sin and perfect him in love; whereas his later hymns still express that earnest *desire* (which all sincere Christians would affirm), but he is mature enough to concede that full realization of this desire awaits the state of glory. Hence I would express the change somewhat differently from Tyson, in that by 1762 Charles had embraced in essence the standard Reformed view of sanctification, albeit retaining a firm emphasis on that deep yearning for perfect holiness—which should be the aspiration of every Christian, as it was a strong emphasis of the Evangelical Revival.

What led to this change of mind? While we can but speculate, a few factors arise. One was his justifiable skepticism concerning those who claimed the blessing: persons full of pride but otherwise living quite inconsistent lives. Even John, though he was prepared to credit these testimonies for a while, also eventually had to concede that many of those who claimed the blessing ultimately fell away. Furthermore, Charles knew all too well his own shortcomings: that his meddling in his brother's marital affairs had caused the latter unnecessary grief; that he himself was given at times to fits of ill-temper; and that he was disposed at other times to resort to belligerence and vehemence of language, e.g., he apologized to the Moravian minister Benjamin Latrobe for his earlier intemperate language regarding him and the Moravians in general.[51] He knew his own heart all too well, and he laments the fact, as again in these verses on Jer 44:4 and Jer 31:33 (from *Scripture Hymns*, 1762):[52]

> *The thing my God doth hate,*
> *That I no more may do,*
> *Thy creature, Lord, again create,*
> *And all my soul renew;*
> *My soul shall then, like Thine,*
> *Abhor the thing unclean,*
> *And sanctified by love Divine*
> *Forever cease from sin.*
>
> *That blessed law of Thine,*
> *Jesu, to me impart:*
> *Thy Spirit's law of life Divine,*
> *O write it on my heart!*

---

51. Dallimore, *Heart Set Free*, 239.

52. Osborn, vol. 10, 44 and 41. Also in 1780 *Collection*, no. 331; and 1933 *MHB*, no. 547.

Part III: Theological Issues and Themes in Christian Experience

> *Implant it deep within,*
> *Whence it may ne'er remove,*
> *The law of liberty from sin,*
> *The perfect law of love.*

Here Wesley identifies with the Apostle Paul in Romans 7, where the latter confesses, "The good that I want, I do not do" (Rom 7:19), and then cries, "O wretched man that I am" (v. 24). Wesley longs, as every Christian should, for that holiness which is "the law of liberty from sin."

Thus by the early 1760s, with this more mature mind, he now believed that any fond imagination that one could climb from the bottom to the top of the ladder of sanctification in one single step—a "second blessing" indeed—was but "a credulous dotard's dream," as he sarcastically mocks such aspirations in the following lines:

> *"But we now, the prize to attain,*
> *An easier method see,*
> *Save ourselves the toil and pain,*
> *And lingering agony,*
> *Reach at once the ladder's top,*
> *While standing on its lowest round,*
> *Instantaneously spring up,*
> *With pure perfection crowned."*

But then he warns that such notions are a delusion, which only bring the Gospel into disrepute:

> *Such the credulous dotard's dream,*
> *And such his shorter road,*
> *Thus he makes the world blaspheme,*
> *And shames the church of God,*
> *Staggers thus the most sincere,*
> *'Til from the Gospel hope they move*
> *Holiness as error fear,*
> *And start at perfect love.*[53]

Clearly by this time Charles had indeed given up on the doctrine, even if his brother John had not. We can but humbly follow him in his Christian pilgrimage, in his willingness to change his views, and to admit that he had

---

53. From *Scripture Hymns*, 1762, no. 3189, on Phil 3:13, in Osborn, vol. 13, 80. John Wesley noted and underlined certain lines in this set of four verses, which were to him offensive. Needless to say, this meditation did not make it into the 1780 *Collection*!

A. Theological Issues

on occasions been in the wrong. Meanwhile, the modern "second blessing" advocates need to heed Wesley's warning.

As to the validity of the Wesleyan doctrine of holiness, Dr. Sinclair Ferguson points out from his Reformed standpoint that he and others of his school do not deny the reality of the experience to which many Wesleyans testify, but that Wesley and many of his followers called this by the wrong name and consequently placed it in the wrong theological pigeon-hole.[54] There is such a thing as the powerful testimony of God's Spirit in one's life, and one does not need to be a Wesleyan to experience this: Romans 5:2–3, 5, 11, together teach this pervasive love of God spread abroad in the heart (see below on the "felt Christ"). Seen from this perspective, Wesley was indeed on to something and we must take this seriously, even if not strictly related to sanctification.

In summary, this conclusion from Dr. Martyn Lloyd-Jones issues a challenge to us all:

> "We are left with the challenge of how to teach our people to live the Christian life. I have criticised these various teachings [i.e., Wesley, Finney, the 'Keswick Movement']; but once more I would pay tribute to the men who taught them. They were men who were concerned about holiness. Are we equally concerned about holiness? ... Let us examine ourselves. It is easy to denounce false holiness teaching; but what is your holiness teaching? Have you the same desire for holiness? These men suffered, and sacrificed much in order to be holy men. They may have been confused about doctrines at times, they may have confused 'things that differ,' but they were zealously concerned to be holy men of God, and many of them were concerned to have a holy and pure church. There, surely, we are with them, and agree with them ..."[55]

In this tribute I believe he has the Wesleys particularly in mind, since as can be seen above, both Charles and John were deeply concerned about holiness in a way that the modern church—sadly—is not. It is therefore hoped that Wesley's hymns will recall us to that deep concern, and willingness, to be holy men and women for the Lord, as Wesley so eloquently expresses it:

---

54. Sinclair Ferguson, "A Reformed Response," in Alexander, *Christian Spirituality*, 123.

55. Lloyd-Jones, "New Developments," 99.

Part III: Theological Issues and Themes in Christian Experience

O for a heart to praise my God,
A heart from sin set free
A heart that always feels Thy blood
So feely spilt for me.[56]

"It is written, 'You shall be holy, for I am holy," (1 Pet 1:16).

---

56. Osborn, vol. 2, 77. The role of feeling, and what he means by "feeling the blood," is discussed more fully in Part III, B.2.

A. Theological Issues

4. Arminianism

The biographical sketch above omitted discussion of the Wesleys' theological differences with George Whitefield over Calvinistic tenets, but it will be convenient to attend to that issue here, in connection with Wesley's early hymns.

Universal atonement and free-will doctrines à la William Laud, along with either rationalist (called "Latitudinarian"), or high-church ritualist views in general became pervasive in the seventeenth century. These views in the Church of England hampered any acceptance of the evangelical doctrines associated with Puritanism, in particular substitutionary atonement, justification by faith, regeneration by the sovereign work of the Holy Spirit, and perseverance of the saints to final glory. Hugo Grotius (1583–1645), the Dutch Arminian, had taught a "governmental" view of the atonement, whereby Christ's death was merely a demonstration of God's moral government of the world, but not an actual redemption of sinners.[57] While this theory was first proposed in Holland, it spread to England and the American colonies. Likewise, the moral influence and moral example ideas from the Middle Ages also became widespread, whereby in the cross Christ's example of love exerts a positive influence on people, leading them to repentance. These views became popular among the moralistic Anglicans of the Restoration period.

When George Whitefield came to conversion through reading Henry Scougal's booklet, *The Life of God in the Soul of Man*, he began to preach the absolute necessity of regeneration, while lying behind this was the teaching of unconditional election by the Father and effectual calling by the Spirit, as taught in Article XVII of the Anglican standards. However, when the Wesleys came to conversion themselves they, like Prisca and Aquila, showed Whitefield the way of God more perfectly by introducing him to justification by faith in the finished work of Christ on the cross. This brought a fullness to his theology and preaching, and served to confirm his Calvinistic position.

Meanwhile, the Wesleys balked at predestination and election, and when John published a sermon against it in 1740, entitled "Free Grace," he set a path to division from Whitefield. To this sermon Charles affixed a series of *Hymns on God's Everlasting Love*, to emphasize God's universal love and Christ's universal redemption. Whitefield replied in a carefully

---

57. Berkhof, *Systematic Theology*, 389–91.

reasoned open letter, which appealed to the usual passages (Rom 8:29–30; Rom 9; John 6, 10, and 17, etc.), and chided both Wesleys for their own lack of appeal to Scripture and their vehement language. Both John and Charles were unmoved, and the controversy escalated, with further pamphlets and hymns by Charles on universal redemption, culminating in a strongly worded letter from John Wesley to Whitefield late in 1741, blaming him for starting the disruption.[58]

These anti-Calvinist views appear—at times in highly polemical mode—in his early hymns, when he was indeed vehemently opposed to Calvinistic views (as he saw them). The following hymn, the first of a series which Charles included with his brother's "Free Grace" sermon, is strongly polemical:

> *Father, whose everlasting love*
> *Thy only Son for sinners gave,*
> *Whose grace to all did freely give,*
> *And sent Him down the world to save.*
>
> *Help us Thy mercy to extol,*
> *Immense, unfathomed, unconfined;*
> *To praise the Lamb who died for all,*
> *The general Saviour of mankind.*[59]

Then in 1741, at the height of the controversy, in a collection entitled *Hymns on God's Everlasting love*, Wesley's rhetoric becomes belligerent against "the Horrible Decree," as follows (emphasis is his):

> *Ah! Gentle, gracious Dove,*
> *And art thou griev'd in me,*
> *That sinners should restrain thy love,*
> *And say, "It is not free:*
> *It is not free for all:*
> *The most, thou passest by,*
> *And mockest with a fruitless call*
> *Whom thou hast doom'd to die."*
>
> *O HORRIBLE DECREE*
> *Worthy of whence it came!*
> *Forgive their hellish blasphemy*
> *Who charge it on the Lamb:*

---

58. The whole sad episode is told, both factually and temperately, albeit from the Calvinist side, by Dallimore, *George Whitefield*, vol. 2, chs. 1–4.

59. Osborn, vol. 3, 3.

> *Whose pity him inclin'd*
> *To leave his throne above,*
> *The friend, and Saviour of mankind,*
> *The God of grace, and love.*

However, these hymns betray both an ignorance of what Reformed teaching on the subject really is, i.e., that the doctrine of election forbids a sincere commendation of God's love and offer of pardon to every sinner who hears the Gospel. They also betray a confusion: e.g., a verse in his hymn "What shall I do, my God to love?" (Published in *Hymns and Sacred Poems*, 1749, but written in 1742 when the controversy still raged), where Wesley extols the love of God in broad, universal terms:

> *Throughout the world its breadth is known,*
> *Wide as infinity;*
> *So wide it never passed by one,*
> *Or it had passed by me.*[60]

If Wesley had stressed the vertical dimension, rather than the horizontal, i.e., the depth rather than the breadth, it would have expressed a vital truth, that the sinner's corrupt nature and "sins of deepest dye" had so alienated him from a holy God, and sunk him into "the miry pit" such that God had to reach to the depths, lift him up, and set his feet upon a rock (cf. Ps 40:2). But in the heat of controversy Wesley felt the need to stress a love "wide as infinity."

Yet for all the controversy and the professed desire to distance himself from Calvinism, Charles's hymns from the outset express man's depravity and the sinfulness of sin in uncompromising language, proclaim justification by faith alone, and "God's grace alone" in regeneration. With the passage of time, however, his views mellowed—and modified—on the subject, such that by 1752 he even offered to join Whitefield's party, an offer the latter politely declined, since he had already relinquished leadership of any party called by his name.[61] Charles even wrote a long poem in his overture of reconciliation (published 1755), and declared that old barriers, if they existed at all, were insufficient to keep them apart:

> *Come on, my Whitefield! (since the strife is past,*
> *And friends at first are friends again at last) . . .*

60. Ibid., vol. 4, 446.
61. Dallimore, *George Whitefield*, vol. 2, 257–59; and Dallimore, *Heart Set Free*, 230–31.

Part III: Theological Issues and Themes in Christian Experience

> *Too long, alas! We gave to Satan place,*
> *When party-zeal put on an angel's face; ...*
>
> *Ah! wherefore did we ever seem to part,*
> *Or clash in sentiment, while one in heart?*
> *What dire device did the old serpent find,*
> *To put asunder those whom God had joined? ...*
> *Soon as the virtue of His name we feel,*
> *The storm of strife subsides, the sea is still, ... etc.*[62]

It is fair to say that Charles's views had changed, at least to a degree. His hymns on Christian pilgrimage triumphantly affirm the Perseverance of the saints, and there is more than a strong hint of electing love in these lines from his well-loved hymn, "Depth of mercy can there be":[63]

> *2. I have long withstood His grace,*
> *Long provoked Him to His face,*
> *Would not hearken to His calls,*
> *Grieved Him by a thousand falls.*
>
> *4. When to me this waste of love?*
> *Ask my Advocate above!*
> *See the cause in Jesu's face,*
> *Now before the throne of grace.*
>
> *8. There for me the Saviour stands,*
> *Shows His wounds, and spreads His hands!*
> *God is love! I know, I feel.*
> *Jesus weeps, and loves me still!*

This first appears early in Wesley's compositions, in *Hymns and Sacred Poems*, 1740, when the Calvinistic controversy first erupted. Yet although titled, "After a relapse into sin," one wonders whether Wesley is also

---

62. "An Epistle to the Rev. Mr. George Whitefield," written in 1755, in Osborn, vol. 5, 65–70.

63. The opening verse of this hymn is as follows:

> *Depth of mercy! Can there be*
> *Mercy still reserved for me!*
> *Can my God His wrath forbear;*
> *Me the chief of sinners, spare?*

This appears early in Wesley's compositions, in *Hymns and Sacred Poems*, 1740 (Osborn, vol. 2, 271–72); 1780 *Collection*, no. 162, under the title, "Convinced of backsliding"; 1933 *MHB*, no. 358, in the section entitled "Repentance and Forgiveness."

A. Theological Issues

describing his pre-conversion experience.[64] There is, I believe, a basic ambivalence in his mind even at this time about the whole theological issue (and experience) of electing love. Certainly for many Methodist converts this hymn indeed expressed their pre-conversion experience, especially in the story of the theater actress who heard this hymn being sung in a house-chapel, and desired a copy. On reading and meditating on Wesley's lines she found Christ, and so forever forsook the stage with all its bawdy performances, to live a Christian life.[65]

Or observe again the same theme expressed in these lines (*Hymns for those that Seek and those that Have Redemption in the Blood of Christ*, 1747; also 1933 *MHB*, no. 376):

> 1. Thou great mysterious God unknown
> Whose love hath gently led me on,
> Even from my infant days.
> Mine inmost soul expose to view,
> And tell me if I ever knew
> Thy justifying grace.
>
> 8. Father, in me reveal Thy Son,
> And to my inmost soul make known
> How merciful Thou art:
> The secret of Thy love reveal,
> And by Thine hallowing Spirit dwell
> Forever in my heart.[66]

Then to put the capstone on all this, what Calvinist could possibly demur at these lines, from *Scripture Hymns*, 1762, on 1 Chronicles 28:4?

> What is in man for God to approve?
> He makes us such as He can love,

---

64. The "recovery from backsliding" becomes explicit in the third verse:

> I my Master have denied,
> I afresh have crucified,
> Oft profaned His hallowed name,
> Put Him to an open shame.

That said, however, the verses could equally well describe his profligate University days, and the rigorist, works-oriented, Holy Club experience.

65. See Price, *101 Hymn Stories*, 15. The story goes that the audience awaited her appearance for some time, and when she finally took to the stage, all she could do was to tearfully repeat the opening verse of this hymn. Then she walked off, never to return.

66. Osborn, vol. 4, 235, 237.

Part III: Theological Issues and Themes in Christian Experience

> *He loved us, not for faith foreknown,*
> *But freely in His favourite Son:*
> *Us to our Head His Spir't unites,*
> *In us as part of Christ delights,*
> *Elected with that perfect Man,*
> *In everlasting bliss to reign.*[67]

In summary, while Whitefield represents a complete break with the Laudianism of his day, Charles Wesley shows an incomplete break, say about 85 percent. That said, however, where it involved the essential things such as justification by faith alone, the finished work of Christ etc., Wesley stands firm, and it can fairly be said that he belongs in the Reformed camp, albeit somewhat left of center. Charles Wesley was no Arminian in the seventeenth century rationalist or "latitudinarian" sense, nor for that matter as we see it in modern "decisionism" and "easy believism."

There is more, however. Wesley's incorporation of the Reformed treatise on the Lord's Supper by Daniel Brevint with his 1746 collection of Communion hymns is possibly indicative of his move in a Reformed direction more generally, albeit to the modified Saumur version. Since Brevint had himself adopted the Saumur position on predestination and redemption (roughly corresponding to what we call today "four-point" Calvinism[68]), which affirmed election but eschewed "limited" atonement, it is quite possible that Wesley had read more widely in the Saumur theology than this treatise alone. If this is so, one could argue that the Saumur position (or something like it) became Wesley's own in his later years, and might well explain the reconciliation with Whitefield. While I cannot prove this, it is a line of inquiry worth pursuing.

For a final comment, Wesley is at his brilliant best when he forsakes polemics, and instead exalts Christ, affirms His deity, proclaims salvation through His atoning blood, rejoices in His resurrection and ascension, points us to His second coming and the heavenly home, and adores the Triune God. Here both Calvinist and Evangelical Arminian can surely concur wholeheartedly, and for this reason his hymns have a supreme, transcendent, and abiding quality.

67. Ibid., vol. 9, 202–3.
68. I realize that I am being somewhat simplistic here (hence the adverb "roughly"), but a full discussion of the Amyraut (or in the Latinized form, Amyraldian) version of Calvinism, taught at the Saumur Academy, is outside the scope of this discussion. For a thorough survey the various aspects of the Amyraut theology of Saumur, see inter alia, Armstrong, *Calvinism and the Amyraut Heresy*.

B. Christian Experience in Wesley's Hymns

1. The Hidden Life

Turning from issues of controversy to the positive features of Wesley's view of Christian life and experience, one recurring theme in his hymns stands out: the importance to him of the text, "You have died, and your life is hidden with Christ in God" (Col 3:3). "The hidden life" on inspection turns out to be a vital concept in Wesley's understanding of Christian life, devotion, union with Christ, perseverance, and anticipation of heavenly glory. It is therefore important to grasp just how he understood this, in the light of the hymns which express it either explicitly or implicitly. These samples will suffice to illustrate the various aspects and nuances as he saw them, while relevant Scripture texts will aid that analysis.

a. From Hymns and Sacred Poems, 1742 (six verses in all)[69]

1. *Christ, my hidden life, appear,*	Col 3:3–4
Soul of my inmost soul;	
Light of life, the mourner cheer,	John 1:3, 8:12
And make the sinner whole.	
Now in me Thyself display,	Col 1:27
Surely Thou in all things art;	
I from all things turn away,	
To seek Thee in my heart.	John 14:17–18, 20
3. *From the world of sin, and noise,*	
And hurry, I withdraw;	
For the small and inward voice	1 Kgs 19:12–13
I wait with humble awe:	Ps 4:4, 33:8, 119:161
Silent am I now, and still,	
Dare not in Thy presence move;	
To my waiting soul reveal	
The secret of Thy love.	Ps 25:14, 91:1

---

69. Osborn, vol. 2, 262–64.

Part III: Theological Issues and Themes in Christian Experience

> 6. *Lord, my time is in Thy hand,*   Ps 31:15
> *My soul to Thee convert;*
> *Thou canst make me understand*
> *Though I am slow of heart.*   Luke 24:25
> *Thine, in whom I live and move,*
> *Thine the work, the praise is Thine;*
> *Thou art wisdom, power, and love,*   1 Cor 1:30
> *And all Thou art is mine.*

In the lines of verse 1, "in me Thyself display," and "seek Thee in my heart" Wesley displays the strong mystical streak he sees in "the hidden life," i.e., "Christ within, the hope of glory" (Col 1:27). The mystical side of the Christian life—Christ residing within the believer—is well stated in the texts from John 14, and Wesley has clearly grasped these, and combines them with the other texts from Colossians and various Psalms. Christ has made His home in the believer (John 14:23), and is hidden within, such that the world cannot know or receive (v. 17), but Wesley as a humble Christian seeks to know Christ more intimately (cf. Eph 3:17–19), and that Christ might sanctify him more fully, making him ever more Christlike. However, for Wesley the hidden life comes not as a result of some "second blessing," which only a privileged few experience; and not something for the Christian to pursue, but the possession of all believers—now!

Furthermore, for Wesley the Christian life is a twofold existence, where on one hand the Christian lives, moves, and works in this world; but because of union with Christ it is also He who works ("Thine the work . . . Thou art wisdom, power, and love"). This helps to resolve an issue with which Christians have often struggled—and at times gone astray, viz., is it Christ in me who lives and works, whereby I am some sort of outfit which Christ wears (the "let go, and let God" approach)? Or is it a matter of cooperation—doing things myself, albeit through Christ's strength (as Phil 4:13 seems to teach)? The answer is, in a sense: both . . . and! Union with Christ supplies the solution, and Wesley has grasped it: "my works in Thee," as he writes in the following verse:

> *The deed, the time, the manner choose,*
> *Let all **my** fruit be found of Thee;*

B. Christian Experience in Wesley's Hymns

*Let all **my** works **in Thee** be wrought,*
***By Thee** to full perfection brought.*[70] (emphases added)

b. From the omitted lines in "Christ the Lord is risen today"

Hid; till Christ, our Life, appear,	Col 3:4; Gal 2:20
Glorious in His members here:	1 Cor 12:27; Eph 5:30
Joined to Him, we then shall shine	Eph 5:15; Dan 12:3
All immortal, all divine![A]	1 Cor 15:52–54

A. Ibid., vol. 1, 186.

Here the theme of the hidden life is union with Christ: "in His members here," and "joined to Him"; and in the context of the hymn this union is intimately associated with Christ's resurrection. Again, this theme opens the gate to the mystical side of the Christian life, which is difficult to express in words. As Deschner notes,[71] John Wesley had little to say about Paul's "in Christ" theme in his sermons, although he does touch on it at times. When he does, he relates it to the Head: we are raised with Him as our living Head. Otherwise he relates "in Him" to the Body of Christ: it is faith which unites the Christian with the Head, as Charles wrote in the famous conversion hymn:

Alive in Him, my living Head,
And clothed in righteousness Divine.

However, Charles in his hymns develops the "in Christ" theme more fully. In the famous resurrection hymn he sees it with the Apostle Paul, as the basis for the spiritual resurrection from death in sin, and the new life in union with Christ:

Second life we all receive,	Rom 6:4–8
In our Heavenly Adam live[A]	1 Cor 15:45

A. Osborn, vol. 1, 186, and so for the next two excerpts.

He sees it as both the basis of and the motive for holy living, "seeking things above":

---

70. Ibid., vol. 5, 11.
71. Deschner, *Wesley's Christology*, 170.

Part III: Theological Issues and Themes in Christian Experience

> *Risen with Him, we upward move;*
> *Still we seek the things above;*   Col 3:1

Hence the hidden life is one in ever closer, mystical communion with the risen Christ, who beckons us forward to our loved abode; but meanwhile that life in Christ is secure.

> *Heaven our aim, and loved abode,*
> *Hid our life with Christ in God!*

c. From "Our life is hid" (1933 MHB, no. 823)[72]

Our life is hid with Christ in God;	Col 3:3–4
Our life shall soon appear,	
And shed His glory all abroad	Rom 5:5; 2 Cor 3:9, 18
In all His members here.	1 Cor 3:27, 12:27
Our souls are in His mighty hand,	Ps 37:24; Isa 41:10
And He shall keep them still;	1 Pet 1:5
And you and I shall surely stand	
With Him on Zion's hill.	Rev 14:1

Apart from its present implications for holy living, the hidden life looks forward to the future, when Christ shall appear at His coming again in glory. Until then believers are "in His mighty hand," i.e., it is God who preserves and keeps the soul.[73] Wesley further affirms that Christ keeps His own until the time we arrive "on Zion's hill." This aligns with John Wesley's comment in his *Explanatory Notes on the New Testament*, where he explains Colossians 3:3–4 as follows:

> "*For ye are dead*—To the things on earth. *And your* real, spiritual *life is hid* from the world, and laid up *in God, with Christ*—who hath merited, promised, prepared it for us, and gives us the earnest and foretaste of it in our hearts." "*Our life*—the fountain of holiness and glory. *Shall appear*—in the clouds of heaven."[74]

---

72. Ibid., vol. 4, 281.
73. See the note in H&B, 600, on this issue.
74. Wesley, *Explanatory Notes NT*, comm. *in loc.*, 748. Italics denote citations of the

B. Christian Experience in Wesley's Hymns

Hence we now have a deposit in advance (an "earnest," Greek ἀρραβων), but because of the merit of Christ who has won this eternal, spiritual life for the Christian, it is thereby a guarantee of holiness and glory at the Second coming. There is a strong note of security here, that our life is, as it were, "laid up," even "locked up" with Christ in heaven, until the grand Consummation. Hence John Wesley's overt denial of Calvinism's "final perseverance"—due to his fear of antinomianism—seems strangely inconsistent with the above lines, as well as his brother's comments above on the hidden life. It would appear that Charles, at least in later life, did not share the same inhibitions and ambivalence on the issue as his brother.

d. From the hymn, "Come on, my partners in distress," final verse:

In hope of that ecstatic pause,	Titus 2:13; Heb 11:16
Jesu, we now sustain the cross,	Matt 16:24
And at Thy footstool fall;	Ps 99:5
Till Thou our hidden life reveal,	Col 1:27;
Till Thou our ravished spirits fill,	Song 4:9
And God is all in all.[A]	1 Cor 15:28

A. Osborn, vol. 5, 169.

In similar vein to the preceding hymn, the Christian's life is hidden, but secure, with Christ during this earthly pilgrimage. Here below he must take up the cross daily (and he knew all about that, what with the mob violence he had to endure, among other things). But when Christ comes in glory that hidden life will be revealed for all to see, and in response there will be that Spirit-filled, emotional joy when his "ravished spirit" is filled in the glory to be revealed. The climax of it all will be that beatific vision of God through Christ, revealed in His full glory:

That great mysterious Deity	Rom 11:33
We soon with open face shall see:	Ps 17:15
The beatific sight . . .	Isa 33:17, 21

Or as in the final verse of Wesley's incarnational hymn:

Scripture text.

Part III: Theological Issues and Themes in Christian Experience

. . . We shall from earth remove,	Phil 1:23
And see His glorious face:	Rev 22:4
Then shall His love be fully showed,	John 17:24, 26
And man shall then be lost in God.	Luke 17:33; John 7:23

In all this we see a thoroughly scriptural understanding of the Christian life: a twofold existence where here below I live and work, but a life which is ultimately mortal; then also the other, all-important one where my eternal life is securely reserved in heaven, awaiting the appointed time.

B. Christian Experience in Wesley's Hymns

2. THE ROLE OF FEELING

Another dominant theme in Wesley's hymns is the emphasis on feeling, or what we would call today the emotional dimension. The following samples illustrate this aspect, whether in respect of Christian assurance, Christian life, or Christian service.

In the following hymn, which first appeared in *Hymns and Sacred Poems*, 1749 (in the 1780 *Collection* in the section entitled "Describing Inward Religion," no. 93; in the 1933 *MHB*, no. 377),[75] Wesley poses the question every believer asks when seeking assurance of salvation:

> *How can a sinner know*
> *His sins on earth forgiven?*

The reply, in part, comes in verse 2:

> *We who in Christ believe,*
> *That He for us hath died,*
> *We all His unknown peace receive,*
> *And feel His blood applied.*

This hymn emphasizes the role of the "inward witness" which Samuel Wesley had stressed to John and Charles from his deathbed in 1735.[76] Wesley further expresses this assurance in the following joyful lines from the hymn, "O filial Deity" (1739):

> *Of life the fountain Thou,*
> *I know—I feel it now!*
> *Faint and dead no more I droop:*
> *Thou art in me; Thy supplies,*
> *Every moment springing up,*
> *Into life eternal rise.*[77]

The "feeling" emphasis comes to the fore also in his hymns on Christian life and holiness; in this connection too, Wesley talks about "feeling the blood," in this hymn based on Psalm 51:10:

---

75. Also in *Hymns for those to whom Christ is All in All*, 1761; see Osborn, vol. 5, 363.

76. "'The inward witness, son, the inward witness,' he said to me, 'that is the proof, the strongest proof of Christianity,'" in John Wesley's letter "To 'John Smith,'" March 22, 1748, in Baker, *Wesley, Letters*, 289. Also cited in Wood, *Burning Heart*, 27.

77. Osborn, vol. 1, 98.

Part III: Theological Issues and Themes in Christian Experience

> *O for a heart to praise my God,*
> *A heart from sin set free,*
> *A heart that always feels Thy blood*
> *So freely spilt for me.*[78]

Wesley further expresses this same theme in following hymn on the Christian as Christ's humble servant as he lives out the Christian life:

> *Behold the servant of the Lord!*
> *I wait Thy guiding eye to feel,*
> *To hear and keep Thy every word,*
> *To prove and do Thy perfect will.*[79]

What are we to make of this emphasis on feeling? One response is to dismiss it out of hand as "pietistic mush," but this is too cavalier and contemptuous, without giving even a cursory consideration of what Wesley might mean. Moreover, evangelical Christianity not only incorporates but insists on this inward, "pietistic" aspect (if one must use such pejorative terms). It will not do to object that "in this scheme 'faith alone' is not enough; there is an addition, that one has also to feel something."[80] This objection can only stand if one has already intellectualized faith in the first place, and thus left no room for the emotional or mystical dimension. Then, of course, feeling would indeed be an "extra." On the contrary, while it can be overdone, we cannot repudiate feeling altogether and thereby beat a reactionary retreat into an arid intellectualism.

Another response is to explain it terms of Wesley's psychological make-up, and observe with Beckerlegge, "John was still essentially a man of reason, Charles a romantic, emphasizing much more the emotions, occasionally to extremes which sadly distressed his older brother."[81] While there is indeed some truth in this, it is not merely a matter of psychology; there still remain the objective issues of both scriptural support and experiential reality. Meanwhile, one thing is certain: Beckerlegge is right that Charles's emphasis on feeling and emotion caused his brother some anguish, hence John Wesley's sermons will be of limited help in this regard.

---

78. Ibid., vol. 2, 77.

79. Ibid., vol. 5, 10.

80. As I have heard from time to time from certain older ministers in the Dutch Reformed tradition. However, such sentiments are by no means restricted to those circles.

81. H&B, 37.

B. Christian Experience in Wesley's Hymns

From the historical angle, we need to understand this emphasis in the context of the time. During the seventeenth century, German Pietism *inter alia* reacted against what was by this time the cold formalism and strong polemics of the Lutheran pulpit—the much-loved German hymn-writer Paul Gerhardt was prominent in this reaction. On the Calvinist side, Dutch and German "Puritans," e.g., Willem à Brakel, also saw the need for reformation of life and devotion as well as doctrine. Furthermore, in this general context, there arose also in the same period various forms of Christian mysticism, both Roman Catholic and Protestant, for which formality and sound doctrine were not enough: there had to be an inward, mystical, and devotional side as well. Hence they would talk of a "felt Christ." We find this *inter alia* in the writings of the Roman Catholics Madame Guyon and Archbishop Fénelon in France, the Lutheran August Francke in Germany, and in England from the Anglicans Jeremy Taylor and William Law. The Protestant mystics in particular exercised a profound influence on the Wesleys, and these in turn formed the basis for John's perfectionist ideas.

However, in the more immediate circumstance, while John was often reluctant to tell of his own feelings and experiences (save for the "warm heart" experience in May, 1738), Charles is more forthcoming, in a way that others can readily identify with. We see this in the hymn entitled "The Marks of Faith" (*Hymns and Sacred Poems*, vol. 2, 1749):

> *What we ourselves have felt and seen*   Acts 4:20; 1 John 1:3
> *With confidence we tell.*^A
>
> A. As Manning observes, see Manning, 28. The hymn itself is in Osborn, vol. 5, 363.

Here, "felt" clearly means his own direct experience of the Savior's pardon and cleansing, but he is not above sharing it with others, as in Psalm 66:12, "Come and hear, all you who fear God, and I will tell of what he has done for my soul." Yet there is nothing contrived or pressured about this, contrary to the "testimony" sessions popular in some circles: Wesley cannot but speak of what he has come to know personally. However, he is adapting to his evangelical experience what in a positive vein the mystics had to offer, but avoiding their errors such as a stress on works and asceticism.

Unquestionably, the one great experience of his life was his conversion in 1738, when he came to know God's pardon and free justification through faith in the blood of Christ. Even in 1762, when he wrote the verse meditations on Scripture passages, the reality and vividness of that experience still

Part III: Theological Issues and Themes in Christian Experience

shone brightly, as he confesses in this verse based on Isaiah 44:26 (from *Scripture Hymns*, 1762):

The blood which hath procured my peace	Isa 53:5; Col 1:20
Now let me feel applied,	
And glorying in his righteousness,	Isa 45:25; Gal 6:14
I now am justified.^A	Rom 3:24

    A. Osborn, vol. 9, 419.

Combined with this reminiscence and experience of conversion is the Wesleys' emphasis on the witness of the Spirit in assurance of salvation. Here John's sermons and letters do give us help, and it is a reasonable assumption that both shared the same view here, since both the hymns and the sermons agree. Apart from the perfection doctrine, they regarded this as their particular contribution to Christian life and experience. I have noted above that "the inward witness" was among Samuel Wesley's dying words in 1735, and it finds expression in many of Charles's hymns. John Wesley defines it in a response to an enquirer in 1740 as ". . . a sure confidence that, by the merits of Christ, [one is] reconciled to the favour of God." He further defines it as a "perceptible inspiration," by which he means that activity of God's Holy Spirit "whereby He fills us with righteousness, peace, and joy, with love to Him and to all mankind."[82] This doctrine of assurance finds expression in these words from the hymn "Come Holy Ghost, all quickening fire," the inward witness in the opening lines, combined with that definite mystical streak in the last two lines:

Thy witness with my spirit bear	Rom 8:16; 1 John 5:10
That God, my God, inhabits there,	John 14:23
Thou with the Father and the Son	
Eternal light's coeval beam;	
Be Christ in me, and I in Him,	John 14:20, 17:23
Till perfect we are made in one.^A	John 17:21

    A. Osborn, vol. 1, 241.

For this understanding Wesley acknowledges a debt to the Moravians who would talk "of a sense of forgiveness," but more particularly he owes his

---

82. Wood, *Burning Heart*, 250–51. In this definition there are echoes of Rom 14:17, and of the famous occasion at Epworth in 1742 when he stood on his father's tomb and preached from this text.

B. Christian Experience in Wesley's Hymns

doctrine to the Puritans of the previous century.[83] Be all this as it may, the central Scripture text for his doctrine of assurance was Romans 8:15–16, "... ye have received the Spirit of adoption, whereby we cry, 'Abba, Father.' The Spirit itself beareth witness with our spirit, that we are the children of God" (KJV). On this both Wesleys placed the strongest emphasis. Our testimony, he taught, is argument and reflection from the fact that we have believed; the Spirit's testimony is immediate and unique, that we are accepted into filial relation with the Father. However, Wesley was also at pains to insist that this persuasion and testimony of the Spirit was not the same as "the ravings of an ecstatic!"

Hence when Charles Wesley talks of "feeling the blood applied" and the like, the reference is both to the doctrine of the Spirit's immediate testimony and the mystical apprehension of Christ à la the Paschal discourses of John 14–17, along with the Pauline statement, "Christ within you, the hope of glory" (Col 1:27). True, mystics like Taylor, Francke, and Law had their influence indeed, but Charles Wesley was above all a man of the Word, and his mysticism is not some vague inward-look or navel-gaze, but, as observed above, a union with Christ according to the terms and teaching of the Gospel. There is a strong note of intimacy with the Savior in his hymns, a dimension which few Christians today know, but this for him is real, and not some figment of his imagination. Observe this again from the hymn, "O filial Deity":

Thou the good Shepherd art,	Ps 23:1; John 10:11
From thee I ne'er shall part;	John 10:28–29; Rom 8:38–39
Thou my keeper and my guide,	Ps 121:5
Make me still thy tender care;	1 Pet 5:7
Gently lead me by thy side,	Ps 23:2–3; Isa 42:16
Sweetly in thy bosom bear.[A]	Isa 40:11

    A. Osborn, vol. 1, 98.

To quote Bernard Manning again,

> "It is Wesley's glory that he united these three strains—dogma, experience, mysticism—in verse so simple that it could be used, by plain men... These three qualities, among others, give such

---

83. Ibid., 254 and n. 4. Wesley cites in particular the Puritans William Perkins, John Preston, and Richard Sibbes as anticipating his doctrine.

Part III: Theological Issues and Themes in Christian Experience

a life to the hymns that they can never grow old while Christians experience God's grace."[84]

Wesley's doctrine of assurance has commended itself to many Christians, both in the English-speaking world and even more widely, and is still held to a considerable extent today in evangelical circles, albeit not universally. In more recent times, Dr. D. Martyn Lloyd-Jones held to a similar view, based again on Romans 8:15–16, but laying stress also on those texts mentioning the "sealing of the Spirit," i.e., Ephesians 1:13 and 2 Corinthians 1:22.[85] This view appears also to have been fairly prevalent in the old Calvinistic Methodist Church of Wales.

Before summing up on this point about the "feeling" emphasis, there is from the modern context a very important caveat: Wesley's emphasis should not be confused or equated with the post-modern obsession with the "feel-good" factor, which not only affects the secular world, but has come into the worship of the church in a flood. Modern lyrics fairly teem with a self-centered faux-mysticism, all about "me and my experiences," "me and my feelings," etc., artificially induced by repeated lines, sensuous music, and bodily movements.[86] This ecstatic and essentially self-oriented spectacle in much of modern worship is a far cry from the Christ-centered and Christ-oriented dimension evident in Wesley's hymns, as for example:

> *Thou hidden source of calm repose,*
> *Thou all-sufficient Love Divine,*
> *My help and refuge from all my foes,*
> *Secure I am, if Thou art mine:*
> *And lo! From sin, and grief, and shame*
> *I hide me, Jesus, in Thy name.*[87]

Here is mysticism, but it is a Christ-mysticism, the mysticism of the Paschal discourses (John 14–17), the mysticism of union with Christ à la Paul's statements, "If Christ is in you, the spirit is alive because of righteousness" (Rom 8:10), or "Your life is hid with Christ in God" (Col 3:3), or in the

---

84. Manning, 30.

85. See Eaton, *Baptism with the Spirit*, where Eaton expounds the teaching of Calvin, various Puritans, Jonathan Edwards, and Wesley on the gift of the Spirit, assurance, and the Spirit's testimony, in regard to such texts as 2 Cor 1:22; Rom 8:16; and Eph 1:13 et al. He then compares this with Lloyd-Jones's similar view, esp. in chs. 8–9.

86. As discussed by P. Masters in his chapter, "Rational or Ecstatic Worship?" in *Worship in the Melting Pot*, 23–31.

87. Osborn, vol. 5, 50.

B. Christian Experience in Wesley's Hymns

repeated "in Christ" theme of his epistles (eg., Eph 1:3, 4, 6, 12, etc.). It has nothing to do with either the self-centered "feel-good" emphasis of contemporary post-modernism, or for that matter with Eastern contemplative pantheism.

It is therefore, the genius of Wesley, as Manning has observed above, that he has combined his mystical outlook with the essentials of the Gospel—justification by faith and salvation by grace—and those quite harmoniously. Too many mystics, lacking this healthy combination and grasp of the Gospel, have veered into excessive introspection, works righteousness, or even a form of outright pantheism. It is my conviction that a proper understanding of the Gospel, and a personal apprehension of the Savior according to the Scriptures, will involve this mystical reach to and union with Christ, a dimension which indeed the world cannot receive or understand, but neither can the merely formal "Christian," who holds to a form of godliness, but denies its power (2 Tim 3:5). Likewise in regard to Christian service, Wesley knew that he needed the Master's touch and leading by His mystical eye and hand. Just as the "felt Christ" was vitally important to Wesley, so it should be to us also.

First Line Index of Psalms and Hymns

THE REFERENCES ARE TO (i) the number in this Collection, (ii) the number in the 1780 *Collection*, (iii) the number in the 1933 *MHB*. Five of the Psalm selections also occur in the 1933 *MHB*, but three others included in the latter are omitted in this volume: Ps 116 (no. 399); Ps 121 (no. 497); Ps 48 (no. 699).

Psalms

	Above	1780	1933
Why do the Jews and Gentiles join (Ps 2)	65		
O Lord, Thy faithful servant save (Ps 16)	31		
The book of covenanted grace (Ps 19:7–11)	6		
My God, my God! I cry to Thee! (Ps 22:1–21)	27		
Jesus the Good Shepherd is (Ps 23)	91		621
Our Lord is risen from the dead (Ps 24:7–10)	37		222
Lord, I will exalt Thy grace (Ps 30:1–5)	1		
My heart is full of Christ, and longs (Ps 45:1–7)	64		270
Sweet is the odour of Thy name (Ps 45:8–17)	17		
O God, Thou art in Jesus mine (Ps 63)	2		
God on us His grace bestow (Ps 67)	23		
I wait to prove Thine utmost grace (Ps 71:14–24)	87		
Jehovah reigns on high (Ps 93)	52		
Sing we to our conquering Lord (Ps 98)	80		
Ye nations, who the globe divide (Ps 117)	24		
Jesus is lifted up on high (Ps 118:22–29)	13		
Lord, Thy word's unerring light (Ps 119:105–12)	7		
Who in the Lord confide (Ps 125)	55		700

First Line Index of Psalms and Hymns

Out of the depths of self-despair (Ps 130)	42		
O God, in whom I trust, appear! (Ps 143:8–12)	59		
Praise the Lord, who reigns above (Ps 150)	101		14

Hymns

All glory to God, and peace . . . (Luke 2:14)	20		
All praise to our redeeming Lord	70		745
All ye that pass by (Lam 1:12)	29		188
Author of life Divine	75		764
Away with our fears, our troubles and tears	44		278
Behold the servant of the Lord!	68	417	572
Break forth into praise! Our Surety and Head	34		
Captain of Israel's host . . . (Josh 5:14–15)	71	317	608
Christ, my hidden life, appear (Col 3:3–4)	99		
Christ the Lord is risen today	32		204
Christ, whose glory fills the skies	3	517	924
Come, all who truly bear	73		
Come, Holy Ghost, all-quickening fire	63	341	553
Come, Holy Ghost, our hearts inspire	62	85	305
Come, let us anew, our journey pursue	88	45	956
Come, let us arise, and press to the skies	89	482	
Come, let us join with one accord	15		
Come, let us with our Lord arise	14		661
Come on, my partners in distress	100	324	487
Doctrines, experiences to try (Isa 8:20)	9		
Drawn by Thy grace the sons of night (Isa 60)	26		
Earth, rejoice, our Lord is King!	66		246
Entered the holy place above (Heb 9:24)	41		232
Except the Lord conduct the plan (Ps 127)	69	512	
Father of everlasting grace	45	366	730
Filled with the Spirit of holiness (Acts 2:4, 6)	46		
God is gone up on high (Ps 68:18)	40		219
God of unexhausted grace	51		

First Line Index of Psalms and Hymns

Granted is the Saviour's prayer	43		277
Hail Father, Son, and Spirit, great (Gen 1:26)	48	248	
Hail the day that sees Him rise	38		221
Hail, Jesus, hail, our great High Priest	39		
Happy the man that finds . . . (Prov 3:13–18)	97	14	360
Hark! the herald angels sing	21		117
Hear, Holy Spirit, hear	60		
I know that my Redeemer lives, and ever . . .	35	373	565
I know that my Redeemer lives (Job 19:25–26)	36		
I would not, Lord, Thy Spirit bind	84		
In Jesus we live, in Jesus we rest	77		
Jehovah, God the Father, bless (Num 6:24–26)	49	250	
Jesu, at whose supreme command	74		
Jesu, Lover of my soul	93		110
Jesu, my strength, my hope	12	292	542
Jesus, the all-atoning Lamb	4		
Jesus, the name high over all	57	36	92
Jesus, we thus obey	76		761
Leader of faithful souls, and Guide	72	69	610
Let earth and heaven combine	19		142
Let Him to whom we now belong	79	416	382
Lo! He comes with clouds descending	83		264
Love Divine, all loves excelling	98	374	431
My soul extols the mighty Lord (Luke 1:46–55)	22		
None is like Jeshurun's God (Deut 33:26–29)	p. 35	395	68
O filial Deity	56	186	97
O for a thousand tongues to sing	58	1	1
O heavenly King, look down from above	54	191	7
O Jesus, our King, Thy glory we sing	33		
O Love Divine, how sweet Thou art	94	141	434
O love Divine, what hast Thou done?	28	27	186
O Thou who camest from above (Lev 6:12–13)	96	318	386
Omnipresent God! Whose aid	5		876

First Line Index of Psalms and Hymns

Pray, without ceasing, pray	11	259–60	541
Rejoice, rejoice, ye fallen race	61		274
Rejoice in Jesu's birth (Isa 9:6–7)	18		
Saviour, Thy sacred day	16		
Sing to the great Jehovah's praise	90		959
Sons of men, behold from far	25		
Spirit of truth, essential God	8	247	1021*
The great archangel's trump shall sound	82	56	
Thee, O my God and King	53	184	
Thou hidden source of calm repose	92	201	98
Thou Judge of quick and dead	85	54	644
Thou Shepherd of Israel and mine (Song 1:7)	95		457
Victim divine, Thy grace we claim	78		771
We believe that Christ our Head (1 Thess 4:14–18)	81	57	
When quiet in my house I sit	10	319	310
Where shall my wondering soul begin?	47	29	361
Who hath believed the tidings? (Isa 53)	30		
Worship and praise belong	50		
Ye servants of God	67		426
Ye virgin souls arise (Matt 25:1–13)	86	64	

*This hymn is not in the body of the 1933 *MHB*, but in the *Australasian and New Zealand Supplement*.

Wesley Hymns in the Wesleyan Hymn Book (USA)

The hymns below are those included in the Collection above, which also occur in the hymn book, *Hymns of Faith and Life*, Light and Life / Wesley Press, 1976, produced for the Free Methodist Church and The Wesleyan Church in the United States of America.

First Line	Above	1933	HFL
All ye that pass by	29	188	225
Christ the Lord is risen today	32	204	172
Christ, whose glory fills the skies	3	924	92
Come, Holy Ghost, all-quickening fire	63	553	320
God is gone up on high	40	219	184
Hail the day that sees Him rise	38	221	182
Hark! the herald angels sing	21	117	117
I know that my Redeemer lives, and ever . . .	35	565	177
Jesus, the name high over all	57	92	104
Jesu, lover of my soul	93	110	277
Lo! He comes with clouds descending	83	264	186
Love divine, all loves excelling	98	431	335
O for a thousand tongues to sing	58	1	1
O love Divine, how sweet Thou art!	94	434	224
O love Divine, what hast Thou done?	28	186	152
O Thou who camest from above	96	386	304
Thou hidden source of calm repose	92	98	375
Thou judge of quick and dead	85	644	238

Wesley Hymns in the Wesleyan Hymn Book (USA)

Where shall my wondering soul begin	47	361	272
Ye servants of God	67	426	80

TABLE OF ARCHAIC WORDS P. 12

Appendix
John Cennick's Hymn on the Second Coming

Biographical Notes

1. *John Cennick* (1718–55): Born in Reading, England, he spent his early life in a lowly home, and because of poor circumstances he was forced to seek an apprenticeship. This took him to London where he fell in with dissolute youths, as he later testified, "I had forgot Jesus . . . loving ungodliness more than goodness." However, through hearing Psalm 32:10 in church one day in 1737, he came to repentance, conversion, and assurance of faith, and subsequently John Wesley appointed him as a teacher in the Kingswood School for colliers' children at Bristol in 1739. However, in the sad division over Calvinism in 1740, Cennick sided with Whitefield and he continued working with Whitefield until 1745, when he went over to the Moravians. He was ordained a deacon with them in 1749; then worked for a while in Germany, and later in Northern Ireland, where a successful ministry introduced Evangelical Christianity to that region. During his short life he wrote some sermons, and collections of hymns—some of great value, but others of indifferent worth. Always a delicate soul health-wise, he finally succumbed to his ailments and died in 1755.

Julian notes that Cennick's original version of his hymn on the Second Coming was first sung by the congregation of the Moravian Chapel in Dublin on April 20, 1750. However, the earliest printed text known to date appeared in the 1752 edition of Cennick's *Collection of Sacred Hymns*, as follows:

> *Lo! He cometh, countless trumpets,*
> *Blow before his bloody sign!*
> *'Midst ten thousand saints and angels,*

Appendix: John Cennick's Hymn on the Second Coming

See the crucified shine,
Hallelujah!
Welcome, welcome bleeding Lamb!

Now his merits by the harpers,
Through the eternal deeps resounds!
Resplendent shine his nail prints,
Every eye shall see his wounds!
They who pierced Him,
Shall at his appearing wail.

Every island, sea, and mountain,
Heaven and earth shall flee away!
All who hate him must ashamed,
Hear the trump proclaim the day:
Come to judgment!
Stand before the Son of Man!

All who love him view his glory
Shining in his bruised face:
His dear Person on the rainbow,
Now his peoples heads shall raise:
Happy mourners!
Now on clouds He comes, He comes!

Now redemption long expected,
See, in solemn pomp appear;
All his people, once despised,
Now shall meet him in the air:
Hallelujah!
Now the promised Kingdom's come!

View him smiling, now determined,
Every evil to destroy!
All the nations now shall sing him,
Songs of everlasting joy!
O come quickly!
Hallelujah! Come Lord, come![1]

2. *Martin Madan* (1726–90): Madan came from an ancestry both military and ecclesiastical, and early on he sought a career in law. However, his life

---

1. Julian, vol. 1, 681. In Hymn 83 above Julian attributes only stanzas 1, 2, 6, & 7 to Wesley, whereas Osborn, vol. 6, 143–45, appears to attribute to him all seven verses as reproduced here. See also Cyber Hymnal, http://www.hymntime.com/tch/htm/l/o/h/lohecome.htm/.

Appendix: John Cennick's Hymn on the Second Coming

turned around when he heard John Wesley preach on the text "Prepare to meet thy God" (Amos 4:12). He sought Holy Orders, and after some difficulty, obtained the post of chaplain at Lock Hospital, Hyde Park Corner. His popularity as a preacher then grew, as also his musical and literary ability. In 1760, he published *A Collection of Psalms and Hymns Extracted from Various Authors, and published by the Reverend Mr. Madan*, which contained 170 hymns, with a supplement of twenty-three hymns added in 1763. This collection exercised a powerful influence on Anglican hymnody for the next 100 years, until John Mason Neale exerted his own high church, Anglo-Catholic influence in the mid-Victorian period. However, it is fairly clear that Madan never composed a single hymn in his own right; his ability was in collecting, and at times altering and improving (in his view) the compositions of others. He did, however, compose some tunes, and one tune at least, viz. "Hotham," made its way into Wesley's *Sacred Harmony* of 1780.

Madan, however, eventually fell under a cloud and had to cease preaching when he published a treatise advocating polygamy.

As observed above, the meter, 8.7.8.7.4.4.7., is the same in both Cennick's and Wesley's version, while Cennick's verses 3 and 5 are quite similar to the corresponding verses in Wesley, and may fairly be attributed to Cennick. Madan also made small alterations of less significance, some of which are incorporated in hymn books of more recent vintage, as follows:

Wesley

Lo! He comes with clouds descending,
Once for favoured sinners slain!
Thousand, thousand saints attending,
Swell the triumph of His train:
Hallelujah! Hallelujah!
God appears on earth to reign!

Now redemption, long expected,
See in solemn pomp appear;
All His saints, by man rejected,
Now shall meet Him in the air:
Hallelujah! Hallelujah!

Madan

Lo! He comes with clouds descending
Once for favoured sinners slain!
Thousand, thousand saints attending
Swell the triumph of His train.
Hallelujah! Hallelujah!
Hallelujah! Amen!

Now redemption long expected
See! In solemn pomp appear!
All His saints, by man rejected,
Now shall meet Him in the air!
Hallelujah! Hallelujah!

Appendix: John Cennick's Hymn on the Second Coming

See the day of God appear!   *See the Son of God appear!*[A]

A. Julian, vol. 1, 681. Cf. the discussion in Glover, *Hymnal 1982 Companion*, vol. 1, 108.

As will be evident, the alterations are slight, and while most hymn books have the version as Wesley wrote it, some incorporate the Madan alterations. Still others render Wesley's verse, *Now redemption* . . . etc., according to a version published by Wigram in 1856:

> *See the Saviour long expected,*
> *Now in solemn pomp appear!*
> *And His saints, by man rejected*
> *All His heavenly glory share.*
> *Hallelujah!*
> *See the Son of God appear!*[2]

Hence this hymn has seen manifold alterations over the years, but it is doubtful that the alterations by either Madan or Wigram constitute improvements, so it is best to sing it as Wesley composed it, with due acknowledgment to the inspiration from Cennick's original. John Wesley's dictum abides (in this case, as in many others), "I desire that they would not attempt to mend them [i.e., his brother's hymns]—for they are really not able."

2. As in http://www.stempublishing.com/hymns/biographies/cennick.html.

Bibliography

Alexander, Donald L., ed. *Christian Spirituality: Five Views of Sanctification*. Downers Grove, IL: InterVarsity, 1988.
Armstrong, Brian G. *Calvinism and the Amyraut Heresy: Protestant Scholasticism and Humanism in Seventeenth-Century France*. Madison, WI: University of Wisconsin Press, 1969.
Baker, Frank. *John Wesley and the Church of England*. London: Epworth, 1970.
Baker, Frank, ed. *The Works of John Wesley*. Vol. 26, *Letters, Vol. II, 1740–1755*. Nashville: Abingdon, 1982. (Abbrev. *Wesley, Letters*)
Berkhof, Louis. *Systematic Theology*. Reprint, London: Banner of Truth Trust, 1969. First published 1939.
Bready, J. Wesley. *England before and after Wesley: The Evangelical Revival and Social Reform*. London: Hodder & Stoughton, 1939.
Bridge, Sir Frederick, music ed. *The Methodist Hymn Book with Tunes*. London: Wesleyan Conference Office, 1904. (Abbrev. 1904 *MHB*)
Center for Studies in the Wesleyan Tradition. *Wesley Texts*. Duke Divinity School. Website: http://www.divinity.duke.edu/initiatives-centers/cswt/wesley-texts. (Abbrev. CSWT)
Dallimore, Arnold. *George Whitefield: The Life and Times of the Great Evangelist of the Eighteenth-century Revival*. 2 Vols. London / Edinburgh: Banner of Truth Trust, 1970–80.
———. *A Heart Set Free*. Welwyn, HRT: Evangelical, 1988.
Deschner, John. *Wesley's Christology*. Dallas, TX: Southern Methodist University Press, 1960. Reprint, Grand Rapids: Francis Asbury, 1985.
Douglas, J. D., ed. *New International Dictionary of the Christian Church*. Exeter, ENG: Paternoster, 1974. (Abbrev. *NIDCC*)
Dunstone, Alan S. *The Atonement in Gregory of Nyssa*. Tyndale Lecture, 1963. London: Tyndale, 1964.
Eaton, Michael A. *Baptism with the Spirit: The Teaching of Martyn Lloyd-Jones*. Leicester, ENG: IVP, 1989.
Ferguson, Everett, ed. *Encyclopedia of Early Christianity*. New York: Garland, 1990. (Abbrev. *EEC*)
Feucht, Oscar E. *The Practice of Prayer*. St. Louis, MO: Concordia, 1956.
Fitchett, W. H. *Wesley and His Century*. London: Smith, Elder & Co., 1906.
Glover, Raymond F. *The Hymnal 1982 Companion*. 2 Vols. New York: Church Hymnal, 1990.

Bibliography

Grace Church. *The Life and Hymns of Charles Wesley*. Lecture created July 9, 2012. Lecturer's name unstated. http://www.youtube.com/watch?v=8TVO1REqSuM.

Harman, Allan M. "The Impact of Matthew Henry's *Exposition* on Eighteenth-century Christianity." *Evangelical Quarterly* 82 (2010) 3–14.

Heitzenrater, Richard P. *Wesley and the People Called Methodists*. Nashville: Abingdon, 1995.

Hildebrandt, Franz, and Beckerlegge, Oliver A., eds. *A Collection of Hymns for the Use of the People Called Methodists*. The Works of John Wesley 7. Oxford: Clarendon, 1983. Reprint, Nashville: Abingdon, n.d. (Abbrev. H&B)

Houghton, Elsie. *Christian Hymn-writers*. Bryntirion, WAL: Evangelical, 1982.

Joint Hymnal Commission. *Hymns of Faith and Life*. Winona Lake, IN: Light and Life / Marion, IN: Wesley, 1976. (Abbrev. HFL)

Julian, John. *Dictionary of Hymnology*. 2 Vols. Reprint, Grand Rapids: Kregel, 1985. First published 1907. (Abbrev. Julian)

Kariatlis, Philip. "A Credible Presentation of Redemption Today." http://www.orthodoxchristian.info/pages/Redemption.htm.

Kimbrough, S. T. *The Lyrical Theology of Charles Wesley*. Cambridge: Lutterworth, 2013.

Lampe, G. W. H., ed. *A Patristic Greek Lexicon*. Oxford: Clarendon, 1961. (Abbrev. Lampe)

Lindström, Harald. *Wesley and Sanctification*. Wilmore, KY: Francis Asbury, 1946.

Lloyd-Jones, D. Martyn. "New Developments in 18th and 19th Century Teaching." In *Living the Christian Life*, edited by David Bugden, 82–99. Warboys, CAM: Westminster Conference Papers, 1974.

Maddox, Randy L., and Aileen F. Maddox, eds. *Scripture Hymns* (1762): The online edition of Charles Wesley, *Short Hymns on Select Passages of the Holy Scriptures*. 2 vols. Bristol, ENG: Farley, 1762. From: https://divinity.duke.edu/sites/divinity.duke.edu/files/documents/cswt/63_Scripture_Hymns.

Manning, Bernard L. *The Hymns of Wesley and Watts*. London: Epworth, 1942. Public Domain reprint, n.d. (Abbrev. Manning)

Masters, Peter. *Worship in the Melting Pot*. London: Wakeman Trust, 2002.

Metzger, Bruce. *A Textual Commentary on the Greek New Testament*. London / New York: UBS, 1971.

Mohan, T. N. *A Heart Set Free: The Life, Ministry, and Lyrics of Charles Wesley*. DVD. Worcester, PA: The Christian History Institute, n.d.

Moule, Handley C. G. *Outlines of Christian Doctrine*. London: Hodder & Stoughton, 1890.

Osborn, George, ed. *The Poetical Works of John and Charles Wesley*. 13 vols. London: Wesleyan-Methodist Conference, 1868–72. (Abbrev. Osborn)

Price, Carl F. *One Hundred and One Hymn Stories*. New York: Abingdon, 1951. (Abbrev. 101 *Hymn Stories*)

Rattenbury, J. Ernest. *The Evangelical Doctrines of Charles Wesley's Hymns*. 3rd ed. London: Epworth, 1954.

Robertson, Archibald, trans. *The Nicene and Post-Nicene Fathers*. Series 2, vol. 4. Reprint, Grand Rapids: Eerdmans, n.d. First published 1891. (Abbrev. NPNF)

Ryle, John C. *Light from Old Times*. First published 1890. Reprint, London: Evangelical, 1980.

Schaff, Philip. *History of the Christian Church*. 7 Vols. Reprint, Grand Rapids: Eerdmans, 1974. First published 1910.

Simon, John S. *The Revival of Religion in the Eighteenth Century*. London: Charles Kelly, [c. 1907].

BIBLIOGRAPHY

Tyson, John R. *Assist Me to Proclaim: The Life and Hymns of Charles Wesley.* Grand Rapids: Eerdmans, 2007.

Van Til, Marian. *George Frideric Handel: A Music Lover's Guide to his Life, his Faith & the Development of Messiah & his other Oratorios.* Youngstown, NY: WordPower, 2007.

Wesley, Charles. *The Journal of Charles Wesley (1707–1788).* The Wesley Centre Online. http://wesley.nnu.edu/charles-wesley/the-journal-of-charles-wesley-1707-1788. (Abbrev. CWJ)

Wesley, John. *Collection of Hymns for the Use of the People called Methodists.* Edited with Tunes, with a New Supplement. London: Wesleyan Conference Office, 1877. (Abbrev. *Collection with New Supplement*)

———. *Explanatory Notes upon the New Testament.* Reprint, London: Epworth, 1958. (Abbrev. *Explanatory Notes NT*)

———. *The Journal of the Rev. John Wesley, A.M.* 4 Vols. London: Wesleyan Conference Office, 1903. (Abbrev. JWJ)

———. *Sermons on Several Occasions: Forty-Four Sermons.* 4th ed. London: Methodist Conference Office, 1787. Reprint, Wesleyan Conference Office, n.d.

Wesley, John, and Charles Wesley. *Sacred Harmony, or a Choice Collection of Psalms and Hymns.* London: s.n., 1781.

Wiseman, Rev. F. Luke, ed. *The Methodist Hymn Book for Use in Australasia and New Zealand.* London: Methodist Conference Office, 1933. [The *Australasian and New Zealand Supplement* of 51 hymns contains one only by Charles Wesley.] (Abbrev. 1933 *MHB*)

Wood, Arthur Skevington. *The Burning Heart.* Exeter, ENG: Paternoster, 1967.

———. *The Inextinguishable Blaze.* London: Paternoster, 1960.

www.ingramcontent.com/pod-product-compliance
Lightning Source LLC
Chambersburg PA
CBHW071243230426
43668CB00011B/1565